D0344935

fP

Also by Daniel Gross

Dumb Money

Pop! Why Bubbles Are Great for the Economy

*Bull Run: Wall Street, the Democrats,
and the New Politics of Personal Finance*

Forbes Greatest Business Stories of All Time

BETTER, STRONGER, FASTER

The Myth of American Decline . . .
and the Rise of a New Economy

DANIEL GROSS

FREE PRESS

New York   London   Toronto   Sydney   New Delhi

Free Press
A Division of Simon & Schuster, Inc.
1230 Avenue of the Americas
New York, NY 10020

Copyright © 2012 by Daniel Gross

All rights reserved, including the right to reproduce this book or portions thereof in any form whatsoever. For information address Free Press Subsidary Rights Department, 1230 Avenue of the Americas, New York, NY 10020.

First Free Press hardcover edition May 2012

FREE PRESS and colophon are trademarks of Simon & Schuster, Inc.

For information about special discounts for bulk purchases, please contact Simon & Schuster Special Sales at 1-866-506-1949 or business@simonandschuster.com.

The Simon & Schuster Speakers Bureau can bring authors to your live event. For more information or to book an event contact the Simon & Schuster Speakers Bureau at 1-866-248-3049 or visit our website at www.simonspeakers.com.

Manufactured in the United States of America

10 9 8 7 6 5 4 3 2

Library of Congress Cataloging-in-Publication Data
Gross, Daniel, 1967-
  Better, stronger, faster : the myth of American decline . . . and the rise of a new economy / Daniel Gross.
     p.   cm.
  Includes bibliographical references and index.
  1. United States—Economic policy—2009-   2. United States—Foreign economic relations.   3. United States—Commerce.   4. Industrial policy—United States.   5. Economic stabilization—United States.   I. Title.
HC106.84.G76   2012
330.973—dc23   2012004764

ISBN 978-1-4516-2128-0
ISBN 978-1-4516-2136-5 (ebook)

For Candi—again

Contents

BETTER, STRONGER, FASTER

CHAPTER 1

The Rise of Decline

The word came down on a hot, muggy August afternoon. And as frequently happens in the financial world, whether announcing bank closures or bankruptcy filings, the messenger dumped the bad news on Friday after the stock markets had closed. Doing so gives investors sixty hours to process the information before trading on it.

On August 5, 2011, Standard & Poor's, the firm that rated Lehman Brothers an investment-grade A credit on the eve of its implosion, that rented out its ancient and venerable name to any investment bank that wanted to shovel junky assets into a credulous market, stripped the United States of its AAA credit rating. In a terse statement, S&P downgraded the credit of the world's largest economy, the unchallenged military leader, the proprietor of the world's reserve currency and guardian of the globe's stability, to AA–. The United States, which first received an AAA score from the credit ratings agency Moody's in 1917, was suddenly judged to be as likely to make good on its debt as . . . *New Zealand*?

The downgrade was just the latest humiliation to befall the U.S. economy in a three-year run of epically bad news. It came a week after the Commerce Department announced that the economy had expanded at a near-recessionary 1.3 percent annual rate for the second quarter. It came at the beginning of a month in which the economy would create no jobs, and two years after the country had officially emerged from a deep recession. It came at a time when Washington was in complete disarray, when Congress and

1

the president were locked in an absurd standoff over extending the debt ceiling. Through fanaticism on the part of Congress and poor negotiating strategy on the part of the Obama administration, official Washington had managed to turn a once-routine formality into a circular firing squad. It came at a time when 14.2 million people were out of work, and when many more seemed to be out of hope. The fact that it was delivered when the markets were closed for the weekend did nothing to soften the blow.

In the fall of 2008 the failure of Lehman Brothers, a lightly regulated, highly incompetent investment bank that had managed to amass $650 billion in debt, triggered a chain of events that transformed the U.S. credit crisis into a global credit crisis. And it seemed to mark the end of a sixty-three-year American-led global epoch—driven by the mighty American consumer, fueled by American banks. For decades American institutions and individuals had provided the moral, intellectual, and financial underpinnings of the world's financial, consuming, and trading system. But when cheap and easy credit disappeared in the wake of the Lehman debacle, the global engine suddenly conked out: 2009 marked the first year since 1944, the height of World War II, in which global economic output contracted. Though the shrinkage was hard all over, the United States seemed to suffer the most grievous physical, financial, and psychological blows. Ghost towns, ghost malls, and ghost office buildings haunted Las Vegas, Nevada, Phoenix, and Miami. Between the end of 2007 and the first quarter of 2009, $9 trillion of American wealth evaporated, making the United States suddenly poorer than Europe. New car sales fell 35 percent from 2007 to 2009. The United States endured a recession that lasted eighteen months, the longest period of economic contraction since the Great Depression.

Nothing was downsized as much as the national ego. The collapse of September 2008 coincided with other foreboding trends: China's relentless boom, $4-per-gallon gas, a falling dollar, an unfathomably large government budget deficit, the soaring price of gold. The largest financial institutions, once the envy of the world, became wards of the state. No entity seemed capable of making a home mortgage except the government. The hardest-working country in the world became Dropout Nation. The unemployment rate spiked to 10 percent in October 2009; an alternative measure of unemployment, which takes into account frustrated part-timers and those who have given up looking for work, soared above 17 percent. A rampant Tea Party, an ungovernable Senate, a seemingly blasé White House, unrepentant banks, and falling home values contributed to a sour mood. An NBC/*Wall Street Journal* poll conducted in September 2010 found that 61 percent of Americans believed the country was in a state of decline and that only 27 percent were confident their children's future standard of living would be better than their own.

Americans who ventured abroad after the Great Panic of 2008 suffered a series of insults and pokes in the eye. At the World Economic Forum in Davos, Switzerland, in January 2010, amid the panels on climate change, green technology, and the need to reimagine capitalism, American voices were conspicuous by their absence. The United States, which had once dominated the forum, occupied negative space in the multilevel Kongresszentrum. U.S. bankers remained in their Manhattan bunkers, reluctant to be seen jetting off on private planes to attend an elite gathering in the Alps. Most of the Obama administration's economic team remained in Washington, prepping for the State of the Union address. The congressional delegation consisted largely of a rumpled Barney Frank, the Democratic representative from Massachusetts, and a sheepish Lindsey Graham, the Republican senator from South Carolina, who was continually forced to account for the antiglobalization rants of his Republican colleagues. In his keynote address, President Nicolas Sarkozy of France, once dubbed *l'Americain* for his interest in bling, long working hours, and generally harder-edged attitude toward economic policy, proclaimed an end to the U.S.-led version of global capitalism and immodestly proposed himself— and Europe—as an alternative leader. "Finance, free trade, and competition are only means and not ends in themselves," he declared. At *Newsweek*'s big Friday lunch, in the sun-dappled dining room of the Hotel Seehof, the White House economic advisor Lawrence Summers was asked to say a few words about the economy. But he was cut off: the queen of Jordan was about to make her entrance. Rania, a radiant vision in a white pantsuit, blew air kisses and made her way to the head table, where Marie-Josée Kravis, the Canadian economist and third wife of the financier Henry Kravis, was nudged aside to make room. Summers crossed his arms and remained on his feet.

Yes, in ways big and small, it was hard to avoid signs of the decline in America's economic status. The data, the trends, and the zeitgeist all began to run away from the country. And that darkened the mood considerably. In 2007 Americans may have invested, lent, and behaved as if nothing could go wrong, but starting in 2009 they began to behave as if nothing could go right. In a nation known for its congenital optimism, declinism quickly emerged as the chic intellectual pose for the new decade. Left, right, center, highbrow, lowbrow, ideological, and pragmatic—you name it. Like Walt Whitman, the American decline caucus contained multitudes.

The vindicated bears, the small group of analysts, economists, and journalists who accurately predicted the financial apocalypse of 2008, roamed the denuded terrain with confidence. Frequently scorned in 2006 and 2007, these prognosticators remained suspicious of the turnaround efforts, believing that the excesses that caused the problems in the first place had yet to be worked off. Peter Schiff, the libertarian money manager who warned of a debt apocalypse in frequent media appearances, proclaimed that the cure was aggravating the sickness. An adherent of the Austrian school of monetary theory, he believed the rescue—cheap money provided by the world's central banks and higher levels of government spending—was a vain effort to reinflate the original bubble. Nouriel Roubini, the bon vivant New York University economist dubbed Dr. Doom, whose blog posts accurately predicted the housing and credit debacle, remained bearish through 2009 and 2010. So long as housing remained an issue, he believed there could be no recovery. "I see one percent growth in the economy in the next few years," he told CNBC in July 2009. "It's going to feel like a recession, even when it ends."

Those who looked backward found ample reason to expect decline. From his perch at Harvard, the historian Niall Ferguson, a nostalgist for the faded British Empire, repeated his case that the once mighty American dreadnought was dead in the water. The weight of history suggested that the United States, overextended and debt-ridden, was likely to suffer the same fate in the early twenty-first century that befell the British Empire in the mid-twentieth. "It's not a thousand years that separates imperial zenith from imperial oblivion," he said in a May 2010 speech. "It's really a very, very short ride from the top to the bottom."[1] Kenneth Rogoff and Carmen Reinhart, economists who data-mined history in *This Time Is Different,* a comprehensive look at financial debacles going back to the 1300s, arrived at a similar conclusion. Centuries worth of data on finance-induced crises suggest the United States won't be bouncing back any time soon, they concluded.

The moment Barack Obama was sworn in as president, a wave of economic declinism swamped the political right. A surprising number of analysts, including op-ed page contributors to the *Wall Street Journal,* George Will, and adherents to supply-side economics, insist on viewing economic and market performance mostly through the lens of politics. Democrats, they are convinced, are bad for markets and the economy, while Republicans are good for both—evidence be damned. "Obama's Radicalism Is Killing the Dow," screamed a *Wall Street Journal* op-ed by George W. Bush's economic advisor Michael Boskin on March 6, 2009, as the Dow touched 6,600—the same level at which it stood in January 1997. As President Obama began to enact his agenda—passing a stimulus package and an ambitious health care plan, appointing officials—Republicans warned darkly against creeping socialism and trillion-dollar deficits. House Minority Leader John Boehner famously shouted in March 2010 that the passage of health care reform would presage Armageddon. Everyone on the right, from Tea Party activists to the Republican economic establishment, regards President Obama as a job-killing, market-wrecking, socialist disaster. When the Federal Reserve chairman, a mild-mannered Republican first appointed by President George W. Bush, tried to do his job, Governor Rick Perry of Texas suggested he was engaging in behavior that right-thinking folks might regard as treasonous. Having voted en masse against the 2009 stimulus package on the grounds that it couldn't work, the right went all out on economic failure, intellectually and politically. Until one of its own is back in the White House, the party of economic sunshine is in the strange position of praying for rain.

Through a different way of thinking the left reached a similar conclusion about the nation's short-term economic prospects. The bailouts of 2008 were conceived in sin, because they provided unjust and unwarranted rewards to the highly paid, malign idiots (i.e., bankers) who nearly destroyed the economy. More broadly, Obama, under the sway of advisors too close to Wall Street banks, was overly concerned with appeasing discredited economic interests. Joseph Stiglitz, the Columbia economist and 2001 Nobel laureate, argued that the collapse and tepid response to the financial crisis and economic downturn had rendered the United States irrelevant. "The point now is that no one has respect for that kind of model anymore," he told the *Washington Post* in October 2008. Obama's repeated and fruitless attempts to reach across the aisle in 2009 and 2010 only deepened the angst. The price of three Republican votes for the stimulus bill in the Senate was reducing its size by $300 billion. And that, argued the Nobel laureate and *New York Times* columnist Paul Krugman, made it too small to be effective, given the steep decline in economic activity. In essence, the government was left with "$600 billion trying to fill a $2.9 trillion hole," Krugman said in February 2009.[2] For Keynesian economists, President Obama was excessively passive. He outsourced the design of vital health care legislation to Congress, failed to fill open positions at the Federal Reserve, tolerated Republican holds on crucial nominees and filibusters of legislation, and focused on deficit reduction at precisely the wrong time in a fruitless effort to garner Republican support. By generally failing to aggressively press his economic agenda and command the legislative stage, he let disputes fester into confidence-sucking faux crises surrounding the debt. Yes we can? No we can't.

Instead of pointing out internal sources of rot and decay, many declinists looked abroad to bolster their case. Take the China Bulls, a group of analysts and journalists awed and impressed by China's rapid growth, such as Thomas Friedman of the *New York Times*. It's hard not to be overwhelmed by the enormousness of

China. Every year of 8 percent growth, each high-speed rail track laid down and solar panel erected, and the steady agglomeration of impressive economic data seem to signal China's rise and America's fall. In the summer of 2008, when America was melting down, China staged the Summer Olympics in impressive fashion. In the fall of 2009, when I visited China for the first time, I traveled to Chongqing, which had been the country's national capital during World War II. In the middle of town stands the Liberation Tower, which was erected to memorialize the war effort. Thirty years ago this ninety-foot-tall structure was the highest in town. Now it sits in the middle of the Jiefangbei shopping district, dwarfed by the office towers, hotels, and apartment blocks that march along the foggy banks of the Yangtze River. Oh, and there's a Rolex ad embedded in the top of the tower.

Massive cities, rampant growth, and stunning scale confront visitors to China at every turn. On a six-hour boat ride through the Three Gorges area, I counted fifteen new bridges that had recently been built over the Yangtze River at the high-water mark. After debarking I toured the immense power plant built into the dam. The world's largest renewable energy generator, the Three Gorges plant has the capacity to produce 18,200 megawatts of energy—about nine times the capacity of a large nuclear power plant. I rode the Maglev train that shuttles passengers from downtown Shanghai to the immaculate Pudong Airport at 250 miles per hour, without subjecting them to bumps. Returning to John F. Kennedy Airport's glum arrivals hall and resuming my commute on Metro North, whose Eisenhower-era cars jostle passengers along at Eisenhower-era speeds, it was hard to avoid the conclusion that the future is happening somewhere else.

The shift in economic energy to the Far East is obvious. In 2010 stock exchanges in Hong Kong and China combined raised three times as much in initial public offerings as was raised in the United States: $119 billion to $42 billion; in 2011 greater China's exchanges staged forty-six IPOs worth $47.9 billion, while the New York Stock Exchange and NASDAQ between them floated forty-seven IPOs worth a combined $20.8 billion.[3] The fearful American reaction to dynamism in China and elsewhere was very similar to the trepidation Europeans felt when visiting the United States during our industrial revolution of the late nineteenth century: *We are sooooo screwed*. Think what visitors from Old Europe encountered when they saw Pittsburgh, or New York, or Chicago—cities that were dirty, bustling, crowded, booming, difficult to understand, and self-confident. The latest technology being put to ambitious use. A sense of purpose and striving. People who just seemed to work harder and want it more. As the economist Arvind Subramanian argued in his 2011 book, *Eclipse: Living in the Shadow of China's Economic Dominance*, Americans had better get used to this feeling of inferiority.

A different cloud of decline drifted over the Pacific from Asia: the cautionary tale of Japan. Less than twenty-five years ago, Americans believed Japan was something like today's China, only with a smaller population and an even more exotic cuisine. By dint of a superior work ethic, better adaptation of technology, military aggression channeled into commercial ambition, and industrial policy, this Asian power was poised to eat America's lunch. But in the two decades since the collapse of its real estate and stock bubbles of the late 1980s, Japan has sunk into deep decline. The proud nation's citizenry seems to have lost the will to procreate, or even to live. Walking around Tokyo, I frequently felt as if I were in a remake of *Children of Men*, the film about a world in which there are no babies. I was on a Shinkansen train from Kyoto to Osaka that came to a sudden stop. After a few minutes an announcement came over the intercom. Somebody had jumped in front of the train, a fairly common occurrence. Nobody batted an eye. About 100 Japanese commit suicide every day; the annual suicide rate was 24.4 per 100,000 people in 2009, more than twice the rate in the United States.[4]

Japan really can't afford to lose people. I received a tutorial on Japan's demographic problems from Kiyoaki Fujiwara, director of the Japan Business Federation's economic policy bureau. Japan's population peaked at 127.8 million in 2004 and has fallen pretty much every year since, to about 126 million in 2010. The forecast called for the population to shrink to 90 million in 2055. Fujiwara was sweating as he described the situation, and not just because it is so troubling. Japan's Super Cool Biz campaign, aimed at saving energy, urges offices to keep the thermostat set in the mid-80s, even in the middle of Tokyo's tropical summers. (If policymakers listen to Cole Porter's "Too Darn Hot," which describes the many ways in which heat dampens men's sexual ambition, they'll understand the connection between high temperatures and low birthrates.) Well-regarded economic analysts believe that Japan's fate could be ours. "I had said that it would be more of an L-shaped, slow recovery," Joseph Stiglitz told the *New York Times* in August 2011, when the economy seemed to hit stall speed and fears of a second recession were rising. "I think the answer now is a Japan-style malaise."

For many pessimists, decline isn't a matter of ideology or faith. It's a matter of simple numbers. The U.S. economy fell into a very deep ditch in 2008 and 2009. To return the ratio of American household debt to gross domestic product, about 92 percent in late 2011, to its historical average of between 40 and 60 percent, consumers will have to pay down a few trillion dollars of principal. For the price of a typical home to return to its 2006 peak, it must rise 40 percent. The output gap—the difference between what the economy is currently producing and what it could produce without significant inflation—was 6.3 percent, or about $1 trillion, in the summer of 2011. Jobless recoveries have been the norm in recent decades. After the previous recession ended in November 2001, companies slashed payrolls for seventeen of the next twenty-one months. In the past, factories closed down and furloughed workers while inventory was depleted, then recalled workers when new orders came in. These days the shuttered factory is likely to reopen in China, forcing Americans to scramble for lower-paying service jobs. To recoup the 8.75 million jobs lost between January 2008 and February 2010, it will take 6.5 years of growth at 150,000 jobs per month. And that's simply not good enough. Thanks to immigration and natural population growth, the U.S. worker base grows by about 150,000 per month.

Worse, the forces that drove job creation in the recent past—the housing boom, easy money, reckless lenders—are no longer with us. In fact, the great forces that propelled so much growth in the past few decades are poised to act as a brake on growth—at home and globally. For sixty years policymakers relied on a series of simple tools for combating slowdowns and promoting growth: the Federal Reserve cut interest rates, the government slashed taxes, and a deregulated Wall Street provided easy money. All of which spurred debt-fueled consumption and the movement of goods and services around the globe. No more. The Federal Reserve can't lower interest rates any further; the overnight lending rate it controls has been close to zero since December 2008. In coming years interest rates will rise, and taxes and spending will be constrained to deal with the massive deficits that sprouted up in the post-bust years. Meanwhile a dysfunctional government continually sows uncertainty and hinders growth. In the absence of a massive new transformative economic force—the next steam engine, the next electricity, the next Internet—it's difficult to see the path to a brighter future. Until the excesses of the past decade work themselves out, the 2001 Nobel economics laureate Michael Spence told me, "we're just going to have to live with some version of the slow-growth employment problem." For companies dependent on the free-spending American consumer, the days of effortless 15 percent earnings growth and easily accomplished expansion goals are over. "Flat is the new up," William Lauder, chairman of the Estée Lauder Companies, told me in early 2010.

So as the economy muddled through, a kind of fatalism pervaded America, as if we had burned the tools necessary for growth. In many cases, even those most heavily invested in success were skeptical of the nation's capacity for renewal and growth. At a dinner in Washington in 2009 convened by the Aspen Institute and the technology company Intel to discuss innovation, I asked Larry Summers, then the Obama administration's chief economic spokesman, what would happen if we all tried a little harder, if we were more careful with resources. Wouldn't that be worth something? Mustering all the diplomacy he could, Summers responded with a patronizing "Maybe." The weak economy, pundits agree, ended Democrats' control of the House of Representatives in 2010 and will seriously damage or maybe even doom Obama's chance of a two-term presidency.

As negative sentiment bubbled up from a variety of sources

in 2009, 2010, and 2011, the conventional wisdom hardened. The United States has a very slim hope of recovering from all the blows it has suffered. And even if we could somehow clear away the obstacles to satisfying growth in the short term, bigger problems loom on the horizon, from the national debt to global warming and the failures of public education. In the space of a few years the American economy had transformed from a fearsome beast into a wounded, lumbering behemoth, shorn of aggression and attacking spirit and vitality. By the time Standard & Poor's, a crew generally known for being the last to know, announced its downgrade, it was like the coup de grâce at a bullfight.

As is so frequently the case, however, the conventional wisdom is wrong.

CHAPTER 2

The Myth of American Decline

The level of pessimism and uncertainty surrounding the decline of the U.S. economy may be unprecedented. And, of course, it may be justified in time. The headlines certainly serve up ample fodder for the decline case.

The bankers failed en masse and sank the economy. The housing market is so bad the government is the only entity capable of making new mortgages. Never mind the top-level statistics, the real unemployment rate is well into the double digits. When reforms were proposed aimed at warding off repeats of the financial meltdown, unrepentant bankers howled and accused the government of socialism. The president of the American Bankers Association declared that "overwhelming opinions of experienced bankers are emphatically opposed" to proposals that "compel strong and well managed banks to pay the losses of the weak." Faced with the glaring need for reform after a meltdown and a series of scandals, the head of the New York Stock Exchange essentially brushed it off. "It's a perfect institution," he said.[1] A president with great rhetorical gifts, a Harvard-educated lawyer who had been elected promising hope and a new era, wasn't able to get much bipartisan support for any of his initiatives, which were derided as half-measures by his left flank. From the right, his outraged opponents accused the mild-mannered president of all sorts of things: he's a fascist, a socialist, a communist; he's aiming to take over and nationalize entire segments of the economy and subvert the constitutional order. The media are filled with rabble-rousers, lunatics, and acerbic commentators trying to rile things up. The president, the most prominent radio commentator says, is "leaning toward international socialism." Many look at the name and policies of the leader of the free world, who was duly elected in a landslide, and conclude that he may not even be American, or a Christian. Overseas there's a lot of instability. There are questions about the intentions and ambitions of the resource-rich, nondemocratic regime that runs the former Russian Empire. Europe seems about to implode as Germany bosses its neighbors around. In Asia a strong, rising, authoritarian regime is flexing its muscles and venting nationalist spleen.

Bad stuff, indeed. But all these developments, which could have been ripped from recent headlines, in fact happened in the early 1930s. In 1933 unemployment was above 24 percent, and the economy had been in recession for more than three years. The American Bankers Association leader opposed to reform? That was Francis Sisson railing against the establishment of the Federal Deposit Insurance Corporation in June 1933. The New York Stock Exchange president who boasted of running a perfect institution? That was Richard Whitney, who later went to jail for embezzlement. Father Charles Coughlin branded President Franklin D. Roosevelt a socialist. In the 1930s Hitler's Germany was threatening its European neighbors, Stalin's Soviet Union was on the march, and Japan was a rising power.

In other words, a widespread sense of decline and hopelessness amid a long period of subpar growth is nothing new. In fact, when it comes to decline, we've been here before, many times. Things have been going south economically in this country since the cruel winter of 1609, when nearly 90 percent of the settlers in Jamestown, Virginia, died. Even after winning independence, the young nation was perpetually starved for capital, easily bullied by the British, unable to control Atlantic sea lanes, and reluctant to invest in public infrastructure. Lacking a central bank, the U.S. financial system lurched from banking crisis to banking crisis and suffered a series of panics and lengthy recessions. The United States was an economic and cultural backwater for virtually all of the nineteenth century, an immature, uncouth cousin that required huge infusions of European capital to build its railroads. In 1875 U.S. gross domestic product per capita was $2,600, below that of Australia, New Zealand, Belgium, the Netherlands, and the United Kingdom.[2]

The sense of insecurity lingered even after industrialism supercharged growth between 1880 and 1920 and the United States seized the mantle of economic leadership after World War I. Progressives who went to Italy in the 1920s saw in Mussolini's fascist regime a country that was far more interested in economic efficiency and effective policy than America was. During the New Deal, bankers and industrialists earnestly fretted that Franklin Roosevelt, an un-American socialist, would ruin the nation's prospects for growth by establishing a new welfare safety net. The USSR's launch of the Sputnik satellite in 1957 inspired fear that the Soviet Union's apparent technological advantage would lead it to triumph in the cold war. In the 1970s there was widespread talk of malaise. Next, Japan went on the attack, this time with exports of electronics and cars and armed with yen to buy trophy properties like Rockefeller Center and Pebble Beach. Despite the triumph of Western capitalism over Eastern socialism at the end of the decade, the United States felt it was losing ground to countries that were more hardcore about schooling, training, and protectionism. "The Cold War is over, and Japan won," as Senator Paul Tsongas, a Democrat from Massachusetts, said during his 1992 presidential campaign.[3]

The history of declinism is like an antiphony to the classic American theme of rising confidence and triumph. Although Americans are optimists and risk-takers by nature, they have frequently been plagued by a sense of insecurity, a presentiment that the enterprise is doomed. Declinism is a virus that lies dormant during expansions, only to break out in a rash of self-flagellating think pieces, gloomy op-ed articles, and dire warnings when defenses weaken. At present the gloom is so thick you can cut it with a (made in China) knife.

But here's the thing: the doomsayers and declinists, the Debbie Downers and double-dippers are too pessimistic by half—in theory and in practice. The talk of America's inevitable, inexorable economic decline is as off-base in 2011 and 2012 as it was at other points in history. And it's not just because we've managed to bounce back from setbacks in the past.

The U.S. economy suffered a wipeout in the Great Recession of 2008–2009, like one of the icons of my childhood, Steve Austin. Played by Lee Majors, Steve Austin was an astronaut who crashed to earth and then became the Six Million Dollar Man. The series started as a television movie in 1973, a year the United States was undergoing a similar dark night of the soul, grappling with a succession of political and economic crises: Vietnam, Watergate, rising inflation, and an oil shock. But from its opening credits the *Six Million Dollar Man* exuded a typically American confidence: "We can rebuild him. We have the technology. We have the capability to make the world's first bionic man. Steve Austin will be that man. Better than he was before. Better, stronger, faster." And like Steve Austin, the U.S. economy can bounce back from its catastrophic wipeout. In fact, the process has already started.

The United States has serious problems, many of which verge on pathologies. Housing could take a generation to right itself. President Obama is not FDR, not by a long shot. There is no denying the raft load of negative data and economic pain. But there is no reason that the expansion that started in July 2009, against all the odds and predictions, can't last just as long as the previous three expansions, which lasted 73 months (from November 2001 to December 2007), 120 months (from March 1992 through March 2001), and 92 months (from November 1982 through July 1990), respectively. When the definitive history of this period is written, it's possible—likely, even—that this post-bust era will go down as a time not of stagnation and decline, but of reconstruction and transformation.

Such an optimistic outlook doesn't come naturally to me. I grew up in Michigan in the 1970s and early 1980s, as auto plants closed and people began to flee the state. As an adult I've studied and written about the history of financial folly and lived and reported through a series of booms and spectacular busts: the dotcom explosion of the 1990s, the housing bubble, and the financial meltdown. A charter member of the gloom-and-doom caucus in 2006 and 2007, I wrote the January 2008 *Newsweek* cover story that suggested the U.S. economy was in recession—a full eight months before the economic establishment came around to that view. My perch at *Newsweek* afforded me a front-row seat at the meltdown of 2008. When I started at the magazine in July 2007, it was a profitable, $300 million-a-year business with four hundred employees. When I left in the fall of 2010, it was a money-losing $100 million-a-year business with a couple of hundred employees that was about to be sold to a ninety-one-year-old man, Sidney Harmon. For a dollar.

I know from decline.

So why am I optimistic that the United States can avoid a lost decade? I have several reasons.

The first is backward looking. As I've noted, the United States has been in similar situations many times before in its lengthy history and has always managed to come back. What's more, much of the hand-wringing of recent years has been freakishly ill-timed. By the time people started complaining about a lost decade in 2010, we had already had one. The time to worry that bad policy, poor regulation, corrupt banks, and a feckless administration would queer growth for a decade was in 2003 and 2005. In November 2011 there were 109.9 million private-sector payroll jobs in the United States—almost precisely the same number there were in October 1999. Stocks went nowhere between 1998 and 2010. Both the number and the percentage of people living below the poverty line rose, from 11.9 percent in 1999 to 14 percent in 2010. The nation's median income fell 5 percent from 1999 to 2009.[4]

The sheer breadth of the decline sentiment also offers reason for hope. If the American economy were a stock, every analyst would have a sell recommendation on it, and every major hedge fund would be shorting it. The declinists could all be right, of course. But that's not likely. When all the forces are arrayed against an asset or an idea and are invested in its falling, that's usually a pretty good sign it's about to rise. Many of the loudest proclamations of decline come from those who thought the period from 2001 to 2008 was a rip-roaring good time, the Bush Boom. The consensus is frequently wrong, especially the consensus of those who predict the near future. As Yogi Berra put it, "It's tough to make predictions. Especially about the future." Looking at their models in 2007, forecasters told us housing prices couldn't fall, the economy wouldn't lapse into recession, and all those subprime borrowers were good credit risks. The fraternity of seers who, in March 2009, saw the stock market rising back to 12,000 within two years was about as small as the exclusive club that saw it plummeting from 14,700 to 6,600 in the space of six months. The fellows who spend their days trying to figure out the direction of the economy always seem to be the last to know about a turn. In the fall of 2008 the professional forecasters surveyed by the Philadelphia Federal Reserve Bank said the economy would shrink at a 1.1 percent annual rate in the first quarter of 2009; instead it shrank at a 6.7 percent annual rate.[5] Oops!

A human factor is at work here. Muscle memory exerts a powerful hold on markets and economic actors. Once bad things happen, there's a natural tendency to think—and expect—that they will happen again. Many people who were burned during the Great Depression never again invested in stocks, thus missing out on powerful bull markets. An engine backfiring in lower Manhattan today provokes a much different set of reactions than it did in, say, September 2000. The deep recession of 2008–2009 has been one such searing, life-altering experience. As Ross DeVol of the Milken Institute noted, "The peak-to-trough decline in real GDP during this recession was 4.1 percent, making it the most severe downturn since World War II."[6]

The majority of people alive today, working, managing, investing, and commenting, have no experience of a recession this long and this deep. In the quarter-century from November 1982 to December 2007 there were only sixteen months of contraction, from July 1990 to March 1991, and from March 2001 to November 2001. These recessions were unusually shallow too, with 1.49 and 0.62 percent declines in output from peak to trough, respectively.[7] The only contraction worse than the one we just lived through was the Great Depression, a forty-three-month doozy that ran from August 1929 to March 1933. Our balance sheets, bank accounts, egos, and psyches simply weren't prepared for the depth and degree of shrinkage. Or for the slowness of the recovery. As Kenneth Rogoff and Carmen Reinhart document in *This Time Is Different*, not all recessions are created equal. Economies recover relatively quickly from downturns that are natural outcomes of the business cycle. Having produced too much or too exuberantly, companies idle capacity until inventories are worked down, and then reopen factories when demand rises again. By contrast, contractions precipitated by financial crises last longer, are slower to dissipate, and can retard economic growth for a decade.

It's common for exuberant projections to be made at the top of economic and market cycles. The book *Dow 36,000*, in which the authors James Glassman and Kevin Hassett proclaimed the Dow Jones Industrial Average could easily triple from its 12,000 level, was published in September 1999—just before the market took a big tumble. Just so, prophesies of long-term decline are usually issued only after we've suffered a catastrophic fall. In the spring of 1933 few New Deal critics believed that a bottom had been reached, that many of the programs and reforms would work, that the nation would rebuild itself and, ten years later, be in a position to lead the world to victory in the fight against tyranny—because nobody could imagine any of those events. From the uprising in Libya to the housing market, we live in an age of continual discontinuity. Predictions about what will happen in the economy over the next ten, twenty, or fifty years generally make their authors look like fools. Imagine a book written in 1990 that tried to look twenty years into the future. Would it have accounted for China? The Internet? 9/11? A $7 billion company named Zynga that involves fake farms on something called the Internet? The Kardashians?

It's tempting to think that history unfolds in a steady, linear path and that events are destined to happen. But as I learned twenty years ago in the basement of Robinson Hall at Harvard University, in a seminar with the great colonial historian Bernard Bailyn, we must regard history—and the present—as contingent. At any moment things can go either way. On the morning of July 1, 1863, it was entirely possible that the Union would falter at Gettysburg. A century later, on November 22, 1963, it was entirely possible that Lee Harvey Oswald's aim would not be true. As late as 2006 it was still entirely possible that the worst of the subprime crisis could have been averted. After the fact we ascribe a pattern and logic to events that were not apparent when they were happening. It's entirely possible the United States is doomed never to recover from the self-inflicted economic wounds of 2008–2009. It is also entirely possible—even more, entirely plausible and probable—that it will get past them in time.

There are also real, observed, fact-based reasons to be skeptical of decline. Although the United States may be in bad shape, the rest of the world stinks too. Japan really seems to be in terminal decline. In 2006 official New York was in a tizzy about concerns that London, with its light-touch regulatory scheme and rampant hedge funds, would overtake Manhattan as a financial center. The consulting firm McKinsey issued an alarming report, commissioned by New York City's mayor Michael Bloomberg and Senator Charles Schumer of New York State. The big recommendation: to avoid losing ground to the Brits, the United States should ease up on regulation of the banks! Two years later London's financial system swamped Britain's economy, which is still waterlogged with bad debt, ownership of major financial institutions, and a government whose austerity measures are promoting stagnation. How about Europe? In 2004 the journalist T. R. Reid published *The United States of Europe: The New Superpower and the End of American Supremacy*. With Europe united in a common trading bloc, he argued, this new agglomeration of power, a force with a population and economy as large as America's, would rule the future. After all, it had better social programs, a high degree of wealth, and the advantages of integration on trade and monetary policy. Why, there was nothing France, Germany, Spain, Italy, and Greece couldn't do. Except, it turns out, create jobs, pay their bills, get along, and stay solvent. The new conventional wisdom, as Floyd Norris of the *New York Times* wrote in the spring of 2011, holds, "It is hard to see how the euro zone can be undone, but it is even harder to see how it will prosper."[8]

In his 2008 book, *The Post-American World*, Fareed Zakaria, editor of *Newsweek International*, convincingly asserted that the developing world will play a greater role in the global economy and in geopolitical affairs. But as impressive as the growth of the BRIC nations—Brazil, Russia, India, and China—has been, they are still way behind the United States, and they are still extremely poor. With a combined population of 2.85 billion, the BRIC countries had a combined GDP of $11 trillion in 2010, about $3,860 per person. The United States, with 311 million people, managed to produce nearly $15 trillion in GDP in 2010, or $48,000 per capita. The gap between the United States and these developing economies is so vast that they will need a few more decades of uninterrupted growth before their citizens' standard of living truly matches that of Americans.

Just as they ignored the weaknesses of Japan in the 1980s, today's fatalists ignore the brittleness of the Chinese juggernaut. China has plenty of problems. The state bailed out many of its largest financial institutions in 2004, and ghost cities built with bad debt are likely to stimulate another round of bank bailouts. Wage inflation is causing a chunk of its manufacturing base to lose its cost advantage. Corruption and theft are widespread, and shoddy standards of business practice prevail in everything from drywall to high-speed rail to accounting. From Ai Weiwei, the artist who was briefly imprisoned, to the villagers of Fukan, who expelled corrupt officials in the fall of 2011, citizens are questioning the regime's legitimacy. China has a set of rather blunt and crude instruments it can use to deal with challenges: when prices go up, it puts in price controls; when the regime fretted about food shortages and overpopulation, it instituted a one-child policy and ruthlessly enforced it for thirty years; in 2011 the government canceled *Super Girl,* China's version of *American Idol,* because the concept of voting for a favorite pop star was dangerously close to the concept of, say, voting for leaders directly. And then there's that whole freedom and human rights thing.

Even the Chinese are pessimistic about the prospects of middle-class people enjoying a decent life. In late 2010 a viral email circulated lamenting how long people would need to work to afford a small apartment in central Beijing, which was then going for about $450,000. "As long as there were no natural disasters, a peasant farmer working an average plot of land would just have been able to afford an apartment if he or she somehow had worked from the Tang Dynasty, which ended in A.D. 907, until now. Prostitutes would have to entertain 10,000 customers."[9]

But the real reason for optimism isn't simply that declinists have been wrong in the past, or that the other economies that are supposed to seize the mantle of leadership from the United States aren't in great shape. No, just as it overlooks the *relative* strength of the United States and its rivals, the case for decline overlooks the *intrinsic, enduring* strengths of the United States. Excuse me while I put on my American Exceptionalism cap. America has been, and remains, unique—politically and economically—in the way it responds and reacts to crisis, in the way its public and private sectors act, and in the way its private sector innovates and find opportunities. In late 2010 I asked Treasury Secretary Timothy Geithner which country's problems he'd rather have: America's or China's. A "duh" expression crossed his faced. "No one's," he replied. That could have been an administration official giving the party line. But there are times when the party line and the truth intersect. This was one of them.

The United States came out of the global recession better, stronger, and faster than most of its peers—and better, stronger, and faster than most observers expected. And it remains the largest, most prosperous, and most interesting economic market. Metrics like business investment, exports, car production, industrial production, retail sales, and savings rate all rose significantly from 2009 through 2011. Default rates, delinquency rates, corporate failures, and bank closings all fell significantly in the same period. Whenever something bad happens in the world—revolts in the Middle East, a tsunami in Japan, a fiscal crisis in Greece—investors around the world rush to dollar-denominated assets. At a time of widespread pessimism, America was still attracting new citizens from abroad and manufacturing them at home. In 2009 and 2010, 1.13 million and 1.04 million immigrants, respectively, obtained legal permanent resident status. But nothing says more about attitudes toward the future than a country's birthrate. In 2011 Japan's fertility rate was 1.21 per woman; in the United States it was 2.05.[10]

The bad news bears presume that America is incapable of rebuilding itself. But the rebuilding has already begun. In getting back on its feet, the country rediscovered the competitive advantages it has long had, advantages that lay dormant during the credit and housing boom. In February 2011 Mary Meeker, who gained fame as an Internet stock analyst at Morgan Stanley in the 1990s and has since evolved into a venture capitalist, issued what was meant to be a 466-page report evaluating the United States as if it were a stock. Meeker is remembered for having slapped buy recommendations on dot-com stocks and never changing her mind even as the market plummeted. As Peter Elkind wrote in *Fortune* in May 2001, "Among the stocks she has never downgraded are Priceline, Amazon, Yahoo, and FreeMarkets—all of which have declined between 85% and 97% from their peak." Meeker concluded that America's liabilities vastly outweighed its assets. But she ignored some of America's tangible assets, such as the nation's holdings of gold and its huge stock market capitalization. And she ignored many of the nation's intangible assets, like the ability to conjure up giant global Internet companies from nothing. In the summer of 2011 I was at a dinner with Tung Chee Hwa, the billionaire shipping magnate and former chief executive of Hong Kong, and a handful of journalists. When one of my colleagues mentioned Meeker's analysis, he was somewhat incredulous. "What about America's earning power?" he asked.[11]

Indeed Meeker's analysis was about as rigorous and as sound as many of her 1990s-vintage reports on dot-com stocks. Still, the bears have their story and they are sticking to it. The miasma of bad news and gloom has permitted a host of assumptions to take root in the narrative surrounding the U.S. economy:

- The United States didn't react with sufficient speed to the collapse of 2008. Policymakers, the private sector, and consumers simply kicked the can down the road, denied reality, and papered over problems.
- The United States is tapped out and lacks the physical, emotional, and natural resources to fund and drive its own renewal and recovery. As other countries enjoy rampant growth and trade with each other, the United States is turning into a forgotten backwater. It is unable to attract investment from overseas and doesn't make anything the world wants.
- The United States has lost the ability to build innovations into global businesses. And Americans lack the cultural sensitivity to integrate into local markets and fully participate in global growth.

- The American consumer is a spent force, incapable of assisting in the recovery of the economy or the development of new business models.
- America is in decline.

As we'll see in coming chapters, none of these statements is accurate.

The reality-based case for optimism rests in large measure on an understanding of America's core competencies and competitive advantages: attitudes, habits, and capabilities that, even in this age of globalization, remain unique. Yes, the United States has proved in recent years that it's better than other countries at blowing systems up. But we've also learned that it is better at recovering, at recognizing and confronting new realities, at developing and executing decisive policies, at processing failure and moving on. The rescue plans and recovery efforts of 2008 and 2009 were conceived on the fly, and they were haphazard and painful. But the bailouts, stimulus, and private-sector restructuring efforts got the country back on the path to growth, unsatisfying as it has been. In fact, U.S. companies and consumers, with an assist from policymakers, proved adept at restructuring rapidly and shucking debt. Jim O'Neill, the London-based Goldman Sachs economist who coined the term BRIC, hasn't given up on the United States. "Crucially, the post–credit bubble collapse doesn't seem to have left some other powerful attributes of the U.S. economy severely damaged," he wrote in the *Financial Times* in January 2011. "Another wonderful attribute of the U.S. is the decisiveness of policymaking, despite frequent evidence to the contrary in Congress." These abilities helped the public and private sectors to put the brakes on the epic fail of late 2008 and early 2009 and propelled the beginnings of a recovery. If embraced more broadly, systematically, and wholeheartedly, they can sustain a lengthy expansion. While growth has been fitful since the recovery began in July 2009, and the economy seems to be in constant danger of slipping back into recession, there's no reason to think that America's ability to grow is permanently impaired.

Modern-day declinism rests on a simplistic view that all the structural forces transforming the global economy are arrayed against us.

But that's not true. In fact, many of them work in America's favor. In viewing global growth as a zero-sum game, declinists underestimate the ability of the United States to benefit from the developments sweeping the world. Far from being a victim of global growth, the country has been a beneficiary of it. Since the recession, the United States has continued to lead the world in foreign direct investment, to lead the world in exports, and to develop new types of exports. American companies have successfully planted their flags in booming foreign markets. In recent years, as in the past, the U.S. private sector has shown a great ability to innovate, to create new business models and take them to global scale, and, most important, to engage with the world. Meanwhile, changes in the global economy are spurring some jobs that left the country to return and are leading a larger number of foreign companies to hire in the United States. American companies are still creating new economic ecosystems that invite and encourage further investment.

The next several years are going to be a period of digging out, cleaning up, and reorienting. There may not be another zero-down mortgage in our lifetime, but as Senator Al Franken would say in his Stuart Smalley voice, that's okay. Markets can move sideways for long periods of time. That's okay too. Between 1929 and 1954, when the Dow Jones Industrial Average essentially didn't budge, the economy nearly quadrupled and the nation won a war, rebuilt Western Europe, and developed, among other things, television, the first computer, and nuclear power. The U.S. economy did just fine for the many decades in which home values rose at the rate of inflation. Without the artificial juice of debt, Americans may have to work harder to get ahead. It's like going from riding an electric bike downhill, with the wind behind you, to pedaling a 21-speed into an incline with the wind in your face. Harder, but definitely possible.

The United States may not have as big a role in the global economy as it had before. That's okay too. In assessing America's economic prospects, it is necessary to differentiate between relative decline and absolute decline. The shape of the world's economic geography is shifting significantly. For much of the twentieth century it did so in ways that were really advantageous to us. World War I led to the transfer of financial leadership and markets across the Atlantic from the United Kingdom. After World War II, during which the rest of the developed world pretty much destroyed itself, the United States was left as the undisputed political and industrial leader. The dominance of communism and socialism in the world's most populous countries had the same effect as force-feeding a couple of generations there with lead paint. In 2000, with only 4 percent of the world's population, the United States accounted for 30 percent of the world's economy, and its principal stock exchanges accounted for about half of the world's stock market capitalization—a stunning achievement that stemmed in large measure from the widespread avoidance of capitalism in many of the world's largest countries. By 2010, however, thanks largely to rampant global growth, the United States, still with about 4 percent of the world's population, accounted for 28 percent of the world's economy and 32 percent of its stock market capitalization. This relative decline is likely to continue.[12]

At some point in this decade, China, whose economy was one-eighth the size of America's in 2000, and about one-third the size in 2011, may well overtake the United States in aggregate economic output. But China has five times as many people as the United States has. And even when it outproduces America, China will remain a poorer place—culturally, financially, socially, and politically—than the United States for decades to come.

This changing economic geography, by the way, should be celebrated. It means that the rest of the world is doing its share of consuming and producing. With each passing year, tens of millions of people around the world are rising from abject poverty to mere poverty, and from mere poverty to a semblance of middle-class life. Far from detracting from America's economic status, this development has the ability to enhance it.

Focusing only on failures of policy, government, and politics can easily lead one down the path of decline. Yes, suboptimal policymakers and incorrigible bankers are holding America back. But it's difficult to think of a period when economists, historians, and political scientists agreed that the fiscal policy, regulation of banking, and financial sector were good and useful. We forget that Chester Arthur served a term as president of this country, that Richard

Nixon ran the show for six years, and that George W. Bush was in charge for eight years. There's much more to recent economic history than mendacious bankers and pathetic politicians.

It's hard to see what will propel the United States forward. And that's okay too. In modern-day recessions the force that drives the economy into the ditch is never the one that gets it out. In fact, that force is, by definition, almost entirely unforeseen, sometimes even unimaginable. Former treasury secretary Larry Summers tells a story about an event in 1992. After the election of Bill Clinton, the best minds in the country assembled in Little Rock to discuss how to get the economy moving again. Having spent twelve years in the wilderness, the Democratic policy elite was plotting a return to greatness. There was talk about education and trade policy, hours of discussion and thousands of papers, much posturing and bloviating. In all the miles of position papers, Summers recalls, one term was conspicuously absent: the Internet.

I believe not only that a recovery will materialize, but that the elements and ingredients for a recovery already exist. I've seen them.

In the past several years, I've been to five continents, two dozen countries, and thirty-five U.S. states. These travels have given me a chance to see firsthand many of the trends that are shaping our world. I've spent time with oil CEOs in Houston and solar panel makers in Boulder. I've visited a Prius factory in Japan and a bustling Chang'an-Ford auto plant in Chongqing, China, gas turbine factories in South Carolina and a business process outsourcing outpost in Bogotá, Colombia. I've chatted about the credit crunch with Warren Buffett and Blackstone Group's chairman Stephen Schwarzman. I've toured thriving fish factories outside Saigon, publishing offices in Istanbul, gas stations in Soweto, and an aluminum smelter on a glacial fjord in eastern Iceland. I've interviewed small-town bankers and private equity magnates, American executives at Indian wind-turbine makers and Indian executives at American computer companies; dined at Davos with Nissan CEO Carlos Ghosn; and interviewed managers of 99-cent stores in Upper Manhattan. I've spent a lot of time rooting around, like a pig in search of truffles, for data, stories, trends, and facts that might point in a positive direction.

And I've turned up plenty. What I've seen around the United States, and around the world, has reinforced my belief in the potential of the U.S. economy to grow and lead. This work has led me to believe that if the United States does enter a period of stagnation and decline, it won't be because of inevitable, vast structural forces. It will be by choice.

CHAPTER 3

Faster: Policy

After an economic downturn and financial crisis that were the worst in at least three generations, the United States avoided tough, swift decisions. Instead of dealing with reality and confronting problems head-on, policymakers, companies, and consumers kicked the can down the road. Faced with a glaring need for what the sociologist Richard Florida called a "Great Reset," America chose to hit the pause button. When the policy efforts came, they were too little (or too much, depending on where you sit ideologically), too late, too slow, and too ineffective. The bailouts and stimulus efforts were expensive, poorly designed failures. Economic setbacks may be nothing new in American history. But the failure to react, bounce back, and improve certainly seems to be.

These assumptions lie at the heart of the case for American economic decline. They're also largely wrong.

The economic and market lows of March 2009 didn't mark the beginning of an era of irreversible stagnation. Rather they marked the beginning of an unexpected and largely unforecasted recovery. Instead of persisting for years, the recession that started in December 2008 ended in June 2009. In the first quarter of 2009 the U.S. economy, we now know, was shrinking at a 6.7 percent annual rate. By the fall of 2009 it was expanding at a 3.8 percent annual rate. That's a change in the rate of annual growth of 10.5 percent in a six-month period—unprecedented in modern history. Objectively speaking, in the aggregate, the United States has come back better, stronger, and faster than its peers. In June 2011 Martin Wolf, the sage *Financial Times* columnist, wrote, "Of the six biggest advanced economies—the U.S., Japan, Germany, France, the U.K. and Italy—only the U.S. and Germany had higher gross domestic product in the first quarter of 2011 than three years before." Three years after the September 2008 meltdown, the United States was leaving its credit mess behind. By contrast, Europe was headed into a fall of discontent, fueled by raging debt and political crises.

Since unemployment was at 9 percent, Wolf wrote, "the fact that the U.S. had the highest GDP, relative to its starting point, of these six countries, may be a surprise to some." There shouldn't be any surprise. America's rapid bounce back was fueled by a resilient private sector that quickly figured out new ways to engage with the world and to innovate. But a rapid, decisive, and effective—or sufficiently effective—policy response was the precondition for a return to growth. During and after the crisis America's *public sector* responded with alacrity. In the years of the credit boom, U.S. policy failures were legion, especially around housing and financial regulation. But practical—and above all, rapid—policy moves had a lot to do with the turnaround of 2009. If the criterion for a successful policy response was a swift return to the prevailing economic conditions of 2006 and 2007—unemployment rates of 5 percent, easy credit, rising house prices—then the post-bust policy response clearly failed. But if the goal was to stop the worst decline in eighty years, ward off a second Great Depression, salvage the financial system and auto industry, and create the conditions that would bring the U.S. economy back to its prior peak, then the bailout and stimulus succeeded. The response was far better than what was seen in the United Kingdom and the Eurozone in this decade, and better than what was seen in Japan in the 1990s.

In the summer of 2009 I met with Kiyohiko Nishimura, deputy governor of the Bank of Japan, in Tokyo. Nishimura, who received his PhD from Yale, noted that there was a "remarkable resemblance in developments between the U.S. crisis and Japan's 'lost decade.'" Having spent a week getting acquainted with the depopulating, self-doubting country, I gulped hard. But Nishimura's takeaway was an optimistic one. In the 1990s Japanese policymakers deliberated and delayed before embarking on a regime of interest rate cuts, stimulus measures, an expansion of bank deposit insurance, a partial nationalization of failed institutions, bank capital injections, a zero-interest-rate policy, quantitative easing, and still more stimulus. The United States, he said, had essentially undertaken the same response, with one significant difference: speed. It took the United States just eighteen months to conduct the aggressive fiscal and monetary actions that Japan waited twelve years to carry out. Whereas Japan's first major stimulus came seven quarters after its commercial real estate bubble peaked, the U.S. policymaking apparatus responded to the downturn much more quickly.

The Bush administration was guilty of many sins of omission and neglect, and it was chronically late to react to the bursting housing bubble and downturn. But it didn't simply sit on its hands as the economy began to contract. In February 2008, just two months after the recession started, President Bush signed the $152 billion Economic Stimulus Act of 2008, a package of individual tax rebates, business tax cuts, and aid to the mortgage market. President Obama's much larger stimulus, the American Recovery and Reinvestment Act, was signed on February 17, 2009, the twenty-eighth day of his administration. Designed to roll out over three years, the $787 billion package of tax cuts for individuals and businesses, aid to states, and spending and investment programs has been widely panned as a failure by both the left *and* the right. But this is largely due to the economic establishment's misapprehension and the depth of the downturn. In early 2009 stimulus advocates argued that, were the bill to be passed, the unemployment rate would peak at 8 percent in 2009 before falling to below 7 percent in late 2010. Instead the unemployment rate lingered at about 9 percent through the end of 2011. This assumption was wrong, in large part because, at the time, the sheer horror of job loss and short-term economic contraction in late 2008 and early 2009 was seriously underestimated. In fact, the worst of the shrinkage was yet to come, with the loss of 3.9 million jobs in the first half of 2009. Projections made three months later would have started from a significantly lower baseline and led to promises that would have seemed less extravagant.

The broad middle agrees that the stimulus achieved a large chunk of its intended goal of boosting demand, growth, and employment. In a November 2010 report on the stimulus, the White House Council of Economic Advisers concluded that the measure had created or preserved between 2.7 million and 3.7 million jobs. The Congressional Budget Office's May 2011 report showed a similar result: real GDP was higher in the first quarter of 2011 by 1.1 to 3.1 percent, unemployment was lower by between 0.6 and 1.8 percentage points, and somewhere between 1.6 million and 4.6 million jobs had been created. The economist Mark Zandi of Moody's Analytics, an advisor to the 2008 Republican presidential candidate John McCain, and Alan Blinder, the Princeton economist and former Clinton administration official, concluded in a joint study entitled "How the Great Recession Was Brought to an End" that in 2010 the stimulus boosted real GDP by 3.4 percent, cut unemployment by 1.5 percentage points, and created almost 2.7 million jobs.[1]

Could the package of tax cuts, spending, and aid to the states have been designed better? Should it have been bigger? And did the projections suffer from poor timing? Yes, yes, and yes. Many on the left, most notably Paul Krugman, argued, correctly, that from the very beginning the effort wasn't commensurate to the task. But the talking point embraced by Republicans—that the stimulus failed, and in doing so delegitimized the whole concept of trying to boost demand through spending and tax cuts—is absurd. Let's assume forecasters believe a flood will crest at twenty feet above the river's normal level, and officials build sandbags to a level of twenty-two feet. When the river instead rises to twenty-five feet and the area remains underwater for months after the flood, we wouldn't conclude that using sandbags to mitigate flooding was misguided and that we should never repeat such a folly. No, we'd conclude that we didn't pile them high enough. Like placing sandbags along the Missouri River, the stimulus was a quick, pragmatic response that achieved its intended result to a significant degree.

Cleaning up the financial mess called for a policy response that was much larger than the stimulus. Like the stimulus, the bailout and rescue efforts have been panned by people all across the political spectrum. And like the stimulus, the government's market interventions and backstops also represented a quick, largely effective, and pragmatic response. Between 2001 and 2008 the distinguishing factor of monetary and financial policy was the triumph of ideology over pragmatism. Once the financial crisis hit, the reaction marked a shift away from ideology and a rediscovery of pragmatism, the original American philosophy. Where Alan Greenspan idolized the libertarian goddess Ayn Rand, his successor, Ben Bernanke, seemed to look to the 1980s TV action hero MacGyver as a role model: he would patch markets together with gumballs, pine needles, and a paper clip. Henry Paulson, the former chief executive of Goldman Sachs who served as treasury secretary in the latter years of the Bush administration, was similarly willing to dispense with ideological purity for the sake of saving the system that had enriched him. His co-conspirator and later successor, Timothy Geithner, who was president of the New York Federal Reserve Bank during the depths of the crisis, hewed to a similar whatever-it-takes creed. The dispensation with ideology in the face of crisis stands in stark contrast to the more orthodox approaches taken by European and British policymakers in 2010 and 2011.

As Wall Street imploded, the Federal Reserve and the Treasury Department engaged in a range of expensive and unprecedented moves. In March 2008 they helped JPMorgan Chase take over an ailing Bear Stearns, with the Fed lending $30 billion to a newly created investment partnership that would acquire dodgy assets from the listing Bear. It was called Maiden Lane I, after the narrow street in lower Manhattan that runs near the Fed's New York branch.[2] In the long, hot summer of 2008 Treasury and the Fed rushed to the aid of AIG, the massive insurer whose reckless extension of credit insurance on mortgage debt threatened to sink it, its counterparties, and the global financial system. In September 2008 Treasury formally assumed responsibility for the trillions of dollars of debt issued by the housing behemoths Fannie Mae and Freddie Mac, a move intended to shore up the banking system. In the weeks and months after Lehman Brothers collapsed in September 2008, the bailout machine kicked into higher gear. Between them, the Fed, the Treasury, the Federal Deposit Insurance Corporation, and, by implication, American taxpayers guaranteed pretty much every credit-related security ever concocted by an MBA with a bent toward financial engineering. The Fed opened its lending windows to all comers: international banks, high-flying investment banks, pretty much every type of bank except blood and sperm banks. Thanks to *Bloomberg*'s intrepid reporting and litigation, we know that the Fed made available up to $7.7 trillion in total credit and guarantees to banks and other financial institutions. The government bought hundreds of billions of dollars of shares in America's banks, took stakes in the nation's largest and third-largest automakers, and put nearly $185 billion at risk to keep afloat one single insurer, the cataclysmic AIG.

The actions represented an enormous risk and a desperate gamble: guarantee everything, hope the panic passes, and give the sectors time to get their house in order. In so doing Bernanke, Paulson, Geithner, and the Bush and Obama administrations put taxpayers on the hook for trillions of dollars in liabilities. The week before Lehman Brothers went down, on September 11, 2008, the Fed's assets were about $925 billion. By the time President Obama entered office in January 2009, its balance sheet—the stated total of its financial obligations—stood at $2.041 trillion.[3]

By and large, however, the bailouts worked, and at comparatively little cost to taxpayers. The swift action essentially stopped the panic. In late 2008 and early 2009 the government morphed into a massive insurance company. And unlike AIG, it turned out to be pretty good at this. It's little known or reported, but virtually all the blanket guarantees offered by the Fed, the Treasury Department, and the FDIC were lifted without being used. The overwhelming majority of the liabilities they assumed melted away.

In March 2008 the Fed lent $30 billion to Maiden Lane, the vehicle created to acquire junky Bear Stearns assets at panic-level prices. As credit markets reflated, Maiden Lane recovered sufficient value and income from those assets to pay down the debt—and turn a profit for the Federal Reserve. By the end of 2011 the $30 billion loan had been reduced to $4 billion, and Maiden Lane still had assets worth about $7.2 billion.

The week that Lehman Brothers failed, the Treasury Department started a program to guarantee the $3.4 trillion money market fund industry. It collected $1.2 billion in fees from operators of money market funds and didn't pay a single claim before the guarantee was lifted in September 2009. In November 2008 the Federal Deposit Insurance Corporation, an independent agency ultimately backstopped by taxpayers, threw a huge lifeline to the banking industry by offering to guarantee the debt of financial services companies—for a fee. Banks took advantage of the low rates and quickly issued more than $313 billion in debt under the Temporary Liquidity Guarantee Program. The FDIC collected $10.36 billion in fees, closed the TLGP to new entrants in June 2009, and through December 2011 had yet to pay out a penny. In the wake of the Lehman Brothers meltdown, the commercial paper market, which companies tap to borrow funds for thirty or ninety days, seized up. In October 2008 the Fed offered to guarantee this vital short-term credit market, in exchange for fees paid by borrowers. The Commercial Paper Funding Facility, which held more than $350 billion at its peak in January 2009, expired in February 2010 and generated $5 billion in profits for the Fed. The Fed backstopped the market for newly issued asset-backed securities like car loans and credit card receivables by creating the Term Asset-Backed Securities Loan Facility in late 2008. TALF's assets peaked at $48 billion in March 2010 and steadily declined to about $9 billion at the end of 2011. In 2009 and 2010, through fees and interest, TALF generated $721 million in profits for the Fed, which didn't pay out a dime in guarantees.[4]

These efforts were short-term emergency interventions to unclog the nation's—and the world's—financial plumbing. Other interventions were made to keep interest rates low and to jolt the economy back into life. After the financial panic passed, the Federal Reserve continued to add new assets to its balance sheet, creating new money to buy $1 trillion in mortgage-backed securities in 2009, in the first round of what came to be known as "quantitative easing" (QE). In late 2010 and early 2011, in a second round of quantitative easing, the Fed bought $600 billion in Treasury securities. But the overall balance sheet didn't expand by anywhere near $1.6 trillion as a result of QE1 and QE2, thanks to the slow-motion erosion of crisis-era facilities and loans. Each week, as people made payments on mortgages and refinanced and sold homes, the mortgage-backed securities portfolio shrank. Holdings of mortgage-backed securities, which peaked on June 24, 2010, at $1.128 trillion, fell to $849 billion by November 2011—without any losses. It's little understood, but the Federal Reserve is like a very profitable bank that turns over profits to the taxpayer. And because virtually all the loans it made in 2008 and 2009 were paid back, and because Fannie Mae, Freddie Mac, and the U.S. government made good on all the bonds they had issued that were bought by the Fed, the central bank turned over a combined $205.5 billion in profits to Treasury between 2009 and 2011.[5]

The scope of the aid to AIG was as breathtaking as it was highly convoluted. In September 2008 the Fed extended an $85 billion line of credit to the company. Meanwhile the Treasury bought $40 billion of preferred stock in AIG in November 2008, and in March 2009 it said it would make up to $30 billion available to the company in the form of new stock. But almost at once plans were made to exit from the interventions. In March 2009 AIG turned over two of its crown jewels, AIA (Asian insurance operations) and Alico (its U.S. life insurance unit), to the Federal Reserve in exchange for converting $25 billion of the funds borrowed from the Fed into preferred shares in the two subsidiaries. The plan was that once markets recovered, AIG would sell these two units and use the proceeds to pay back the Fed. It made good on these promises. In October 2010 it executed an initial public offering of AIA, raising $20.5 billion, and in November 2010 it sold Alico to MetLife for $16.2 billion. AIG used the proceeds to pay down $20 billion in credit to the Fed in January 2011. In the interim the Treasury paid back the remaining loan AIG had taken from the Fed and then converted its interests in AIG into common shares worth 92 percent of the company. Next AIG set about returning cash to the Treasury. Over the course of 2011 AIG raised cash from selling subsidiaries and common shares and turned over some of the proceeds to taxpayers. By the end of 2011 Treasury had received $15.45 billion of the $67.84 billion it put into AIG, and still owned 1.455 billion common shares of the company.[6]

Separately, in November 2008, the Fed created two investment vehicles to remove toxic assets from AIG's balance sheets. The first, dubbed Maiden Lane II, borrowed $19.5 billion from the Fed and bought $20.8 billion in mortgage-backed securities at half of their original price. The second, Maiden Lane III, borrowed $24.3 billion from the Fed and bought a portfolio of collateralized debt obligations from former AIG customers, also at about half their face value. As the credit markets recovered, the investment vehicles — essentially hedge funds with concentrated positions — generated enough income to pay off the loans, and the Fed sold off chunks of the assets held by the Maiden Lane entities. The upshot? By the first quarter of 2012 Maiden Lane II had paid off the entire $19.5 billion loan, and Maiden Lane III was down to $8.9 billion in debt to the Fed, supported by assets worth $17.7 billion. Together they are likely to return profits to the Federal Reserve of between $4 billion and $5 billion, which will be turned over to the Treasury.

The taxpayers are still likely to notch a loss on their investment in AIG, but it'll be a small fraction of the total laid out — and much smaller than anticipated.

Make no mistake: AIG, and the larger bailout program of which it was a component, the Troubled Asset Relief Program, was a debacle, a travesty, and a mockery of all that is good and true. TARP has been widely dismissed as a $700 billion fiasco. But here again, the policy succeeded more quickly than anticipated and at a direct cost to taxpayers that was much less than advertised or feared. Just look at the numbers: while around $700 billion was authorized, only $413 billion went out the door. The parts of the program that were designed to be loans and investments were generally repaid — with interest. And the components that were designed as pure expenditures weren't all spent. Of the $30 billion earmarked for mortgage modification, for example (essentially checks written to banks to help them write down mortgage principal), only $2.5 billion was actually spent.[7]

In 1930 and 1931, in the absence of comprehensive backstops, banks liquidated and destroyed their shareholders, creditors, and depositors. This time around, banks would be given several quarters to rebuild balance sheets by boosting earnings (and retaining them), or by raising new capital. The participants in the Capital Purchase Program, the central component of the TARP, didn't just sit around after receiving cash. After all, the CPP funds came with carrots and sticks. The investment took the form of preferred shares, which required banks to make 5 percent annual interest payments. Banks also had to give Treasury warrants that entitled the holder to buy shares at a set price, as a kind of sweetener. The government told banks they couldn't pay dividends or unjustly enrich their executives until they shored up capital, which is a little like telling five-year-olds they can't have candy unless they clean their rooms. And so the banks moved faster. In 2009 and 2010 they slashed dividends, raised capital, took losses, and changed the way they did business. Instead of letting banks put off the day of reckoning (as Japan had done), in the spring of 2009 the Treasury Department insisted on stress tests—just seven months after providing the capital. Similar to stress tests for heart patients, these tests were designed to gauge the ability of banks to withstand difficult conditions. Banks were required to run exercises under which they and federal examiners would assess how their balance sheets would perform under adverse economic conditions, and figure out what they would need to do to survive the next downturn. Between May 2009, when the Treasury announced the stress tests, and November 2009, nine of the ten large banks ordered by the Fed to raise capital boosted cash by a combined $70 billion. On June 17, 2009, ten months after the program started, ten huge banks, including Chase, Goldman, Morgan Stanley, and Wells Fargo, showed up on Treasury Secretary Geithner's doorstep to repay $70 billion—about 29 percent of total CPP funds.

Even the worst managed of the big banks, the institutions that had the toxic combination of massive size and massively incompetent managers, were able to right themselves. Citigroup and Bank of America, the two largest banks in the United States before the crisis, with a combined $3.7 trillion in assets in 2008, were so horribly exposed to bad loans that they were in danger of being nationalized. Citigroup took $25 billion in initial CPP funds in October 2008 and another $20 billion at the end of December. In addition, Treasury agreed to insure a chunk of Citigroup's assets in exchange for fees totaling about $2.2 billion, which at the time seemed a little like selling life insurance on a Stage 4 cancer patient. It took a while, but Citigroup made good on these investments. It paid back the $20 billion in December 2009. In July 2009 the Treasury converted its $25 billion initial investment into common shares, which it sold into the market between April and December 2010 at a substantial profit, bringing in $31.85 billion. The taxpayers also pocketed the insurance premiums. In all, $45 billion went out to Citigroup, and $54.6 billion came back. Bank of America had a similar happy ending for taxpayers. It took $15 billion in CPP funds in the first round in October 2008 and another $30 billion in early January 2009. In December 2009 it paid back the entire $45 billion, and Treasury reaped another $1.56 billion from selling the warrants it had received.

In August 2009 not even the most cockeyed optimists could have projected that, within four months, Bank of America, Citigroup, and Wells Fargo would return nearly $100 billion in borrowed funds to the taxpayers. But that's what happened. And the process of recovery and repayment continued. By the end of 2011, while several large banks still owed sizable chunks—they included Regions Financial ($3.5 billion), and Zions Bank ($1.4 billion)—the Capital Purchase Program was winding down. Total up the dividends, interest, and funds received from selling warrants granted to the Treasury, and the CPP turned in a better three-year performance than many hedge funds. Between the CPP and the extra aid to Citigroup and Bank of America, $245 billion had gone out. Of that, by the end of 2011, $225 billion of capital had been returned, with only $2.58 billion written off as losses. Dividends, shares, and warrant sales brought in another $33 billion in cash, leading to a profit of $14.4 billion. There was still $17 billion in capital outstanding and more dividends arriving each month. The central component of the TARP had clearly turned a profit.

Compare that with what happened in Europe. In Ireland three massive banks required a bailout equal to about one-third of the country's 2009 GDP. In November 2008 the United Kingdom formed its version of TARP, U.K. Financial Investments, to take stakes in the Royal Bank of Scotland, Lloyds, and two other, smaller banks. In 2008 it injected £37 billion, about $60 billion, into RBS and Lloyds. A year later a second round, of £31.3 billion in public funds ($51 billion) for the two banks, brought the total to $111 billion and left the state owning 84 percent of RBS and 43 percent of Lloyds. But England's banking system didn't bounce back as rapidly as the American system—not by a long shot. RBS and Lloyds were unable to repay the funds, leaving the British taxpayers underwater on the big stakes they held in the banks. At the end of 2011 the combined value of U.K. Financial Investments' share in RBS and Lloyds was £37.5 billion (about $60 billion) *below* the sum paid for them.[8] France and Germany bailed out many of their banks in 2008 and 2009, in part because of these banks' exposure to U.S. subprime loans. But in 2011 the European powers were poised to bail out their banks again, this time because of the banks' exposure to European debt.

Consider the turnaround in the fortunes of the U.S. banking system. Institutions insured by the FDIC racked up a colossal $37.8 billion collective loss in the fourth quarter of 2008. Buoyed by government aid and shocked into action, the sector returned to profitability in the first quarter of 2010, and it hasn't looked back. In the second quarter of 2011 institutions insured by the FDIC earned a combined profit of $28.8 billion. In 2008 only twenty-five banks failed. But since that number included the mammoth Washington Mutual, which had $307 billion in assets, 2008 was a record year for bank failures when measured by assets. In 2009 the 140 banks that failed had combined assets of $170 billion. In 2010 the pace of bank failures picked up, to 157. But the systemic and macroeconomic impact of these failures was significantly smaller. The average bank that failed in 2010 was about half the size of the average bank that failed in 2009. Together the 157 banks that failed in 2010 had assets of $92 billion. In 2011 both the number and the size of banks that failed fell further still. For the full year, only 92 banks with combined assets of $34.7 billion failed.[9]

In 2009 and 2010, as the pace of bank failures picked up, the FDIC's deposit insurance fund went into the red. But the banks effectively funded their own bailouts by replenishing the fund, in part thanks to another quickly implemented policy that was largely overlooked: the October 2008 decision to put higher premiums into place. At the height of the crisis, the FDIC told the wayward banks that they'd have to pony up more to fund their own bailouts; for banks in decent shape, the average premium rose from 6.3 cents per $1,000 of deposits to 13.5 cents. Bolstered by these higher premium payments and receding payouts for failed banks, the FDIC deposit insurance fund returned to a positive balance in June 2011. Once the panic passed, banks quickly restored their ability to avoid failure, to avert massive losses, and to replenish the fund that would insure them against their own future failures. While the banks remain dependent on cheap money from the Federal Reserve, the era of direct aid has largely ended.

Aid to the auto industry was one of the smaller components of the TARP, but it was perhaps its most controversial. The aid to General Motors and Chrysler caused a great deal of political ruckus and debate, in part because it involved only two companies and an intense government involvement in the bankruptcy process. Ideology and orthodoxy would have recommended cutting the companies loose and letting creative destruction work its wonders. But simply letting General Motors and Chrysler go into unsupervised bankruptcy and an almost certain liquidation in 2009 would have been irresponsible and disastrous—not just for the employees of GM and Chrysler, but for the companies' supply chains, vendors, and dealers. There wasn't any capital standing in the wings waiting to turn the firms around. At the time, the economy was losing several hundred thousand jobs per month. Here again, speed was a distinguishing factor. And here too a large chunk of the industry was preserved at a relatively low cost to taxpayers.

In all, the government provided $80 billion to Chrysler, General Motors, and GMAC, the auto financing arm of GM that was reborn as Ally Financial. Although the problems that laid them low had built up for decades, the reaction was relatively swift. General Motors filed for Chapter 11 on June 1, 2009; emerged from bankruptcy forty days later, on July 10; and went public in November 2010. Chrysler filed for bankruptcy protection on April 30, 2009, and was acquired by Fiat, which tapped into government loans. Chrysler emerged from bankruptcy protection on June 10, after just forty-two days. In bankruptcy, the two companies slimmed down, ripped up contracts, shucked benefits, lopped off a combined $109 billion in liabilities, improved their cost structures, and established new business models and new owners. In the case of Chrysler, the government controversially forced bondholders to accept a smaller amount of recovery on their loans than they might have expected in a normal bankruptcy case. The cash injections forestalled the liquidation of both firms and prevented them from becoming massive drags on the economy and symbols of failure. Both companies were put into a position where they could be functional, regain market share, and introduce new products.

In the fall of 2010 I joined a caravan of Chevrolet Volts driving from New York City to Pittsburgh. I have to say that, as an electric car, the Volt still has a long way to go. Shortly after we emerged from the Lincoln Tunnel, and about thirty miles into the trip, the battery was drained and the Volt shifted over to the gas engine. But the symbolism of the drive was arguably more important than the ability of this vehicle to make it deep into Essex County solely on electric power. Here was a bet on the future, a GM product getting noticed on the streets of Manhattan, a sign of innovation from a company that had been left for dead fewer than eighteen months before. As the *Wall Street Journal* reported in June 2011, since GM and Chrysler emerged from bankruptcy, the U.S. auto industry had created 115,000 jobs. Thanks in part to the growth of GM and Chrysler and the production problems in Japan due to the March 2010 tsunami, by the end of 2011 the Big Three had recovered to the point where they held about half of the U.S. car market. GM and Chrysler quickly turned from economic drags to economic contributors. GM earned $7.4 billion in the first nine months of 2011. Chrysler, left for dead in 2008, earned $212 million in the third quarter of 2011. Combined, GM and Chrysler sold 3.87 million cars in the United States and directly employed 133,000 workers, making a substantial contribution to the nation's rising industrial production.

The accounting isn't yet complete, but the final price to the taxpayers is likely to be much less than expected. In May 2011, when Chrysler repaid its loan, the government formally closed the book on its Chrysler investment. It put in $12.37 billion, got $11.12 billion cash back, and took a loss of $1.33 billion, or about 11 percent. Having put $51 billion into General Motors, by the end of 2011 the government had received $24 billion back and still owned 500 million shares in the company, which had a market value of about $11 billion at the end of 2011. The books are still open on Ally Financial, formerly known as GMAC. Between December 2008 and December 2009 the government injected $16.3 billion into GMAC. By the end of 2011, $5.3 billion had been returned through stock sales and dividend payments, and a chunk of the investment had been turned into a 74 percent stake in the company. An IPO would create a vehicle for further returns. Assuming a relatively poor performance for General Motors' stock, the total cost of the auto bailouts is likely to be $14 billion, which is about what the federal government spends every thirty-three hours.[10]

There is, of course, a giant asterisk in this accounting of rapid response and rapid payback: housing. The cost of taking over Fannie Mae and Freddie Mac—saving the financial system by stepping in and guaranteeing their debt—has been a huge financial blow to taxpayers. In 2008 taxpayers formally assumed control and responsibility for Fannie and Freddie. Essentially the U.S. government began to write checks so the two companies could make up for the bad mortgages they had made and keep paying interest on bonds they had issued that were held by private banks and central banks around the world. The rescue, which has the money-losing institutions paying the Treasury 10 percent dividends with money it is already borrowing from the Treasury, hasn't always been a picture of rationality. Through the third quarter of 2011, the two entities had collectively drawn down $181 billion, while returning $32 billion in dividends, for a net of $149 billion. But by late 2011 there were signs that even this bailout could be coming to an end.

These companies' profiles change with every quarter, as bubble-era loans pay off or default and they continue to make new loans. Since the beginning of 2009 the two agencies and a third government-sponsored enterprise, Ginnie Mae, have accounted for about 80 percent of the market for newly issued mortgages. But their post-bust loans were made more intelligently: on cheaper homes, to higher-credit borrowers, and with more money down. By the third quarter of 2011 both institutions reported that 49 percent of their single-family loans had been made since the beginning of 2009, with Fannie Mae reporting a 68 percent loan-to-value ratio for the new loans, meaning the typical borrower was making a down payment equal to 32 percent of the home's value. For both institutions, about 11 or 12 percent of the loans made in 2007 and 2008 were seriously delinquent in late 2011. But of the mortgages made in 2009 and 2010, fewer than 1 percent were in trouble. Today both government-owned institutions are effectively pretty good new banks lashed to truly pathetic old ones.[11]

The point of this accounting is not to argue that the bailouts were a great idea or that they were handled perfectly. Rather it is to note that the quick implementation and winding down of the efforts was a positive for the economy—and a factor that distinguishes the United States from its peers in the developed world. Despite the apocalyptic tone in which they are generally characterized and the political conflict that they give rise to, the policy responses worked as intended to a large degree. And they worked at a much lower cost than even the most optimistic observers might have projected at their inception. The total net cost of the auto, banking, and housing bailouts is likely to be $220 billion, or about 1.6 percent of 2009's gross domestic product. That compares with $146 billion spent to bail out the savings and loans industry after its meltdown in the late 1980s, a sum equal to 1.7 percent of 1992's gross domestic product.[12] Rather than being a cause of further decline, the actions likely helped stave it off. The interventions were the necessary precondition for halting panic and reversing the downward trajectory of the U.S. economy. The extraordinary policy efforts helped spur a significant reflation in the U.S. stock and credit markets, and a less significant one in the real economy.

Although they were necessary, however, the policy measures were not sufficient. In order for the economy to stabilize and move forward against powerful headwinds, the private sector would have to fix imbalances, mend errant ways, change habits, and shore up balance sheets.

CHAPTER 4

Better: Restructuring the Nation

It is a core tenet of the declinist faith that the U.S. private sector, like its public sector, wandered around in a daze after the crash of 2008. But that's not what happened. The speedy public policy response helped stave off a second Great Depression, and at a relatively low cost. And in the face of the worst financial and macroeconomic crisis in eighty years, the *private sector* moved with more impressive speed. Despite protestations to the contrary, the United States has a business and consumer culture that processes failure quickly and reacts swiftly to new challenges. Restructuring is a core national competency, an industry American management experts effectively invented. "Restructuring, whether it is done out of court or bankruptcy, is an accepted genre in the U.S., whereas overseas it still carries much more of an onus," said Stephen Cooper, founder of the restructuring firm Cooper Zolfo, which saw its business boom in 2009 and 2010. The bankruptcy system, armies of turnaround artists, vulture investors who aim to profit by investing in busted companies, and experts who spend their days figuring out how to restructure companies' operations and balance sheets were important internal resources that the U.S. economy could tap into as it tried to recover from its nasty fall.

After years of complacency, penny-pinchers and cold-eyed restructuring mavens chugged Red Bulls and began to pull all-nighters. At first the widespread embrace of restructuring at the depths of the crisis only seemed to make things worse. Restructuring efforts exacerbated the downturn and added to the growing sense of gloom and decline. The U.S. economy is congenitally procyclical. In their enthusiasm and haste, Americans tend to amplify existing, rising trends, adding momentum to vehicles as they gain speed. We tend to add jobs, leverage, and risk at a time when growth, leverage, and risk are already high. And we tend to cut jobs, leverage, and risk soon after we reach the peak. Debts aren't written off during the boom, when balance sheets can handle the pain. Rather they are consigned to the dustbin after the pop, when banks and investors can least afford to mark them down or sell them off at depressed prices. During economic contractions, when employment is already falling, American companies have no qualms about throwing people out of work. In Germany, by contrast, companies responded to slower demand with *Kurzarbeit* initiatives, asking workers to share jobs and work fewer hours. The American tendency to add fuel to the fire helps explain the epic, unexpected job losses of early 2009. In six months, between November 2008 and April 2009, the U.S. economy shed 4.4 million jobs, an average of 738,000 per month, or about 25,000 a day.

But after the worst of the downturn, procyclicality can also hasten recovery. In the months after the collapse of Lehman Brothers in September 2008, companies were ruthless about cutting payroll, idling factories, wiggling out of commitments, and shirking burdens. Borrowers turned over factories, hotels, and office towers to lenders, who in turn wrote off debts. Companies diluted shareholders' existing holdings as they raised new capital, jettisoned long-cherished assets, and didn't hesitate to seek the shelter of bankruptcy protection. Bankruptcy court is like some dreary old bus station of American capitalism: a grimy, low-end place, filled with unfortunates who would be elsewhere if only they could afford it. It's a place where few people want to linger. Once there, many companies liquidated, while others reorganized and emerged in better shape. Individuals and consumers attacked debts with similar alacrity, walking away from mortgages, seeking bankruptcy protection, and shoring up their savings. The net result? Rather than sinking deeper into a financial morass in 2009 and 2010, the American private sector emerged better: better equipped to meet obligations, to save, to invest, to spend, and, ultimately, to grow.

The bailouts may have sustained some undeserving firms, but they did so at an extremely low cost to taxpayers. And the notion that government efforts somehow prevented corporations from failing is a moldy, hoary myth. Between January 2009 and September 2011, 345 banks failed and another 482 were taken out through mergers and acquisitions. The number of banks insured by the FDIC fell from 8,562 at the end of 2007 to 7,513 in June 2011. Although the auto industry was bailed out, its largest members weren't spared the indignity of bankruptcy. In 2008 and 2009 General Motors and Chrysler were joined in Chapter 11 by Delphi, the largest U.S. auto parts company, and by plenty of large, well-connected corporations, including General Growth Properties, a shopping mall pioneer that carried $27 billion in debt; Lehman Brothers, the fifth-largest investment bank; and Washington Mutual, the fourth-largest bank. Total business bankruptcy filings spiked from 28,322 in 2007 to 43,546 in 2008 and 60,837 in 2009—an increase of 113 percent in two years. Chapter 11 filings by businesses rose from 5,736 in 2007 to 13,683 in 2009. Chapter 7 filings, which generally result in liquidation, soared from 18,757 in 2007 to 41,962 in 2009. Among the liquidated were well-known brands like Circuit City, Linens 'n Things, and Borders. In 2009 a record 191 U.S. companies, with a combined $516 billion in debt, defaulted on their bonds, up from 16 with $7 billion in debt in 2007, according to Standard & Poor's.[1]

These business failures took a toll on the national psyche in the first two years after the Lehman Brothers meltdown. In the economy, as in baseball, failure begets a loss of confidence, which in turn begets further failure. Baseball players batting under .200 tend to step meekly into the batter's box. But just as was the case with the Internet boom of the 1990s, the failures tell only half the story. Throughout American history it has always mattered how the system copes with failure, cleans up the mess, and moves on. And financial failure in the United States tends to get worked out much more quickly than it does in other developed countries. That can be ascribed in large part to America's distinct financial culture. In Britain, where debtors' prisons persisted until the 1860s, financial failure is still heavily frowned upon. In Italy until 2005 people who ran companies that went bankrupt could lose their right to vote. In the 1990s Japanese banks permitted zombie companies to stumble around for years without paying their debts because they wanted to allow managers to save face and didn't want to admit failure on their balance sheets. In the United States, the land of second chances for so many people over the centuries, financial failure doesn't carry much of a stigma. In fact, we *expect* that people won't pay a portion of their debts.

American lenders exhibit a Jekyll-and-Hyde attitude. When times are good, they dole out credit freely to anyone who wants it, no questions asked. But when borrowers run into trouble, American creditors morph into ruthless badasses, sending out aggressive lawyers, angry letters, and repo men. Then, once a borrower pleads for mercy, lenders heed the version of the Lord's Prayer that appears in Matthew 6:12: "Forgive us our debts, as we also have forgiven our debtors." Every day in 2009 and 2010 thousands of deals were cut between creditors and debtors, owners and renters, leaseholders and tenants, in and out of court. If you stood on Park Avenue in Midtown Manhattan in 2009 and listened closely, that whooshing noise you heard was the sound debt makes when it gets flushed out of the system.

CIT Group, the large small-business lender, is a poster child for rapid debt write-down. Jeff Peek, a former Merrill Lynch executive, took the helm of the company in 2003 and tried to turn the sleepy lender into a turbocharged investment bank. Like the rest of Wall Street, CIT shifted into subprime at exactly the wrong time. In the face of mounting losses, it became a bank holding company, which allowed it to gain access to assistance from the Federal Reserve and Treasury. CIT took $2.3 billion in TARP funds in December 2008. It was all to no avail. On November 1, 2009, when it filed for Chapter 11 bankruptcy, CIT represented the largest wipeout of the Capital Purchase Program.

But CIT didn't stay in bankruptcy for long. Just as it was willing to forgive the loans it had made to others, it was able to get others to forgive loans they had made to it. "During bankruptcy CIT wrote down about 28 percent of its $44 billion loan portfolio," Jack Willoughby wrote in *Barron's*. The sentiment was reciprocated by creditors. When it emerged from bankruptcy on December 8, after just five weeks in Chapter 11, CIT had reduced its total debt by about $10.5 billion, reduced its assets from $71 billion to $60 billion, and transformed itself from a no-hoper into an institution with cash equal to a solid 15 percent of assets.[2] For its second act, CIT found a CEO seeking a third act: John Thain. A star at Goldman Sachs, Thain left the firm in 2004 after he lost out in the CEO sweepstakes, and he took the top post at the New York Stock Exchange. Next he stepped in to lead Merrill Lynch after its CEO, Stanley O'Neal, became an early casualty of the credit crisis in November 2007. At Merrill, Thain didn't have time to do much more than install a $350,000 antique commode in his office suite. When the deluge came in the fall of 2008, he sold Merrill to Bank of America on September 15, and went running—literally. The last time I saw Thain he was scurrying out of the Bank of America building on Forty-second Street and Sixth Avenue after the press conference announcing the deal, as if from a burning house.

After Thain joined CIT as CEO in February 2010, he set about cutting costs and rationalizing and restructuring the business. With the global and local economy and capital markets recovering, life was getting a little easier for lenders like CIT. In the first quarter of 2010, thanks to its improved cost structure, including significantly lower interest payments on debt, CIT earned $97 million. In short order it tapped into the Fed's TALF to raise capital, and in April 2010 it sold its businesses in Australia, New Zealand, and Canada. Over the next several quarters CIT refinanced billions of dollars of debt, on which it had been paying interest of 10 percent or more, at sharply lower rates, reducing its annual interest bill by hundreds of millions of dollars. In 2010 the company earned more than $500 million, shed $7 billion of high-cost debt, dumped $5 billion of assets, and funded more than $4.5 billion in new business. Two years after filing for bankruptcy CIT was a smaller, safer, more manageable company. And a more useful one. Because it had quickly restructured its business, CIT could play a role in enabling growth rather than detracting from it. It started to make loans again to American businesses needing capital: the grocery store chain Piggly Wiggly, the apparel company Sean John, and the storage technology giant

EMC. And it began to contribute to the economy in more significant ways by funding the large-scale purchase of capital goods. In
July 2011, for example, CIT's rail unit ordered 5,000 railcars. By the
fall of 2011 its expensive long-term debt had fallen to $27 billion,
from $36.7 billion the year before, and the company was sitting on
an $11.2 billion cash cushion.

CIT's experience wasn't unique. The credit markets have seen
more workouts than the Crunch chain. In the spring of 2009 I went
to Boston to see the aftermath of one such deal. The John Hancock
Tower, the sixty-two-story sliver of glass designed by I. M. Pei,
looms above its brick neighbors in Boston's Back Bay. It had just
come under the control of its fourth owner in six years. Michael
Loughlin, the new manager, was learning his way around the building. We went through the marble lobby and up to the vacant thirty-
ninth floor. Free of desks, cubicles, partitions—and tenants—it
offered stunning 360-degree views of Boston Harbor to the east
and the State House and Beacon Hill to the northeast. "There's the
Citgo sign," Loughlin noted reverentially, pointing to the billboard
that looms over Fenway Park.

In 2003 the building and its surrounding complex, including two
adjacent buildings and a parking garage, were sold by the original
owner, John Hancock Mutual Life Insurance Company, to a local
developer, Alan Leventhal, for the then-stunning price of $910 mil-
lion. Four years later Leventhal flipped it to an investor who rode
the credit wave and got crushed when it broke. Scott Lawlor of
Queens, New York, the son of a cabdriver, graduated from Columbia University and leveraged his way into real estate prominence.
His first deal was the 2000 acquisition of a $4.8 million office build-
ing in Westchester County, New York. Between 2000 and 2007
Lawlor's firm, Broadway Partners, bought $15 billion in real estate,
and he began to amass the trappings of a real estate mogul; Lucite
tombstones memorializing consummated deals lined shelves in his
office in the Seagram Building, the Mies van der Rohe office tower
on Manhattan's Park Avenue. In January 2007 he paid $3.3 billion
for a nine-property portfolio offered by Beacon Properties, which
included the Hancock Tower. Lawlor immediately flipped three of
the buildings, and by the time the dust settled, the Hancock Tower,

appraised at $1.4 billion in June 2008, was effectively saddled with two mortgages totaling $1.36 billion. The mortgage was chopped up into pieces and sold—because that's what people did back then.

No sooner had Lawlor acquired the building than the financial services companies that had been the mainstay of the world's high-end office market began to contract. The advertising agency Hill Holliday, balking at higher rents, vacated its four floors in March 2008. When the crunch hit, Broadway Partners tried to sell other buildings in its portfolio, aiming to raise money to pay off $733 million tied to the Hancock Tower that was due in January 2009. But there were no buyers. Meanwhile pieces of the loan began to trade hands at discounted prices, as investors realized they might not be able to collect. Normandy Real Estate Partners, a New Jersey–based landlord, and the Connecticut-based investment fund Five Mile Capital bought chunks of the second mortgage for pennies on the dollar. In January 2009, with the loan balance paid down to $525 million, and just twenty-four months after purchasing it, Lawlor defaulted. On the morning of March 31 a few dozen people showed up at an anticlimactic foreclosure auction staged in a large conference room at the New York law firm Skadden Arps. Normandy/Five Mile, which offered the only bid, assumed control of the building; given the discounted price the two parties paid for the loan, about $400 million of debt officially vanished. The building was now valued at about $700 million, half the amount of a year before.

Thanks to the quick elimination and write-down of a large chunk of debt, the new owners were in a position to improve the building. Normandy spent $40 million renovating the lobby and upgrading heating, cooling, water, and waste-management systems so the building could earn a Gold LEED certification, the standard for green buildings that often proves attractive to upscale tenants. Because of their lower cost basis, the new landlords could offer aggressive discounts to lure tenants into empty floors. In November 2009 Bay State Financial agreed to take over the entire nineteenth floor. Six months later Bain Capital, the firm that Mitt Romney started, signed on for seven floors, including the vacant thirty-ninth floor with the sweeping views of Fenway, totaling about 210,000 square feet. Within a year the building had been transformed from a money-losing, partially empty, tenant-repelling loser into a cash-spinning winner that was at 95 percent capacity. In December 2010, after the credit and property markets had reflated, the new owners sold the tower to Boston Properties for $930 million, a 33 percent gain in about twenty months.[3]

Other companies managed to restructure without inflicting significant damage on their stakeholders. In the early decades of the twentieth century Henry Ford provided one of the original and paradigmatic stories of U.S. business engineering: scaling up cottage manufacturing to mass production and continually reimagining and restructuring the business. A century later, in the years before, during, and after the financial crisis, Ford provided another great case study in engineering. But this time it was financial engineering. Under the leadership of Alan Mulally, who joined the company from Boeing in September 2006, Ford borrowed $18 billion from banks and investors. Doing so was like taking out a huge home equity line of credit to remodel the house. But unlike most bubble-era homeowners, Ford spent the cash wisely. It used the funds to modernize factories and create global platforms that could produce the same car in different locations around the world, and then stowed the remaining cash under the mattress. When the deluge came and U.S. car sales fell dramatically in 2008 and 2009, Ford, unlike General Motors and Chrysler, was able to avoid bankruptcy, but just barely. At the end of 2008, a year in which it lost $14.6 billion, $25.8 billion in debt rested on Ford's automotive operations and the company had just $13.4 billion in cash. Debt on its automotive operations soared to $34.4 billion in 2009, as the company drew down its credit facility in an effort to stay afloat. The stock, which stood at about $8 at the end of 2006, hit a low of $1.59 in February 2009.

While General Mothers and Chrysler were able to shed vast amounts of debt in bankruptcy court, Ford produced and earned its way out of trouble. Eschewing a bailout, it ground out a recovery, embracing foreign markets, holding the line on compensation, and aggressively slashing costs. In 2009 Ford set a goal of reducing its overhead by $4 billion; through the first nine months of 2009 it exceeded that goal, cutting $4.6 billion in structural costs. The company earned a profit in the third quarter of 2009, and has done so in every successive quarter. In 2010 alone it paid down $14.5 billion in debt on its automotive business. In late 2010 Ford went cash positive, meaning it had enough cash on hand to pay all its debt. By the third quarter of 2011, when it had $20.8 billion in cash and just $12.76 billion in debt on its auto business, Ford was on the cusp of regaining an investment-grade credit rating. In December 2011 it reinstated a 5-cent annual dividend on its shares.

Like the U.S. economy at large, in early 2009 Ford's stock had been priced for utter failure. After an impressive rally, the stock topped out near $18 in January 2011, a 1,013 percent rise from the $1.59 low of February 2009.[4] Ford's experience has been matched by the rest of corporate America, albeit not always in such dramatic turns. At companies large and small, executives made heroic efforts to avoid bankruptcy and preserve value for owners and shareholders, taking tough measures to cut costs and fix unsustainable balance sheets, adjust to new realities, and return to profit. Industrial and financial services companies, manufacturers, and retailers pulled off their own bailouts. All this meant that as economic pessimism rose, corporate America began to post impressive profits. Pretax corporate profits, $1.25 trillion in 2008, soared to $1.8 trillion in 2010, and through the first half of 2011 were running at an annual rate of $1.9 trillion. Companies used these profits to make their balance sheets better and stronger. Thus U.S. companies' cash holdings, which fell to $1.4 trillion in 2008, rose in pretty much every quarter since the late 2008 face-plant—to $1.86 trillion at the end of 2010 and $2.05 trillion in the second quarter of 2011. In other words, in the three years in which the United States was supposed to be declining, its companies boosted profits by 50 percent and increased the cash holdings on their collective balance sheet by 40 percent.[5] Not bad for a has-been.

Rather than entering into a phase of decline, the U.S. private sector reconstituted itself—payment by payment, default by default, restructuring by restructuring. In the process, excessive debt, the cause of the crisis, was driven out of big chunks of the global private financial system. In the United States the species of unregulated investment bank capable of amassing hundreds of billions of dollars in debt has become extinct. Lehman Brothers and Bear Stearns are gone, and the rest of the precrisis big five (Merrill Lynch, Goldman Sachs, and Morgan Stanley) evolved into staid commercial banks with much higher capital levels. Citi, the bank formerly known as Citigroup, once sported a trillion-dollar balance sheet teetering on a phyllo-thin equity layer. In late 2011 Citi reported that it had 11.7 cents of what regulators call Tier 1 capital for every dollar of assets it held—a remarkably high ratio. According to the Federal Reserve, financial sector debt stood at $13.7 trillion in the third quarter of 2011, down 20 percent from $17.1 trillion in 2008. Total corporate debt outstanding fell 2.7 percent in 2009, rose 0.4 percent in 2010, and grew at a 1.8 percent rate in the first half of 2011. By the end of 2011 the corporate sector on the whole reported greater profits, far more cash, and less debt than it had in 2008. That's a recipe for greater financial success. And in fact, business bankruptcy filings fell 7.5 percent in 2010 and another 16 percent in the first nine months of 2011.

This would be great news if the United States were an industrial and business economy. Unfortunately, consumers account for about 70 percent of U.S. economic activity. Thanks to the mortgage boom and the collapsing housing and employment markets, in 2009 consumers found themselves in a much more difficult debt situation than corporations did. But here again the data don't support the narrative of terminal decline. While personal restructuring has been significantly slower and less dramatic than the corporate version, consumers have confronted their debts and begun to chip away at them.

Consumers helped to create the global credit crisis, especially in the United States. The expansion that began in November 2001 and ended in December 2007 would not have been possible without the vast increase in consumer indebtedness. From the first quarter of 2001 through the third quarter of 2008, consumer debt rose by nearly 50 percent. Between December 2003 and December 2007 revolving credit rose from $768 billion to $941 billion, or 22.5 percent. In the same period, according to the Census Bureau, monthly retail sales rose from $308 billion to $377 billion, or 22.4 percent. In

2006 alone some 7.9 billion credit card solicitations were sent out, or about twenty-six for every person in the country. That was just the beginning. As housing prices rose, and as the mortgage industry rushed to cash in, consumers borrowed against their homes to finance consumption through home equity loans and refinancings and extracted more value by selling into inflated markets. The cash reaped through these efforts, which came to be known as mortgage equity withdrawal (MEW), accounted for a rising share of consumption. According to the Federal Reserve, net MEW rose from $234 billion in 2000 to $723 billion in 2004. Between 2004 and 2006 Americans extracted a net $2 trillion from their homes. In those three years MEW accounted for between 6.9 and 8.3 percent of disposable income. As for savings? Forget about it. Stowing money away was for chumps and survivors of the Great Depression. In 2005, at the height of the housing boom, Americans' personal savings rate, as measured by the Commerce Department, was a mere 1.5 percent.[6]

The combination of stagnant wages, low savings, and high levels of mortgage and consumer debt left Americans poorly equipped to deal with a sudden downturn in housing prices and employment. In the third quarter of 2008, on the eve of the Lehman Brothers failure, American consumers owed a collective $12.48 trillion in debt. So when the recession came and employment fell off a cliff, consumers took a collective pratfall. People began to fall behind, default, and walk away—on home equity lines of credit, mortgages, and credit cards. But here again the presumption that the system avoided pain and didn't respond rapidly is something of a myth.

The scale of the housing bubble was so vast, so out of proportion to historic norms, and so chaotic that it has defied rapid solutions. Mortgage modification efforts have been feeble, halting, and pathetic. Less than $2 billion of the $30 billion that Treasury was allowed to spend under TARP's home mortgage modification program, under which the Treasury wrote checks to banks that would reduce principal on mortgages, was spent. But Mitt Romney's October 2011 assertion that "the Obama Administration has slow-walked the foreclosure processes that have long existed" is likewise off the mark. Amid the burst bubble, many consumers made heroic efforts to stay solvent, selling excess property, raising cash, borrowing from friends and families, paying down debt, and reducing balances. Not all succeeded, of course. The proportion of mortgages on which borrowers were thirty days late rose from 4.95 percent in late 2006 to 9.5 percent in the fourth quarter of 2009. According to the data provider RealtyTrac, the number of properties receiving foreclosure notices soared from 1.29 million in 2007 to 2.33 million in 2008, 2.81 million in 2009, and 2.87 million in 2010. Between 2007 and 2011 more than 4 million homes were repossessed by banks. After peaking at 69.1 percent in late 2005, the homeownership rate in the United States began to fall; it stood at 66.5 percent in mid-2011. Through a combination of default, pay-downs, and shifting to rentals, Americans have shucked nearly a trillion dollars in mortgage debt since the crisis. According to the New York Federal Reserve, by the third quarter of 2011 the outstanding totals of household mortgages and home equity lines of credit were off 9.6 percent and 10 percent, respectively, from their peaks. But housing was just the beginning. According to the credit card research firm Card Hub, the delinquency rate on credit cards rose from 3.9 percent in the second quarter of 2007 to 6.61 percent in the first quarter of 2009, leading the credit card companies to write off tens of billions of dollars in balances. Individual bankruptcy filings rose from 1.074 million in 2008 to 1.412 million in 2009 and 1.536 million in 2010.[7]

Like businesses, individuals restructured their balance sheets, cutting costs, raising cash, and restructuring or paying down debt. As with housing debt, a lot of consumer debt was written off. It turns out that many of the sales recorded in 2005, 2006, and 2007, financed with store credit or housing credit that went bad, weren't real sales. According to Card Hub, in 2006 and 2007, when unemployment was low, card companies wrote off $32 billion and $38 billion, respectively—about 4 percent of outstanding balances. But write-offs soared to $53.5 billion in 2008, $83 billion in 2009, and $75 billion in 2010. In two years alone, retailers effectively gave back about $158 billion in previously registered sales. According to the New York Federal Reserve, on September 30, 2011, total consumer indebtedness came to $11.66 trillion; that's down 6.5 percent, or $820 billion, from the peak of the third quarter of 2008.[8]

The consumer's balance sheet has improved in other ways. During the recession Americans rediscovered their inner hoarder. The savings rate spiked from close to zero at the height of the credit boom to more than 6.2 percent in the second quarter of 2009, before settling back into a range of between 4 and 5.5 percent. That translates into $2.1 trillion in savings in the period from the beginning of 2008 to September 2011. The figures are even more impressive since Americans had to stop tapping into home equity to fuel consumption and instead put money into their homes to stay current. Mortgage equity withdrawal, which had fueled so much consumption during the boom, turned negative in the second quarter of 2008. That means that rather than taking money out of their homes, Americans began to sink money into them. MEW has remained negative in every quarter since then. In the first quarter of 2011, rather than take money out of their homes, Americans essentially sank a net $107 billion *into* them, a sum equal to about 3.7 percent of disposable personal income.

But this didn't mean a decline in consumer activity. Far from it. In late 2008 mounting job losses and the market collapse knocked the wind out of American shoppers. Monthly sales plummeted from $373.2 billion in August 2008 to bottom out at $336.2 billion in March 2009. Buoyed by debt reductions, write-offs, higher savings, and, ultimately, job growth, shoppers returned to malls and e-commerce sites. By the end of 2010, to the perpetual surprise of analysts, monthly retail sales surpassed precrisis levels, and they set new records in 2011: $399 billion in November 2011. And here's the surprising thing: this growth came as credit card debt declined sharply. Revolving credit peaked at $974 billion in August 2008 and has fallen 18 percent since then, to $798 billion in November 2011. The highest level of monthly retail sales in history, in other words, was supported by the same level of credit card debt as in October 2004.

The divergent trends in consumer credit and retail sales are not contradictions. They make complete sense in a restructured and restructuring environment. Simply put, having reshaped their balance sheets, American consumers were in a better position to stay current on their debt—and to spend. Between 2008 and the first quarter of 2011, total financial assets rose 20 percent (from $37.8 trillion to $45.5 trillion), while total liabilities fell 3.9 percent (from $20.1 trillion to $19.3 trillion). The household debt-service ratio—the amount of disposable personal income devoted to making debt payments—fell sharply, from 13.96 percent in the third quarter of 2007 to 11.09 percent in the second quarter of 2011. That ratio hadn't been that low since the fourth quarter of 1994.

These numbers tell a story of reaction, change, and improvement. In 2006 and 2007 the American consumer was like a weightlifter who uses only his arms and back: he can produce decent results for a while but winds up with horrific injuries. In 2010 and 2011 the consumer was more like a weightlifter who has strengthened his legs and core and has learned how to use them. As a result the vicious debt circle of 2008 and 2009 was increasingly replaced by a virtuous circle in 2010 and 2011. Higher demand—led by global growth, rising government expenditures, and a recovering private sector—spurred job creation starting in February 2010. And this process gained steam even as the effects of policy and public spending withered. The Federal Reserve's quantitative easing helped keep interest rates low in 2010 and 2011, but petered out in the second half of 2011. The stimulus and government assistance, so vital to averting a Great Depression in 2008 and 2009, began to wane in 2010. Meanwhile states and cities were acting as brakes on growth by cutting spending and employment. In what's been dubbed "the conservative recovery," the private sector persistently added jobs even as the public sector just as persistently cut them. Between May 2010 and January 2012 the government sector reduced employment by 1 million. Between February 2010 and January 2012, by contrast, the private sector added 3.66 million jobs.

With more people working at higher wages and devoting a smaller portion of their income to debt payments, and with more companies clocking higher sales and sitting on large cash balances, the serial economic failures of 2008 and 2009 gave way to serial economic successes in 2010 and 2011. Mortgage delinquencies fell, to 7.99 percent in the third quarter of 2011, down from 10.06 percent in the first quarter of 2010—the lowest level since the fourth quarter of 2008, according to the Mortgage Bankers Association of America. Card Hub's data show the delinquency rate on credit card debt fell from a high of 6.61 percent in the first quarter of 2009 to a nontragic 3.47 percent in the third quarter of 2011. The charge-off rate, the percentage of debts credit card companies gave up on collecting, plummeted from 10.97 percent in the second quarter of 2010 to 5.63 percent in the second quarter of 2011. Through the first nine months of 2011 bankruptcy filings fell 10 percent from the first nine months of 2010, with business filings off 16 percent and consumer filings down 9 percent. In 2011, according to Standard & Poor's, forty companies with a combined $73 billion in debt defaulted, compared with sixty-one companies with a combined $95 billion in debt in 2010.

Procyclicality, it turns out, can also have positive effects on the economy. The performance of credit, which did so much to sandbag growth in 2008 and 2009, has shifted from a drag to a potential contributor. The decline in defaults of all sorts had a salutary effect on corporate profits, helping to close the virtuous circle of growth. When economic cycles shift into reverse, companies and banks put aside rising sums of cash to prepare for bad debt. When default rates decline, they start setting aside less money, and, if performance improves rapidly, they can release cash from reserves set aside in prior years or quarters. Which is precisely what happened in 2011. Target reported that in the first quarter of 2011, it had to set aside just $12 million for bad debt expenses in its credit card operations, down from $197 million in the fourth quarter of 2010; the reduction provided a nice boost to profits. The credit card giant Capital One also had more in its wallet because of reduced charge-off rates: they fell from 8.23 percent in the third quarter of 2010 to 2.52 percent in the third quarter of 2011. Across all its businesses, JPMorgan Chase set aside $2.18 billion for credit losses in the third quarter of 2011, down from $3.04 billion in the previous year's quarter. That meant an extra $860 million available for CEO Jamie Dimon to use as he saw fit.[9]

The combination of rapid policy response and swift private sector reaction put the U.S. economy on a better financial footing. Americans' collective financial batting average rose, not to the .350 level of 2005 and 2006, which brought on dangerous overconfidence—more like a solid .250. By 2011, three years after the onset of the crisis, the U.S. economy was larger than its prebubble peak but less dependent on private sector debt for consumption and employment. The moves were largely defensive and were necessary to ensure survival and to forestall further contraction.

But the transformation of the post-Lehman economy wasn't simply a matter of pinching pennies and walking away from debts. As we'll see, the United States proved highly adept at tapping into internal and external sources of growth. In the months following the bust American businesses discovered new reservoirs of strength lying in plain sight.

CHAPTER 5

Stronger: The Efficiency Economy

Timely policy and impatient restructuring got the ball rolling. But the recovery wasn't simply a matter of writing off debts. If the top line isn't growing, as was the case for most businesses and the economy at large in 2009, or if it's growing haltingly, as it was in 2010 and 2011, it's imperative to figure out how to lower the bottom line. That often means cutting costs relentlessly. But in the absence of a big new force boosting demand, and in an environment in which flat is the new up, it means much more. Slashing overhead is just the beginning. Companies have to tap into internal resources to figure out how to produce the same amount of output with fewer inputs, think about how to make the most of what already exists rather than build from scratch, and generally do more with less. In a word: efficiency.

At first blush, efficiency would seem a slender rope on which to hang the hopes of a $16 trillion economy. After all, much of the U.S. economy is built around excess, waste, and profligacy: all-you-can-eat buffets, Big Gulps, giant SUVs, three-car garages, a vast military whose budget can never be cut, a disposable society. Fat and lazy, Americans are simply too stupid and mindless to adopt the types of efficiencies that are routine in other developed economies. In fact, we're downright hostile to them. Sophisticates who travel to Japan and Europe see intelligently designed policies that seek to maintain the quality of life amid constrained resources. Japan's Super Cool Biz mandate keeps the temperature in Tokyo office buildings above 80 degrees in the summer as part of a national effort to curb energy use. London's traffic-battling congestion-pricing scheme, under which motorists pay for the privilege of driving into central London, was rejected in New York, where such a plan could do wonders. Germany's passive-solar homes, which maintain constant temperatures without using heat or air-conditioning; Scandinavia's aggressive gas and carbon taxes, which encourage fuel efficiency and the development of alternative energy—the *bien pensant* view all of these small-living initiatives as necessary to avoid economic erosion. All are alien to, and politically impossible in, America's consume-at-all-costs society.

But the notion that Americans simply can't do better, that they can't do more with less, is a myth. When they put their minds to it, Americans are quite good at looking to internal resources for stability, and for growth. And as declinists fingered their worry beads and warned of a permanent depression, the private sector was figuring how to do things better and faster, laying the groundwork for a stronger economy. The pursuit of efficiency has long been a hallmark of American economic success.

Management consulting, it should be recalled, is an American invention and a field in which U.S. firms dominate. It started with Frederick Winslow Taylor, who may have been America's first management consultant. Starting in the 1890s the inventor of "scientific management" walked around factories with a stopwatch, timing the activities of workers and suggesting ways they could speed up their processes. The efficiency revolution continued with Henry Ford, whose perfection of the assembly line at the vast River Rouge plant enabled him to transform the automobile from a custom-built toy for the 1 percent to a highly practical tool for the 99 percent. In the halcyon years after World War II, with most of the world's manufacturing capacity having just been destroyed, U.S. industry didn't fret too much about improving operations. W. Edwards Deming, the chief evangelist of the gospel of quality, had to go to Japan to find a receptive audience in the 1950s. But after a couple of tough decades in which foreign competition began to erode American advantages, U.S. manufacturers rediscovered efficiency with a vengeance in the 1980s and 1990s. Total quality management, the discipline of reengineering, and the glories of business-process outsourcing transformed the manufacturing industry. In services, Walmart's insanely efficient supply chains relentlessly drove costs out of the system and set a global standard for rational logistics. McKinsey's armies of whip-smart technocrats roamed the globe, peddling expensive advice on how to rationalize operations.

In the happy expansion of the 2000s, efficiency and internal resources were easily overlooked. Manufacturers realized they could save more money simply by relocating production to Shenzhen, China, than they could by dispatching Six Sigma ninjas to improve operations. With debt flowing like a mighty stream and prices and asset values rising to the sky, what was the point of worrying about operational efficiencies? The discipline of business engineering was subordinated to *financial* engineering, as elite business schools created degrees and concentrations in the dark art. Productivity growth actually was quite weak during the credit boom, rising just 1.8 percent in 2007 and 2.1 percent in 2008.

But in the wake of the Lehman Brothers crash, the U.S. economy retrenched, rebooted, rebuilt—and rediscovered the virtue and power of efficiency. In the face of declining demand, the single most important factor that drives profitability (or, in extremis, survival) is the ability to do more with less. Rather than throw in the towel and surrender to Chinese competitors, U.S. companies discovered a range of internal resources and found the funds and mechanisms necessary to invest. In a way, the response was similar to the procedure used in the nascent geothermal energy industry: drilling down below the surface to tap into a powerful, cheap, long-dormant fuel source. From the fourth quarter of 2008 to the fourth quarter of 2009, productivity rose 5.4 percent. That's typical for the months immediately following the end of a recession. But the gains continued as the expansion took hold. Productivity rose 2.4 percent in 2009 and an impressive 4.1 percent in 2010.

Exalting productivity as an impetus for growth may seem counterintuitive. In 2009 and early 2010 the ruthless pursuit of efficiency translated into the uncomfortable dichotomy of sharply rising corporate profits and falling employment. With labor unions weakened and an astonishing amount of slack in the labor market, the rapid economic downdraft of 2008 and 2009 left workers defenseless in the face of corporations' frenzied pursuit of survival. As a result much of the productivity growth came from management beating the living daylights out of workers: firing people and making those who were left work harder for less. The number of private sector payroll jobs fell 7.6 percent, from the peak of 115.6 million in January 2008 to the trough of 106.8 million in February 2010, as companies continued to shed jobs for several months after the economy began to grow in the summer of 2009. Unit labor costs—the amount of labor it costs to produce a dollar of output—fell in both 2009 and 2010, the first time that metric had fallen for two straight years in a half century. The United States produced about as much output in the third quarter of 2011 as it did in the third quarter of 2007, albeit with about 6 million fewer workers on the payroll.[1]

But sticking it to workers was only one part of efficiency. Companies and sectors were ingenious about doing more with fewer resources across the board. At businesses big and small, memos went out about using fewer paper clips, printing on both sides of the paper, replacing travel agents with online travel-planning tools, canceling newspaper subscriptions, using Google rather than 411 to search for phone numbers, dispensing with fancy coffeemakers, and ending free meals and holiday parties. These productivity efforts may seem to come straight out of the manual of Dunder Mifflin, the fictional workplace in *The Office*. But I saw all of them and more at my employers in 2009 and 2010. Empowering bean counters and rummaging through the couch for pennies enabled balance-sheet repair and helped companies do a better job of keeping up with debt payments. Efficiency provided a vital form of ballast for the economy, staving off failure in the depths of the slump.

What starts as a purely defensive move can evolve into a powerful engine for growth. Cutting waste and adapting a more intelligent approach to the way resources are used have produced meaningful results—beyond those seen in the official productivity statistics. Gains reaped through efficiency become a form of recurring revenues. Such investments can reflate the value of assets left for dead and reposition damaged properties and businesses. More significantly, efficiency and the ability to tap into internal resources can become the models for smart businesses, for products and services that enable customers to improve their own cost structures.

In September 2008, as the nightmare was unfolding on Wall Street, BigBelly Solar was on the verge of a breakthrough.[2] In a nondescript office park in Newton, Massachusetts, the eight-year-old company was developing a product that could reduce budget deficits, take a meaningful bite out of global warming, reduce the trade deficit, curb excessive fuel use, improve the prospects for sidewalk cafés, demonstrate the commercial viability of green energy, and revive American manufacturing, all in one $4,000 package. Not since the iPhone has a collection of plastics, metal, and computer chips promised to solve so many social woes. The product: a solar-powered trash compactor.

BigBelly was the brainchild of Jim Poss, a native of Jamaica Plain, Massachusetts, who majored in geology at Duke and got his MBA from Babson College. Poss worked at several alternative energy ventures, including a solar equipment manufacturer and an electric vehicle components maker, before founding what became BigBelly in 2003. Poss's insight was a relatively prosaic one: most of what goes into public garbage baskets, and hence into garbage trucks and landfills, is air. Coffee cups, paper bags, and food containers are essentially plastic envelopes containing air. Stomp the mass down, and a container that might seem full in two days can hold a week's worth of refuse. While an urban garbage can costs about $20, high labor and fuel costs mean emptying and managing it can cost up to $2,000 each year. Reduce the number of times a can needs to be emptied, and you vastly reduce the number of trips garbage men make. In so doing you significantly lower the cost and impact of waste removal. BigBelly believed it had a product perfectly designed for the penny-pinching era. Virtually every institution managing a large number of garbage cans was under financial stress. "Cities and institutions like universities and park systems are eager to do more with less," Poss told me.

The BigBelly is a stumpy-looking garbage receptacle with a thin-film solar panel embedded in its molded top, a twelve-volt battery, and a small engine. An infrared beam flashes across the interior every thirty seconds, and when the light encounters an obstacle, it triggers a compaction cycle, bringing 1,200 pounds of pressure to bear on the refuse. Lights on the panel indicate whether it is full (red) or close to it (yellow), and the machine sends a text to headquarters to indicate when it is 70 percent full. All powered by the sun. "It controls litter, it controls rodents, it has a carbon impact, and it's green," said Jack Kutner, a veteran of the financial services industry who became an early angel investor in 2004, after meeting Poss at an investor fair, and became CEO in 2005. "But it is really a cash-savings device," he adds.

At about $4,000, the BigBelly isn't cheap. But if it can halve the cost of emptying a garbage can, it pays for itself in three and a half years. Cut the cost by 75 percent, and the payback period falls to thirty months, after which the product becomes a cash dispenser for the rest of its twenty-year life. The higher and more intractable the cost structure for waste removal, the more rapid the payback. "We can sometimes produce returns on investment that are under two years," said Kutner. In a world of low yields, BigBelly offered customers a return of up to 50 percent per year on their investment.

In late 2008 Philadelphia was staring at a five-year deficit that could rise to as much as $850 million, so the city was prepared to try devices on a large scale. It planned to purchase five hundred BigBelly compactors for about $2.3 million, in three lease payments spread out over a few years. Unable to find a bank to finance production—"We literally talked to everybody on the planet," said Kutner—BigBelly took one-third of Philadelphia's money up front and deferred its profits until future payments came in. That was a big leap of faith for a small company. When the deal was formally announced in April 2009, employees cracked open bottles of Jose Cuervo Reserva de la Familia Tequila that had been sent by BigBelly's Mexican distributor.

The Philadelphia deal was one of several moves made at the depths of the economic meltdown that would alter the company's trajectory. In May 2009 the trash-collection giant Waste Management came on board as a minority investor and agreed to help distribute the products, and BigBelly raised $3.2 million in equity from outside investors. (Waste Management is itself a pioneer in turning America's inefficiency—generating lots of junk and disposable material—into a valuable product. At 130 of its landfill sites, the company captures the methane gas released by decomposing garbage to produce enough electricity to power about 440,000 homes.)[3]

The rollout in Philadelphia provided a case study of BigBelly machines being used in a network. Philadelphia focused first on Center City, where thirty-three people working three shifts had been making seventeen collections a week on seven hundred waste bins. The bins were replaced with five hundred BigBelly units. By 2011, with the wireless text-messaging system ensuring that no bins were emptied before their time, some of the cans were down to two collections per week. Deploying BigBelly compactors allowed Philadelphia to reduce the number of truck trips, slashing wear and tear on its $250,000 vehicles. Money-saving efficiency led to cash-generating efficiency. The city redeployed workers from trash collection and began a public space recycling program, which by mid-2011 was redirecting twenty-three tons of garbage into recycling every month. That translates to $45,000 in annual savings. The city bought five hundred more units in 2010. Within two years Philadelphia was saving $900,000 a year on garbage collection through the use of BigBelly solar compactors.

In the first quarter of 2010 BigBelly's sales tripled compared with the first quarter of 2009, in part because big cities took to its products in bulk. Boston has embraced BigBelly with the ardor it typically reserves for homegrown sports heroes. Thanks to federal grants and interest from nonprofits and businesses, there are seventy compactors in the Downtown Crossing area alone. The Boston Red Sox bought ten units for Fenway Park and painted them green. There are ten on narrow Hanover Street in the North End, and a few stand sentry on the Freedom Trail. The city boasts around 250 in all. The Massachusetts Department of Conservation and Recreation, the agency responsible for state parks within Boston, has planted a dozen on the Charles River Esplanade, where the Boston Pops plays on the Fourth of July.

There's one in the shadow of the Old South Meeting House, where, in a pocket park stocked with statues dedicated to survivors of the Irish famine, I met Timothy McCarthy, an aide to the commissioner of the Boston Public Works Department. McCarthy, his close-cropped hair gleaming with a little product, described how these changes in a city loath to embrace change had worked out. The BigBelly, whose door snaps shut, is a significant improvement on the old cans. "With the open barrels that we had in the past, a good windstorm could make a mess," said McCarthy, a twenty-year veteran of city government. Besides, for urban areas, garbage collection is disruptive. "If you're in the South End on Tremont Street, and you're having a nice dinner, the last thing you need is a guy running a diesel truck dragging a bag and running the compaction cycle on the garbage truck." Though BigBellys are expensive, they're low-maintenance. "We've had a couple of soldiers go down, but other than that, very little problem," said McCarthy. In areas where BigBellys have been deployed, the frequency of trash collection has declined by about 75 percent.

It seems like the type of device you'd find in the Tokyo showroom of Sharp, alongside low-flow toilets and no-drip faucets. But the ingenuity behind BigBelly is strictly American. And so is the device itself. While the solar panel comes from China, the motor, the single most expensive piece, is made by Bison Gear & Engineering in Saint Charles, Illinois. The machines are built by two contract manufacturers: Mack Molding in Arlington, Vermont; and Creation Technologies in Lexington, Kentucky. BigBelly increased employment by about 50 percent from the beginning of 2009 to the end of 2011. Its head count is fewer than fifty, but the company supports more jobs elsewhere. At Mack Molding thirty-five employees are kept busy on two shifts producing compactors. "When you add the employees at the more than fifty component suppliers, this work is supporting another 180 jobs," said Joan Magrath, vice president of sales and engineering at Mack Molding. In 2011 BigBelly said that, including its supply chain, it is responsible for 250 jobs.

Between 2005 and 2010 BigBelly's revenues essentially doubled each year. And halfway through 2011 they were poised to double again. In March 2011 the company nailed down its largest contract, a deal with Chicago for up to 1,600 units. In May 2011 it sold its ten thousandth unit to the Los Angeles Community College District. The company is still small, but its ambitions are big. "The U.S. market alone is $900 million," said Jack Kutner, who, like everybody else at the company, has a trim figure, as if metabolic efficiency is a requirement for employment. Kutner and Poss envision putting two compactors in front of every Walmart in America. If it could crack the Holy Grail of garbage—New York City, which has 25,000 public waste bins on city streets and many more in its park system—it would really take off. In 2010 BigBelly, which has sold units in forty-nine states and twenty-five countries, struck a deal with Plastic Omnium, a Paris-based company, to distribute in Western Europe, and in June 2011 it opened a sales office in France.

BigBelly won't single-handedly revive manufacturing or solve the fiscal woes of American cities. But the company's value doesn't lie in its sales, or in the multiple that might be placed on its potential earnings in a future IPO. The entire market it seeks to address, $900 million, is about what Walmart rings up in eighteen hours. Rather, the value lies in what BigBelly enables its customers to do: to be more efficient and improve the management of core operations in an era of constrained resources. BigBelly takes an everyday, unavoidable fact of human life (the generation of garbage) and a process thought to be immune to rapid improvement (the collection of garbage) and makes it run better, stronger, and faster. What would the labor, fuel, and landfill savings be if every large municipal and institutional producer of garbage were to adopt it or a product like it? What would you pay to have fewer garbage trucks rumbling down Main Street? Kutner told me, "What we're fighting is inertia. Our competitor is inertia."

Replacing old, dumb garbage cans with smarter ones is a no-brainer and doesn't take much to accomplish. But retrofitting commercial buildings is a much more expensive proposition—and this is an area that offers far more promising returns and efficiencies than garbage collection. In the United States, commercial buildings account for about $108 billion in energy use and 17 percent of greenhouse gas emissions each year. In New York City, buildings consume 80 percent of the energy. And the efficiencies embedded in the existing skyline produce anxiety. As China sprouts new skyscrapers equipped with the latest gadgets and standards for sustainable living, we're stuck with the limestone, brick, and steel structures that were put up sixty, seventy, or a hundred years ago. Most of the buildings that will be in New York in 2040 have already been built, and most of them are the equivalent of gas-guzzling pickup trucks. But simply allocating a few billion dollars to a cash-for-clunkers scheme won't magically transform America's building fleet from a Hummer into a Prius. It makes much more sense to transform existing buildings than to build energy-efficient ones from scratch.

Focusing on energy efficiency can help reflate and reinvigorate damaged, declining assets. That is exactly what happened at the Empire State Building.[4] Several years ago the Empire State Building was perhaps the most famous office building that nobody wanted to be in. When it rose in sixteen months amid the gloom of 1930–1931, the Art Deco spire was an example of entrepreneurial gumption, a blossoming of can-do spirit amid the Great Depression. But the building didn't keep up with the times. Superseded by the World Trade Center as the tallest building in New York, and by pretty much every postwar building as more modern and desirable, it was hamstrung by small floor plates and narrow windows. A partnership of Harry Helmsley (best remembered for being Leona's husband) and Malkin Properties, led by the founder Lawrence Wien and his son-in-law Peter Malkin, bought the Empire State Building in 1961. Entangled in long-running litigation, the feuding partners were collecting B-list rents from B-list clients.

In August 2006 a settlement left Malkin Properties, now led by Peter Malkin and his son, Anthony Malkin, in control as managing agent and owner. Faced with a choice of selling the trophy asset or fixing it up, the Malkins chose to look inward, embarking on a $550 million effort to spruce up the building and make it a more attractive destination for tourism and business. Malkin Properties restored the Art Deco lobby, reengineered the tourist experience, replaced all the elevator cabs, and spruced up the bathrooms and common area hallways. "We were really bringing the building into the twenty-first century," said Anthony Malkin. As with any significant building project, this effort had to be green. But Malkin was frustrated. LEED standards, the accepted criteria for a building's relative greenness, are more about marketing than metrics. The LEED measurements award more points for installing bike racks than for quantifiable efforts to cut energy use. "The concept of green is very well and good, but what really matters is energy efficiency," Malkin told me.

For Malkin, making the Empire State Building more efficient was in part a marketing exercise, but it was also an effort to help tenants do more with less. When it comes to the three main costs for tenants—salaries, rent, and utilities—the last is the only one where the landlord can make a big difference. Malkin had already been thinking about using one of the smaller buildings in his portfolio as a demonstration project for how to retrofit an older structure. W&H Properties, one of Malkin Properties' subsidiaries, owns nine large prewar buildings in Midtown Manhattan. But in a meeting in the summer of 2007, Ira Magaziner, the architect of the failed Clinton health plan of 1993, suggested that Malkin use the Empire State Building instead. The company was already plotting a gut renovation, and any work done there would attract attention. Malkin Properties began to work on a plan with the Rocky Mountain Institute, a Colorado-based think tank that focuses on energy issues. Engineers had plenty of ideas on how to improve operations and reduce energy use. But there was no accepted methodology for calculating the results. For nine months they reviewed sixty-seven different energy-efficiency measures and applied the tools of modern industrial management: benchmarking the energy consumption, monitoring, verification, and writing contracts with suppliers that guaranteed specific energy-reduction performance. The practical approach led them to avoid showy items like solar panels and instead focus on replacing windows; reimagining the lighting scheme; using components, fixtures, and appliances that received Energy Star ratings from the Department of Energy; redoing the air-conditioning systems; and recycling. In 2008, as Manhattan's property market spiraled downward, Malkin hired Milwaukee-based Johnson Controls to carry out the plan. "The incremental cost of doing the retrofit, or what I call the Empire State Rebuilding program, from an energy-efficiency perspective, was a 3 percent increased cost," said Malkin. In other words, the energy efficiency add-ons cost an extra $13 million. But the owners figured they'd get it all back within three years through reduced energy use.

When the work on the base building was completed in the spring of 2011, the Empire State Building cut the same profile in the New York skyline, but it was slimmer in some crucial ways. The contract with Johnson Controls guaranteed that the remodeled building uses 39 percent less energy than it did before, and it earned the LEED Gold certification. But the return and impact don't come from lower electricity costs alone. With a more effective internal recycling system, the building recycles all tenant waste and diverts more than 75 percent of internal construction and demolition waste from landfills. The building turns junk into gold. "It's gotten to the point where we get paid to remove our waste rather than paying to have it removed," said Malkin.

When Malkin Properties formally took over the building in 2006, the average rent was $26.50 per square foot, which was at the low end of the market for Manhattan. But even at that knockdown price, it wasn't anywhere near full. "We're about 20 percent vacant," Malkin said in the spring of 2011. But after the renovation it appealed to more upscale tenants. "In addition to redoing the building, we're redoing the tenancy," Malkin said. The French cosmetics company Coty took most of two floors in 2008 for its U.S. headquarters and more than doubled its space in June 2011. An Italian accounting firm, a Swedish conglomerate, Turkish Airlines, and the *People's Daily* of China have all checked in, paying significantly higher rents. "We're now doing leases at the base of the building that average $49 to $50, and at the top we're getting into the $60s," said Malkin. In May 2011 the Empire State Building scored its biggest coup: LinkedIn, the Silicon Valley networking startup, whose growth demonstrates the ability of the U.S. economy to develop highly valuable, global companies at warp speed, took the entire twenty-fifth floor at a "high $40-per-square-foot range." "Five years ago, I never would have believed we would have had a tenant like this," Malkin told *Crain's New York Business*. And the investments have yielded other returns. Part of the goal of the redesign was to improve the experience for tourists, with faster elevators to better designed observation decks. And that allowed the owners to tap into an internal gold mine. With tourism to New York boom-ing, driven in part by foreign arrivals, the Empire State Building in 2011 generated about $60 million in income from tourism alone, as Charles Bagli reported in the *New York Times.*

Like BigBelly, the efforts at the Empire State Building are small in the scheme of things, but they have the potential for scale. And they are a good example of the way an owner can strengthen and ultimately use existing assets to much greater effect. The Malkins created value and new revenue streams by more intelligently man-aging what already existed. "If we only succeeded at the Empire State Building, we failed," said Malkin. Malkin Properties is apply-ing the lessons it learned to the other old office buildings in its port-folio and is pledging to offer its findings to other building owners.

A study by McKinsey & Co. conducted in the summer of 2009 concluded that the United States could cut energy use outside the transportation sector by 23 percent by 2020, slashing $1.2 trillion in waste, "well beyond the $520 billion up-front investment (not including program costs) that would be required."[5] That $520 bil-lion in up-front investments is the sticking point to making effi-ciency investments in a time of slow growth. You've got to spend money to save money. Anthony Malkin, the third-generation owner of an eighty-year-old building, had the perspective and free-dom to invest $550 million in the Empire State Building. But most executives have short-term perspectives. And when they're fearful about the future and concerned about debt payments, it's hard to make the internal case for big up-front energy investments. "Tradi-tional energy efficiency is characterized by big-ticket capital expen-ditures. You pay a lot for equipment, and it takes a few years for the investment to pay back," said Tim Healy, the CEO of EnerNOC.[6] The Boston-based company has been able to turn this proposi-tion on its head. It has two main lines of business, each of which depends on delivering energy savings to—and through—buildings with little or no up-front costs. Between 2007 and 2010 its revenues quadrupled, from $60 million to $280 million, while the size of the virtual power plant it runs grew sixfold.

Electricity is a highly procyclical business. On hot days, when a lot of people are already using a lot of electricity to power air conditioners, more people crank up the air-conditioning. And when few people are using electricity, at night and on cool days, there's little extra demand. That poses a challenge for utilities. The old response was to build spare capacity that would sit idle most of the time and could be called into action at peak times. But that's a highly inefficient and expensive proposition. And in many areas of the country, the market price of the extra electricity goes through the roof at times of peak use. The resulting volatility causes customers and utilities to suffer in periods when the system is already producing all it can.

Utilities like to say that the most efficient power plant is the one that doesn't have to be built. So what if, instead of keeping a real power plant on standby, utilities could construct a virtual power plant? Rather than produce energy, this virtual plant would reduce the need for electricity use. It's far better to invest in measures that can cut use by 5 or 10 percent at peak periods (90-degree days in August) than to build and maintain a standby power plant that will be called into action for just a few days per year. The concept of encouraging some users to dial down their electrical loads at a time when other users are ramping it up is called "demand response." In recent years, information and communications technology has enabled much greater use of demand response.

Utilities negotiate deals with big users, who agree to dim lights and turn down air-conditioning or heating when asked. They also pay companies like EnerNOC to do it for them. EnerNOC has effectively created a very large virtual power plant by obtaining commitments from companies that let it reach into their systems and dial down energy usage. But EnerNOC doesn't simply flip a switch. When EnerNOC signs up big users—hospitals, colleges, office buildings—it installs software that analyzes the facility's energy use in minute detail. The company then calculates how much energy each office, hallway, closet, nook, and cranny is using and analyzes the airflow through every piece of equipment. "When we submeter a facility, we can receive 6,000 to 10,000 data points on a building's management system in real time," said Healy. "As a result, we can see where air is being moved unnecessarily." It then calculates how buildings can shed load quickly without disrupting operations, by turning off the lights in a rarely used hall, or maybe running air-conditioning a few degrees higher when called upon to do so. There's no installation cost for the user. EnerNOC shares the payments it gets from the utilities with customers who agree to be part of the plan to reduce usage. When customers actually cut their usage, they receive additional payments. The demand-response model has proved attractive in a recessionary environment of pinched capital spending. EnerNOC's demand-response program grew from 800 customers with 2,200 sites at the end of 2007 to 4,750 customers at 11,150 sites by September 2011.

From the beginning of 2008, when the recession started, to the third quarter of 2011 EnerNOC expanded its ability to supply power nearly sixfold without stringing up a single line. Its "megawatts under management" rose from 1,100 at the end of 2007 to more than 7,000 in September 2011. For comparison's sake, the Indian Point nuclear power plant outside New York City has a capacity of 2,000 megawatts. That's equivalent to the energy produced by three and a half nuclear plants, enough to power about 7 million homes. Time and again this plant has been called into action by utilities—300 times in the first three quarters of 2011 and 225 times in the summer alone. On July 22, 2011, EnerNOC's network "delivered approximately 1,230 megawatts of demand response capacity," helping to reduce the risk of blackouts and lessening the need for utilities and power users to buy electricity on the spot market. EnerNOC has expanded operations to Canada, New Zealand, and Australia.

EnerNOC has a second, smaller line of business that pivots off its main line of demand response. It sells software that analyzes buildings and generates ideas on how to cut energy use. In effect it promises that the service will be free to customers. "We're guaranteeing that they'll be able to identify energy savings opportunities worth at least twice what they pay us on an annual basis," said Healy. EnerNOC contracts to reduce energy use by 8 to 10 percent and shares the savings. At Morgan Stanley's New York headquarters, it identified more than $100,000 worth of savings "from operational energy efficiencies, such as refining automated schedules to better align with actual occupancy behavior." (Translation: turning off lights and cranking down the air-conditioning on the trading floor when fewer people are around.) Like BigBelly, EnerNOC is a relatively small business. Its revenues in 2010 were about $280 million. But the market it addresses is a huge one, and its contribution can't be tallied on its sales or from the taxes it pays; it comes from its potential to save utilities and utility customers from large expenses on a recurring basis. A widget on EnerNOC's home page tracks, in real time, the amount of money customers have saved by using its services. On the afternoon of January 5, 2012, the total stood at $410,399,537. Like BigBelly, EnerNOC has shown an ability to scale up rapidly in a very harsh financial climate and to take its model abroad.

Energy consumption is about 8 percent of gross domestic product, but it has outsize implications for foreign policy, national security, and the environment. In the twentieth century the United States constructed a society geared around low-cost and plentiful energy that doesn't work as well in an era of high-cost energy. Driving a Hummer fifty miles to Walmart from an exurban 4,200-square-foot McMansion, which costs a ton to heat, didn't make much sense in the first place; it made even less sense in 2009 and 2010, with unemployment high and gas and heating oil at $4 per gallon. The addiction to foreign oil, and our inability to quickly remake the systems that rely on it, contribute to the sense of helplessness in the face of decline. And yet the American economy has shown a significant capacity to do more with less, even in the absence of a carbon tax or other government mandates. All we have to do is try a little.

Large businesses have found they can reap significant savings from efficiency when they focus on it. In recent years Walmart, the nation's largest retailer and its largest private sector employer, has hit a wall in the United States.[7] Its lower-end consumers, who were hit hard by the recession, haven't participated fully in the recovery. It has long since saturated rural and exurban America and is finding it difficult to penetrate urban markets. Walmart's same-store sales, the key metric for the health of retailers, fell in 2009, again in 2010, and once more in the first two quarters of 2011. The company's monthly sales figures became so depressing that Walmart stopped reporting them in 2009. So, in an age of diminished prospects, the company began to look for other profit levers. If sales were stuck at current levels, it would have to find other ways to reduce recurring costs. In 2005 Walmart, which has always been evangelical about cutting costs, started to tackle gas usage. It set a goal of doubling the efficiency of its vast trucking fleet, from 5.9 miles per gallon in 2005 to 13 mpg by 2015. Walmart didn't reinvent the wheel or the semitrailer or even the culture of driving. Instead it took what was out there: putting wind skirts along the bottom and sides of the trailers to change the airflow, installing power units that enable a small diesel engine to replace the main engine for heating and cooling the cab, and replacing clunkers with new, more efficient trucks. In 2008 and 2009 Walmart replaced about two-thirds of its fleet with newer models. By 2008 the fleet was up to 7.1 miles per gallon, an increase of 20 percent. But the company also focused on areas that had nothing to do with energy and everything to do with making incremental improvements: route mapping, logistics, and packing schemes that eliminated unnecessary driving. Driving less produces the same amount of cost savings as driving more fuel-efficient rigs and doesn't require as much up-front investment. Between 2008 and 2010 the company increased the number of cases of goods it delivered to its U.S. stores by 134 million, while eliminating 149 million miles of driving. Fewer miles, more goods, and less gas used per mile translate into significant savings. Walmart is a case study in continuous improvement in efficiency.

Energy efficiency is all well and good, but people in the business of delivering goods can also gain efficiencies from software that monitors drivers and from continually redesigning work processes and tools. Logistics companies have figured that they can squeeze more profit dollars out of the same amount of business by just being a little bit smarter. Designing routes more effectively and making incremental improvements in the way packages are handled, loaded, and stacked can yield significant results. A May 2011 research report by Justin Yagerman, a Deutsche Bank analyst, noted that between the first quarter of 2009 and the first quarter of 2011 UPS drivers clocked 10 percent fewer miles, even though the number of packages they delivered was roughly the same. This improved efficiency came about thanks to "increasingly leveraged

.IT, Package Flow Technology, and network optimization." One of UPS's secret weapons has been the elimination of left turns. For a decade UPS has been using software that generates routes without the dreaded left turns. The aversion has nothing to do with politics and everything to do with time and money. "You have a safety factor of crossing traffic, and you have a delay factor on commercial roads," Bob Stoffel, senior vice president of UPS, told Geoff Colvin of *Fortune*. "We figured it saves about 20 million miles." With gas at $4 a gallon and trucks getting 10 miles per gallon, that's about $8 million in fuel savings, by my calculations, per year. "That's why I love the engineers, they just love to continue to figure out how to make it better," Stoffel said.[8]

Engineers have done some of their most important and significant work in the auto industry. Americans' reliance on cars for mobility, and the proliferation of gas guzzlers, has been an economic drag on the country. But in the past several years the combination of rising prices, incentives for the purchase of more fuel-efficient vehicles, and competition has pushed manufacturers to improve. The imposition by the Obama administration of new mileage standards, which mandate that cars sold in the United States average 54.5 miles per gallon by 2025, has provided another stick. Again, as with the Empire State Building and EnerNOC, progress has come less from reinventing the wheel and more from tweaking existing systems and technologies. Engineers have focused their efforts on aerodynamics, more efficient combustion engines, start-stop technology that turns the engine off when cars idle, and adapting elements of the hybrid drive train to propel vehicles. Largely unseen, these efforts amount to a quiet revolution. New passenger cars sold in 2010 averaged 33.7 miles per gallon, up from 30.1 in 2006, an improvement of more than 10 percent. For light trucks, the average went from 22.1 mpg in 2005 to 25.1 mpg in 2010, a 13.6 percent increase.

As news channels obsess about gas prices and politicians call for more drilling, the U.S. auto fleet grows less reliant on oil every day. Every month, tens of thousands of Chevy Cruzes, Ford Escapes, and Hyundai Sonatas, vehicles that get 35 to 40 miles per gallon on the road, are sold, most likely replacing cars that were notably less efficient. Each month, about 30,000 hybrids leave car lots. Large sedans like the 2012 Buick LaCrosse, equipped with eAssist, which employs a small electric motor, check in at 25 miles per gallon in the city and 36 miles per gallon on the highway, a huge increase from the 2011 figures of 19 and 30 mpg. Between 2007 and 2010 gasoline consumption in the United States fell from 3.39 billion barrels to 3.3 billion, off about 2.7 percent, while miles driven fell 1.1 percent, from 3.03 billion in 2007 to 3 billion in 2010. Part of the decline can be traced to the downturn and decline in employment. But the data show the decreases continued even as growth returned and accelerated. Through November 2011 gasoline consumption was down 2.8 percent from the first eleven months of 2010, and through October 2011 miles traveled were down 1.4 percent from the first ten months of 2010.[9]

The restructuring of all three large U.S. automakers meant that in 2011 they relied less on SUVs and pickups and had funds available to invest in new platforms. Policy has played a role beyond the new fuel standards. Part of the reason the U.S. car industry became so reliant on SUVs and pickup trucks was because the carmakers needed the fat profit margins of these big, expensive cars to help meet overhead, pension, and labor costs. But the bankruptcy of General Motors, Ford's self-imposed restructuring, and the government-brokered deal to sell Chrysler to Fiat have changed the situation. Less debt and new deals with unions have left the three automakers able to make profits on the smaller, more efficient cars that are more in tune with the post-bust consumer zeitgeist. And the government's deal with Fiat was structured so that Fiat could increase its stake in Chrysler significantly by building a fuel-efficient engine in the United States and by bringing to market a U.S.-produced car that gets more than 40 miles per gallon. Fiat achieved both of those milestones in 2011 with the launch of the Fiat 500.

Another important development has taken place in the auto industry. The ethos of efficiency spurs companies and industries to make the best possible use of existing resources. Rather than dismantle production capacity vacated by General Motors, new users have taken it over, with different cost structures and with different types of vehicles in mind. In April 2010 a large factory in Fremont,

California, belonging to NUMMI, a joint venture of GM and Toyota, was closed, putting 4,500 people out of work. But Tesla, the Silicon Valley start-up that makes high-end electric sports cars, took it over in May 2010. In July 2009 GM closed the Boxwood Road plant in Newport, Delaware, where it had been making vehicles since 1947. In June 2010, armed with a $528.7 million loan from the U.S. government and $175 million of its own money, Fisker Automotive, an electric vehicle manufacturer based in Anaheim and founded by two former BMW executives, bought the plant for $10 million. It plans to make the Nina sports car there.

Hybrids and electric cars make up a tiny fraction of U.S. auto sales, and they may never be anything more than marginal components of the overall auto market. But they put pressure on all the others in the market to step up their game. Infrastructure may be falling down, and public investment in roads lags. But private investment in more efficient vehicles has been significant and has produced results.

American drivers are stopping to fill up less frequently thanks to the renewed focus on efficiency. And when they do stop, they're more likely to be filling up with domestically produced oil than they were at any time in the past decade, thanks to another successful effort to tap into internal resources. As we'll see in upcoming chapters, the advent of hydraulic fracking—drilling down, and then across, and using high-pressure water to break apart rock—has led to huge discoveries of natural gas and oil. Thanks to new production techniques, U.S. reserves of natural gas grew 40 percent between 2004 and 2009, and fracking has set off an investment boom in the Marcellus Shale in Pennsylvania and in the Barnett Shale in Texas. Fracking kindled an oil boom in North Dakota, which, we'll see later, has grown from an oil backwater into a producer the size of a small OPEC nation. Elsewhere technology is being put to new use to get at existing sources and to reflate and find value in assets that were thought to be played out. In California, in the fields in the San Joaquin Valley first tapped in the era of *There Will Be Blood,* tired oil fields are being given new life by the application of technology: injecting steam into the ground to force more oil to the surface. In a hundred-year-old oil field in McKittrick, California, GlassPoint

Solar and Berry Petroleum have set up a venture in which an on-site solar array generates a portion of the energy that creates the steam. Since 2009 oil production has reversed its decades-long decline. In 2011 the United States produced more oil than in any other year since 2002.

Think about these examples: the festering piles of garbage on city streets, an old skyscraper, the intractable problem of peak power, logistics companies struggling to make headway amid slack demand, a largely bankrupt heavy manufacturing industry, massive discoveries of valuable new resources. Here is a whole set of core U.S. businesses and business models that stopped making sense in the chastened post-bust environment, and whose apparently inevitable decline would drag America down with them. Each was given new life and created big economic benefits by focusing on efficiency and tapping into internal resources.

Government policy, restructuring, and efficiency have helped the economy recover better, stronger, and faster. These efforts, which helped stave off collapse and helped place key sectors of the economy on sounder footing, were all generated internally. But they alone can't help the U.S. economy regain all the ground it has lost or avoid decline. And while these efforts were vital and useful, the main forces that have helped propel growth came from *external* sources, not internal ones. While the United States was getting its economic house in order, it was also engaging with the world in a new way, showing that it could compete and attract resources in an age of rampant global growth.

CHAPTER 6

The Myth of International Irrelevance: Foreign Direct Investment

In the aftermath of the financial crisis, the United States began to recapitalize its economy. The process began with substantial assists from the government. The Federal Reserve put the financial system on life support by guaranteeing assets and giving free money to banks. Government stimulus funds helped substitute for vanished private sector money. These efforts bought time for the private sector to get its house in order. Banks recapitalized by increasing profits, companies restructured and focused on efficiency and productivity, and consumers repaired their balance sheets. This painful and hard work put the private sector in a much better position. But it wasn't nearly enough.

The country still needed vast new sources of capital to repair, rebuild, and make up for the equity lost in the housing and stock market busts. Where would it come from? Declinists commonly argue that we're broke and claim that the smart money is continuing to search for opportunities all over the globe, *except* in America. Well, a lot of it will come from the same source that helped fund the development of the colonies in the seventeenth century, the Revolutionary War in the eighteenth century, and the railroads in the nineteenth century: foreigners.

Colonists didn't just plunder the virgin New World; they invested here. Americans forget that European powers—France, the Netherlands, Russia—funded the lengthy rebellion against

King George III. The construction of an extensive railroad network in the decades after the Civil War bound the country together, created a national market for goods, established New York as a financial center, and supercharged growth for a half century. Between 1865 and 1980 Europeans bought about $2.5 billion in American securities; virtually all of these were railroad bonds. And when one-third of the railroads ended up going bankrupt after the panic of 1893, guess who got stuck holding the bag?

Though they've been burned in the United States during many earlier episodes, from the railroads in the 1890s to dot-com stocks in the 1990s and subprime debt in the 2000s, foreign investors continue to look to the United States. Since the collapse of 2008, a frequently overlooked attribute—America's openness and attractiveness to the world—has stood the country in good stead. As American companies went into survival mode and slashed jobs and investment, foreign capital continued to stream in from all over. In the post-bust era the United States has retained its title as the world's leading destination for foreign direct investment.

Foreign direct investment (FDI), which totaled $1.7 trillion in the decade from 2001 through 2010, fluctuates with the business cycle. It hit a low of $64 billion in 2003, surged to a historical peak of $328 billion in 2008, and then collapsed to $134.7 billion in 2009. In 2010 FDI rose to $194.5 billion, and it was $155 billion through the first three quarters of 2011. I'm not referring to the investment that arrives when, say, the Chinese Central Bank buys U.S. government bonds, or tourists spend on hotels and restaurants, or a London-based hedge fund buys shares of IBM. No, I'm talking about carefully considered, strategic investments. In the globalized economy, companies and individuals around the world have a vast array of choices as to where they can deploy capital, and more of them choose the United States than any other market. Swiss companies buy American companies, Brazilians buy apartments in Miami, and Japanese and German carmakers build brand-new factories in Tennessee and South Carolina. The flow amounts to several hundred million dollars a day, and it sustains a significant portion of the labor force, about 5 million jobs in any given year. Since foreign companies tend to invest disproportionately in manufacturing, the jobs supported by FDI tend to pay significantly more than typical U.S. service jobs. While U.S. companies hold earnings offshore in the hopes of a tax holiday, foreign companies often invest their earnings here. "Reinvested earnings more than tripled from $28.5 billion in 2009 to $93.1 billion in 2010," according to the Organization for International Investment (OFII), a Washington-based group that represents large foreign companies.[1]

If the United States is in terminal decline, if it is irrelevant, a spent economic force, why are foreigners so interested in investing here? There are several reasons. Even in the depths of self-pity and despair, the United States remains the largest, richest, most secure market in the world, full of attractive, valuable resources. Big American companies are right to invest overseas. Coca-Cola, McDonald's, Intel, Procter & Gamble, and other companies have long since saturated their home market. Household names can grow only as rapidly as households do. The statement that the United States contains 4 percent of the world's population and about 30 percent of the global economy is something of a Rorschach test. Americans look at it and conclude, correctly, that most of the world's activity is happening overseas. Foreigners interpret it, also correctly, to mean that the United States punches well above its weight and there's lots of business to be done here. For millions of companies and billions of people, the United States remains virgin turf, terra incognita. Foreigners are investing here because they want to tap into the resources, technical expertise, human capital, and large customer and consumer bases—and because they just like being here. In an age when competition can come from anywhere, so too can the capital that will revive a company, save jobs, or take that condo off the overleveraged hands of a relieved seller.

Consider real estate. The origins of our current malaise lie, in part, in the millions of poor decisions Americans made about spending and borrowing on real estate between 2002 and 2007. Millions of people bought houses they couldn't afford, builders built developments they had no business building, and banks spread loans around recklessly. The inability to clear the thicket of poorly timed purchases and investments is one of the factors holding the economy back. Which makes it very difficult to sell trophy properties such as the Aaron Spelling mansion in Los Angeles. After the television mogul's death, his widow tried to unload the *90210*-size abode, listing the 57,000-square-foot mansion in March 2009 for $150 million. Like many houses, the mansion, which sprawls over five acres in Holmby Hills and sports gift-wrapping rooms (yes, that's gift-wrapping *rooms,* plural), a bowling alley, and fivescore parking spots, lingered on the market. Who would want such a beast of a home? A British heiress, it turns out. In June 2011 Petra Ecclestone, the twenty-two-year-old daughter of the Formula One magnate Bernie Ecclestone, bought the house for an undisclosed price.[2]

There's nothing wrong with the high-end housing market that a few dozen oligarchs, heiresses, dissolute royals, and ambitious strivers can't solve. A century ago, when Americans made it big, they went back to their ancestral countries and made big statements through gaudy real estate purchases—think of Andrew Carnegie buying Skibo Castle in Scotland in 1898. Now it's the other way around. When people make huge sums of money elsewhere, they buy a piece of the new sod. Yuri Milner, the unassuming Russian Internet entrepreneur, has channeled large chunks of his fortune into expensive plots of Silicon Valley real estate. He's bought a stake in Facebook and a chunk of the online gaming company Zynga, and in March 2011 he bought a 25,500-square-foot French château in Los Altos Hills, the stomping and bicycling grounds of America's technological elite, for a reported $100 million.[3]

In Manhattan, where people routinely pay stupid money for much smaller trophy properties, foreigners from volatile countries are parking cash in the bedrock. The activity gives new meaning to the term "safe house." In July 2011 the *Wall Street Journal* reported that Barbara Garza, a director of a Mexican Coca-Cola bottling company, paid $19 million for two adjoining units at the Plaza Hotel. That was chump change compared with the $48 million that the Russian composer Igor Krutoy paid for a condo in the famed property. (Aren't composers supposed to be impoverished artistes living in garrets?) The Plaza's transformation from hotel to condominium, by the way, was financed by an Israeli developer. When news broke in December 2011 that former Citigroup CEO Sandy

Weill had successfully sold his apartment at 15 Central Park West for the unprecedented price of $88 million, the only question was: Which Russian oligarch was behind the purchase? It was Dmitry Rybolovlev, who bought it for his twenty-two-year-old daughter, Ekaterina.[4] Lower down on the luxury scale, Chinese buyers are pouring cash into condominiums around New York. Meanwhile money from Brazil, Argentina, and Colombia is pouring into the bottomless pit of south Florida real estate.

Foreigners find all sorts of U.S. trophy properties irresistible, and in turn are helping to put defunct properties to new use. A Malaysian casino company bought the headquarters of the *Miami Herald* from the McClatchy Co. for $236 million in May 2011, with plans to redevelop it as a casino. When Bruce Ratner, the owner of the New Jersey Nets, a franchise with a long history of futility, was forced to scale back his dream of building a huge arena and mixed-use complex in Brooklyn, he put the basketball team up for sale in 2009. The usual buyers of sports teams—hedge fund managers, private equity magnates, media moguls—weren't exactly lining up to purchase the New York area's second hoops team. But in 2010 Mikhail Prokhorov, a six-foot-five Russian natural resources and banking oligarch, plunked down $200 million for the privilege of owning the franchise. When the New York Times Co. ran into trouble in 2009 and concerns over the paper's viability inspired panic on the Upper West Side and in Park Slope, Brooklyn, where many of its employees live, the Sulzberger family turned to a Mexican investor, Carlos Slim Helú, the world's richest man. In January 2009 Slim lent the *Times* $250 million at a fat 14 percent interest rate to tide the Gray Lady over. The *Times* then cut costs, laid off workers, and paid back Slim in 2011, three years ahead of schedule.[5]

Foreigners don't simply take assets off the hands of overextended Americans or bail them out at usurious rates. They invest for growth. Because wind turbines are large and unwieldy devices, it makes sense to build them close to where they are going to be used. Since opening its first U.S. manufacturing facility in Windsor, Colorado, in 2008, Vestas, the Danish wind turbine maker, has become a significant presence in the Plains states. Its tower factory in Pueblo, one of four facilities in Colorado, is one of the largest such facilities in the world. Vestas employs 3,300 people in North America, with operations in twenty-eight states. Its factories represent a total capital investment of about $1 billion. And Europe-based suppliers such as Bach Composite, a Danish manufacturer of wind turbine components, have followed Vestas to Colorado.

Foreign companies also deploy capital in the United States to get access to technology and expertise. As we've seen, America still has much to show the world about how to tap into existing internal resources. It has led the world in developing new techniques for liberating natural gas and oil from shale. Foreign energy companies, eager to get a piece of the U.S. action and, more important, to learn how to bring hydraulic fracking to their own substrata, have invested in U.S. companies. In October 2010 CNOOC, the Chinese state oil company, agreed to invest more than $2 billion in a Texas oil and natural gas project with the natural gas titan Chesapeake. Reliance Energy, a unit of one of India's largest conglomerates, has plowed more than $3 billion into North American natural gas companies. Royal Dutch Shell, the Anglo-Dutch energy company, dished out $5 billion to get a foothold in the Marcellus Shale.[6]

They come to America for the natural resources—and for the human resources. It often seems that every American business leader wants to talk about his China, or India, or Persian Gulf strategy. Mumbai, Dubai, or bye-bye, as the saying goes in investment circles. But when I met with Sunil Godhwani, chief executive officer of Religare Enterprises, an Indian financial services company, in the lobby of the Morosani Posthotel in Davos, Switzerland, in January 2011, he wanted to talk about his U.S. strategy. With 2,200 offices in six hundred cities and $15 billion in assets under management, Religare is perfectly situated to cash in on the rising tide in India, where the population of high-net-worth individuals (those with over $1 million in assets) rose 80 percent between 2008 and 2010. Why would anyone want to go elsewhere? Well, in February 2010 Religare paid $200 million for a majority stake in Northgate Capital, a private equity firm based in San Francisco. In December 2010, just weeks before we met, Godhwani had bought a 55 percent stake in Landmark Partners, a fund of funds based in Simsbury, Connecticut, for $171 million. He wants to build an emerging-market investment bank, and he can't do that without American human and financial assets. "There is a lot of capital in America that will get deployed in emerging markets for better returns," said Godhwani, who has a master's degree in industrial engineering and finance from the Polytechnic Institute of New York. "The fact is the talent of managing money and the liquidity lies in the U.S. And when it comes to the mannerisms of working and businesses and analysis, they have superior models. They just need to be tweaked." Religare's board has authorized up to $1 billion for U.S. acquisitions.

One of the most depressing visions I've seen was the dismantling of a furnace from a decaying steel plant in Cleveland that belonged to LTV and was to be shipped to China. The process of U.S. industrial facilities migrating to Asia is still taking place. But in many areas FDI is now helping to revive abandoned American production capacity and create new factories. After Chrysler's brush with death in the fall of 2008, Fiat, an Italian company, stepped in, helped to avert liquidation—with a helping hand from the U.S. government—and injected new life into the automaker. CEO Sergio Marchionne, who has set up shop in Detroit, is using the investment as a platform to reintroduce the Fiat brand into the world's largest, and richest, auto market. Dozens of Chrysler dealers shut down in 2009, but in 2011 Fiat-Chrysler announced it was going to build a network of Fiat dealers in forty-one states. Since the 1980s foreign car companies—BMW, Toyota, Honda, Kia—have invested tens of billions of dollars in new U.S. factories, mostly in the South and Midwest. In 2011 foreign car firms produced 3.5 million vehicles in the United States, compared with 5.16 million from the erstwhile Big Three. In the fall of 2010, at a time when the economy was slipping back into a low-growth mode, BMW announced it would invest $750 million to expand its plant in Greenville, South Carolina. As Jeff Bennett reported in the *Wall Street Journal,* the facility will be "the largest U.S. car plant by number of employees" and will further tie "the German auto maker's future to the U.S." After the expansion, the plant, which was first opened in 1994, will employ 7,600 workers (and a multiple of that number at suppliers) and be able to produce as many as 240,000 vehicles per year.[7]

Investments in new facilities are known as "greenfielding."

Though greenfielding accounts for only about 20 percent of FDI (the rest tends to take the form of corporate acquisitions and the purchase of units), it packs a larger economic and emotional punch. I saw this firsthand on a visit to Dublin, Virginia, where an unlikely investment from an unlikely source in an unlikely place has provided a significant injection of capital—and hope.

Pulaski County lies so far west in the long finger of the state that extends underneath West Virginia and Kentucky that it is almost due south of Youngstown, Ohio. This is not the well-heeled, ethnically diverse Virginia of Alexandria and Fairfax County. But it's also not Appalachia. In nearby Blacksburg, home to Virginia Tech, a large research university, you'll find Middle Eastern markets and women in hijabs walking around town. Dublin has a population of about 2,300 people, 89 percent of them white, and a median family income of about $37,000. If more people lived in Pulaski, just a few miles down Lee Highway, it would be quaint. Instead, with its tiny Confederate war memorial, an old movie theater (that once had a separate entrance for blacks), and the massive, now vacant Pulaski Furniture factory, it looks forlorn.

In recent years the region has been heavily reliant on foreign companies for employment. A large Volvo truck operation employed 3,000 people and kept many local suppliers busy. But in 2008 Pulaski County's employer base started to disappear. Pulaski Furniture, which employed about 1,000 people, closed down. Volvo axed 2,000 employees. In May 2009 Findlay Industries, which made components for Volvo truck cabs, left its 110,000-square-foot building in a county-owned industrial park outside town, firing 100 workers. TMD Friction Group, a brake-pad manufacturer that was a tenant of the same park, shut down.

But in the spring of 2011 the former Findlay Industries facility was a beehive of activity, thanks to a significant investment by Grupo Phoenix, a plastics company based in Bogotá, Colombia. "We are here to bring jobs back to America," Alberto Peisach, Grupo Phoenix's president and chief executive officer, said at the formal opening on March 30, which featured state and local dignitaries, including Governor Robert McDonnell. Aric Bopp, the executive director of the New River Valley Economic Development Alliance, choked up as he spoke: "We know how important these types of jobs are to the community and I, personally, know how important these jobs are to the people who are out of work. . . . It's what keeps us up at night." Grupo Phoenix had already begun to invest $25 million to create 240 jobs in its first phase of operations and was considering adding another $15 million expansion that would result in a total of 350 jobs.

Of all the places Alberto Peisach was likely to end up, an industrial park in the shadow of Knob's Peak was pretty low on the list. His grandparents were immigrants from the Ukraine, Romania, and Poland who fled from pogroms in the 1930s and made their way to Colombia. A University of Pennsylvania engineering graduate, Peisach helped build Grupo Phoenix into a midsize plastics company in the 1990s. But Colombia was proving to be increasingly inhospitable. His grandmother, then seventy, was abducted. In 1997 gangsters killed his brother-in-law during a kidnap attempt. In 1996, when he was informed of a plan to kidnap his six-year-old son, Peisach turned to the Colombian intelligence agency. With police concerned they could not protect his children, Peisach moved his family to Miami the next day. The business remained, survived through Colombia's dark years, and thrived as the country made its stunning comeback. In 2010 Grupo Phoenix had sales of about $150 million, with ten facilities spread throughout Colombia, Venezuela, and Mexico. It boasted 4,000 employees and a reputation for supplying innovative plastic containers. Peisach is a polymath with a large personality; he's been involved in real estate and private equity, helped start a magazine for Hispanic businesspeople in the United States, and is interested in libertarian ideas. "Life is too short to drink bad wine," he said over dinner in New York.

Grupo Phoenix has ridden several hot American consumer trends. It makes inverted yogurt cups for Yoplait, containers for one of the biggest manufacturers of Greek yogurt, and the plastic coffee pods for the increasingly ubiquitous Keurig machines. It developed a seven-layer cup with a twelve-month shelf life for Green Mountain Coffee and was making these cups in Colombia. That was fine when Green Mountain was ordering 4 million per month, but as consumers and office managers latched onto the pods as a more effective caffeine delivery system than Starbucks, volumes ramped up to 50 million, then 100 million per month, and Green Mountain suggested that Grupo Phoenix locate production closer to the U.S. market. So the company hired a consulting firm in Chicago, and Peisach and his colleagues toured a couple of dozen sites. Dublin offered proximity to a railroad (the better to bring in raw supplies and reduce freight costs), cheap electricity (about 5 cents per kilowatt-hour), and a ready workforce. State and local authorities in Virginia chipped in with aid: an $850,000 grant from the state to build out the plant, a $650,000 loan from the county, and a $450,000 grant from the Virginia Department of Rail and Public Transportation to construct a railroad spur, plus funds for training workers.

In May 2010, when Grupo Phoenix agreed to invest $25 million to build out the plant and announced it would hire 250 people, it was a big deal. "When I came down to the actual plant to look into putting in my application, there were two hundred to three hundred people waiting in the parking lot," said twenty-four-year-old Fred Davis, who works in quality control at the plant. "At our local employment agency in Radford, it was a half-mile line of people to get in to apply."

The Grupo Phoenix plant is an inversion of much of the light manufacturing and processing industries in this part of the country. Jaime Lederman, a forty-six-year-old sandy-haired former Colombian national tennis champion, is the CEO of the U.S. unit. He wears a training watch, jeans, and a blue polo shirt. When we met, a whiteboard in his office was filled with a matrix describing the progress of equipment installation: *Maquina, Plan, Quien, Estado.* In a nearby conference room, a dozen small-statured, dark-skinned Colombians pored over laptops; these were the executives and managers responsible for shared services, human resources, IT, and accounting. On the shop floor, a clean expanse dotted with large machines and presses, the managers and the people who know how to work the thermoforming equipment speak Spanish, while the Anglos are the rank and file. Many of them are women in their fifties who used to work at places like Walgreens.

The juxtaposition of worldly Colombians and rural Virginians

90

is poignant at times. "This is not Bogotá. This is not Miami," said Lederman. "One shock to us is that we're used to people, if they're doing something at five o'clock, you continue doing it. Here, if the shift is eight to five, at five you leave. We learn that this is part of the culture." When Fred Davis, who has lived in Pulaski County his whole life, traveled to Bogotá in 2010 for ten days of training in plastics forming and maintenance, it was the first time he had left the United States other than a trip to the Bahamas. Of the five other new hires who traveled with him, two had never flown before, and four had never left the country. Grupo Phoenix had to help them get passports.

Davis came back with straw hats, coffee, and emeralds for his girlfriend and mother, and an appreciation for Colombia. "A lot of people want to think it's a Third World country, a horrible place to be. You only knew the things you heard about Colombia—drugs, Pablo Escobar," he said. "We went down there and felt very safe." On the weekend colleagues took them sightseeing to Monseratte, the hill overlooking Bogotá, and to Zipaquirá, the underground salt cathedral. "This is the first company I've worked for where I can pick up the phone and call the CEO and talk to him about a problem," said Davis. "We have dinner. We sit down like a family at the table. You don't see that out of American companies."

In May 2011 Grupo Phoenix was up to a hundred employees in Virginia and adding ten to fifteen per week, and work was about to start on a 120,000-square-foot expansion. When the payroll reaches 350, this company will be one of the top ten employers in the region. The jobs pay $13 to $15 an hour, which is not princely, but Grupo Phoenix offers health insurance, participation in a 401(k), a subsidy for gym membership, and training assistance. "One of the things that Phoenix is going to do is pay for me to finish my engineering degree," said Davis. But the economic impact extends beyond payroll. The factory buys boxes locally and is providing work for another small firm owned by an immigrant in the same industrial park, L.H. Corp., a small machining company owned and run by Clemens von Claparede, a native of Germany who immigrated in 1983. L.H. Corp. saw its revenues scythed in half during the recession. But they've bounced back. The company, which has fourteen employees, helps fix Krispy Kreme doughnut cutters and equipment for Flowers Baking. Now L.H. has a new customer. "They moved in, and almost the next day they came with the first little project," von Claparede said. "Whenever they have breakdowns, four of them come over, and they absolutely love us, because I speak Spanish. This past month was probably the second month in which we had a substantial amount of work from them."

In crippled industries where Americans see only doom and gloom, foreigners frequently see opportunity. In May 2010 the Canada-based TD Bank (formerly Toronto-Dominion) took over three failed Florida banks with a combined sixty-nine branches and $3.9 billion in assets. In January 2011 ICBC (Industrial and Commercial Bank of China) bought Bank of East Asia, a Hong Kong bank with thirteen branches in New York and California, for a price said to be $100 million. According to the FDIC, eight banks that are affiliates of foreign firms have acquired eleven failed institutions.[8]

From Circuit City to Borders, U.S. retailers are contracting and vacating acres of space. But foreign retailers are taking up some of the slack, paying record prices for storefronts in prominent areas. Uniqlo, the rapidly growing Japanese chain owned by Fast Retailing, opened its first U.S. store in New York's Soho in 2006. In October 2011 the Japanese apparel retailer opened its three-story, 89,000-square-foot flagship store on the corner of Fifth Avenue and Fifty-third Street in Manhattan. In 2010, when it signed the $300 million, fifteen-year lease for the space, formerly the location of a Brooks Brothers store, it was reported to be the most expensive retail lease in New York's history. While Uniqlo occupies pride of place on Fifth Avenue, a few blocks down from Bergdorf Goodman and Tiffany, hyperluxury retailers whose sales bounced back quickly in 2009 and 2010, the store aims at different customers. The clothes are affordable, but not necessarily cheap; cashmere sweaters, a line designed by Jil Sander, go for up to $149. There's so much cashmere stacked from floor to ceiling at the store, which employs 650 people, that it makes one wonder if Uniqlo means "corner on the goat market" in Japanese. (In fact, it's an amalgam of the words "unique" and "clothing.") Uniqlo knows that people are spending money in the United States, or at least in New York. The Soho store is the chain's highest-grossing outlet. Establishing a major presence smack in the middle of Manhattan allows retailers to service the local market, and gives them exposure to tens of millions of visitors. "Fifth Avenue is the best shopping street in New York, and it was very important to us to have a great location here," Shin Odake, Uniqlo's U.S. CEO told me.

And this is just the beginning. "As a brand, we want to be as ubiquitous in the U.S. as we are in Japan," Odake said. "We are looking at real estate in different cities throughout the United States, and our intention is to open stores in every major city." The company has spoken of its desire to open two hundred stores in the United States. Founded in 1984, Uniqlo isn't put off by concerns over stagnation in the country. "We also had an economic struggle in Japan, but during those difficult times we were able to grow," Odake told me. What does Uniqlo, which has 840 stores in Japan, see in the United States that few locals do? "The U.S. is obviously an extremely important market for us, because it's the number one economy in the world," said Odake. "We'd like to grow our business to $50 billion by 2020, and in order to do that we have to gain market share in the United States." The company's founder, Tadashi Yanai, wants to beat out Gap and Spain's Zara as the biggest retailer in the world. Company officials have spoken of boosting U.S. sales alone to $12 billion by 2020. That means it will need to open a lot of stores. The company is focused less on the economy's cyclicality and more "on the fact that the U.S. is the biggest market in the world."

Chinese banks too have taken up residence on Fifth Avenue. ICBC opened a New York branch in 2008, taking the twentieth floor of Trump Tower, and let it be known that the Chinese are interested in more than treasury bills. In June 2010 ICBC closed its first commercial property loan in the United States, lending $150 million to help refinance a twenty-seven-story office and retail tower in Midtown, at 650 Madison Avenue. The building that occupies the corner of Fifty-seventh and Broadway in Manhattan was a classic story of New York bubble-era exuberance. Since the 1990s the building had housed the offices of *Newsweek*. But in 2007 and

2008 the building's owner, the Moinian Organization, decided to kick out long-standing tenants, borrow tens of millions of dollars, sheath the building in glass, and jack up rents. By 2009, when the renovation was to be complete, hedge funds would be lining up to pay megabucks for the high floors, which offered unobstructed views of Central Park. The timing couldn't have been more wrong. In April 2011, with rival investors circling to take control of the troubled building, the Bank of China lent the owners $250 million to refinance 3 Columbus Circle. Seven months later it lent $800 million to Brookfield Office Properties to refinance 245 Park Avenue. "Many of the largest loans, the large property financings that we've observed over the last few quarters, have depended on the extension of credit by international lenders that are active in the U.S.," said Sam Chandan, the chief economist at Real Capital Analytics.

All things considered, it would be better to have Chinese entities financing the private sector than the public sector. And you'd rather have them investing on an equity basis than on a debt basis. That is happening too. According to the Rhodium Group, in 2010 Chinese companies pumped $5.2 billion into U.S. companies; in the first nine months of 2011, forty-nine deals involving Chinese companies resulted in $4.2 billion in new investment. "The U.S. gets much more foreign direct investment than China, and it could get even more," says Karl Sauvant, executive director of the Vale Columbia Center on Sustainable International Investment at Columbia University. (That institute was itself the recipient of foreign direct investment. In 2008 it was endowed by and named after a Brazilian mining company.)

In a sign of how the United States is successfully engaging with the world in new ways, emerging markets that benefited from the U.S. offshoring of its industrial base have emerged as a source of new investment. "Look out for the Brazilians and the Indians," the CEO of a large Fortune 500 consumer products company told me in 2010. He wasn't talking about the World Cup. Driven by a rising middle class, robust commodity markets, and trade with China, Brazil's domestic economy powered through the economic crisis and the recession. In March 2010 a KPMG survey of executives from seventeen countries found that "Brazilian businessmen are the most optimistic in the world" about the future of the global economy. The acquisitions have centered mostly on large-scale, old-economy industries, the type that first gained national scale in the United States on the backs of the railroads in the 1890s: beer, meatpacking, oil, and chemicals. InBev, the Belgian-Brazilian beer company, led the way in 2008 by acquiring Anheuser-Busch. JBS, the giant Brazilian meatpacker, bought Pilgrim's Pride for $800 million in the fall of 2009 and then in January 2010 acquired Swift for $1.4 billion. It now has a very large presence in the United States. The same month, Petrobras, Brazil's oil behemoth, bought a chunk of Devon Energy's stake in the Gulf of Mexico's Cascade field. Marfrig agreed to acquire Keystone Foods for $1.25 billion, turning the Brazilian firm into a key supplier to all-American fast-food chains like Subway and McDonald's. Speaking of fast food, in September 2010 Burger King was bought by a Brazilian private equity firm for $3.3 billion. In February 2010 the Brazilian resin producer Braskem acquired the polypropylene business of Sunoco Chemicals for $350 million. In April 2010 Banco do Brasil, the big bank largely owned by Brazil's government that has outposts in Miami, New York, and Washington, D.C., received permission from the Federal Reserve to set up retail banking operations in the United States. It bought a small bank with three branches in Florida as a beachhead. "In five years, we want to have 20 branches in the U.S.," Allan Toledo, Banco do Brasil's international business vice president, told reporters in the spring of 2011. "We will invest close to $25 million [to do so]."[9]

And so on. Every day several hundred million dollars of capital pours into the United States. Though not as high as it was during the boom years, FDI is clearly a BFD. The Organization for International Investment says U.S. subsidiaries of global companies employed 5.6 million Americans at the end of 2010, up from 5 million in 2008, with a collective annual payroll of $408.5 billion. And these numbers are just scratching the surface. In general, FDI derives primarily from developed markets. In 2010, 84 percent of FDI derived from six European countries, Canada, and Japan. The lead investor in 2010 was Switzerland at $35.6 billion, followed by the United Kingdom ($31 billion) and Japan. No developing countries were in the top twenty. Which means there is much more room for growth.

The process of foreign investment in the United States is not without its hiccups. The Committee on Foreign Investment in the United States, the federal body that reviews prospective deals, has blocked investments such as the Chinese technology firm Huawei's 2008 efforts to purchase the listing networking company 3Com. Dubai Ports World's effort to purchase a company that ran ports in Baltimore and other cities inspired a great deal of ire back in 2006. And for reasons that are difficult to nail down, the prospect of Budweiser being owned by a foreign beer company instilled a high level of angst. It shouldn't. Regardless of its ownership, the company makes the same watery beer. The agita is somewhat reminiscent of what we went through in the late 1980s, when Japan Inc. was seen as an economic aggressor. But foreigners aren't any worse bosses or stewards of iconic brands than Americans are. And they are no more likely to take our trophy assets back to home markets than Japanese buyers were to disassemble Rockefeller Center and Pebble Beach and cart them off to Japan when they acquired control of those assets in the 1980s. By and large, foreign investors come to the United States for the right reasons.

As economic development spreads throughout the world, a standoffish attitude toward FDI is a luxury the United States can't afford anymore. America still leads the world in direct investment, said Nancy McLernon, president of the OFII. "But our share is going down. We used to get 40 percent, and now we get about 20 percent. Looking at the trends, we have to work harder." American companies must be open to foreign investment, ownership, and partnerships. We have to be prepared for higher levels of FDI, not just in terms of policy and trade, but psychologically. "As American businesses, we should not be fearful of partnering with foreign investors. This is something we need to do." That's what Brad Williams, the chief executive officer of MVP RV, a recreational vehicle manufacturer based in Riverside, California, told the *Wall Street Journal* in March 2011. The recreational vehicle industry was hit hard in the recession. But in 2011 MVP RV was poised to boost its annual production from 10,000 in 2010 to 40,000, and to add

1,200 employees. The company had been fortified by a $310 million investment from Winston Chung, a Chinese businessman whose company, Winston Global Energy, makes batteries for electric cars. "It's almost something out of a fairy tale," Williams said.[10]

It's no fairy tale. Foreign capital has been on these shores, in one form or another, for four centuries. Now that there's so much more capital sloshing around the world, there's likely to be more foreign capital washing up on our shores. We'd be better off welcoming it than shooing it away. We don't need foreign investors just for their cash; we need them for their ability to help American workers and factories break into foreign markets and forge connections to a growing world. According to the OFII, U.S. subsidiaries of foreign companies account for about 18 percent of total exports. BMW's factory in Greenville, South Carolina, for example, sends 70 percent of its production overseas. And therein lies the key to debunking another enduring myth about America's economic present—and future.

CHAPTER 7

The Myth of Not Making Stuff the World Wants

To hear declinists tell it, the United States doesn't make anything anymore. It can't compete on wages. It has outsourced, offshored, and dismantled its way to economic oblivion. Americans are like the humans in the film *Wall-E*, consuming everything, producing nothing: useless, obese spectators. While the rest of the world's nations are getting rich, trading with each other and selling stuff to Americans, a mere 1 percent of American firms manage to export.

But that's a myth too.

In fact, as Donald Trump might say, the United States is a world-class exporter. We may be a nation of isolationist homebodies—only about 30 percent of Americans have passports—but even as the talk of decline has grown, exports have risen, in real terms and as a percentage of GDP. In fact, the United States is the top exporter in the world.[1] And most of the stuff it exports is stuff. In 2009 exports stood at $1.53 trillion ($1.06 trillion in goods and $470 billion in services), compared with $1.36 trillion for Germany and $1.33 trillion for China. Other countries do better on some metrics. Germany certainly punches above its weight, with exports at 44 percent of GDP. Australia, an island nation, has exports equal to about a quarter of its economy. China has become the world's factory. Yet no country exports more services than the United States, and only China and Germany ship more manufactured goods beyond their borders. The United States remains the category killer in food, airplanes, chemicals, and missiles. As a percentage of gross domestic product, exports may be comparatively low, about 14 percent. That's a long way from the high of 18 percent in the 1790s, but it is up substantially from a decade ago. And the low ratio can largely be ascribed to the fact that the United States is a rich country with a very large domestic market, surrounded by smaller countries. We haven't exported all that much because we had relatively few places to which we could easily ship goods.

The misperception about exports and America's ability to engage with the world economically has helped fuel rampant pessimism. But since the cries of decline began to ring out amid the Great Recession of 2008–2009, exports have in fact been rising. Demand from foreign consumers—companies and individuals alike—began to fill in for the pinched domestic market. U.S. exports, which had soared to $165 billion in July 2008, fell rapidly after the Lehman Brothers crash. After bottoming in April 2009 at $124 billion, they ticked upward, helping to lead the recovery. President Obama's March 2010 proclamation that the country should strive to double exports by 2015 seemed like a pipe dream. (If we read between the lines, he was saying the United States should set a goal of doubling the monthly export total from its low of April 2009.) But by October 2011 monthly exports had already risen to a record $179 billion, an increase of 44 percent from the bottom in April 2009. That's almost halfway toward doubling.

The shape of the economy has shifted, from agriculture to manufacturing in the first half of the twentieth century and from manufacturing to services in the second half. Since the Great Recession of 2008–2009 it has shifted from an economy led almost exclusively by domestic growth to one in which foreign trade plays a larger role. From April 2009 to July 2011 monthly exports rose nearly 44 percent, while the economy probably grew about 4 percent. Exports have been a bright spot in job creation. In 2010, a year in which the economy added 1.03 million new jobs, the number of jobs supported by exports rose by 500,000 from 8.7 million to 9.2 million. That year, the Commerce Department estimated that each

$181,000 in exports supported one job. Apply that ratio to 2011, and by the end of the year, exports were supporting up to 10.6 million positions.

In *The Next Convergence*, the Nobel laureate Michael Spence convincingly argues that the world is in the middle of a century-long third industrial revolution, in which the 85 percent of humanity that missed the first two centuries of modernization will finally climb aboard the growth train. China is done living in the eighteenth century, India is done living in the sixteenth century, and Brazil is done living in the nineteenth century. (Russia, I'm not so sure about.) Canada and Mexico, which have historically been America's largest trade partners, are good ones to have. They're pretty big, share a large border with the United States, and aren't desperately poor. But with each passing year, new trading partners are boosting their ability to buy more U.S. goods. Exports to China soared from $41.2 billion in 2005 to $92 billion in 2010, and to $104 billion in 2011. If we want to prosper, Americans must figure out how to sell to more people around the world.

The good news is that we're already doing it. Foreigners may not like us much, but they sure like all the stuff we make. The world literally can't live without us.

In April 2011 David Wessel, the normally mild-mannered *Wall Street Journal* columnist, sounded an alarm: "The Chinese want our nuts." Gulp! Wessel wasn't talking about some strange new Eastern fertility treatment. He was talking about pecans. The United States grows about two-thirds of the globe's supply of pecans, mostly for domestic consumption. But the Chinese have taken a shine to the nuts, which they regard as brain-friendly health food. From virtually nothing in 2006, China "bought one-quarter of the U.S. crop" in 2009. Between 2005 and 2010 "exports of pecans rose more than 20-fold." And it's not just pecans. In 2010 the *New York Times* reported that China's purchase of American tree nuts had risen eightfold in the previous five years, from $89 million to $737 million.[2]

More people around the world are eating better. That's good, because the United States is to food what Saudi Arabia is to oil. In 2010 the United States produced about 480 million metric tons of agricultural products, followed by China (450 million metric tons), India (220 million), the European Union (210 million), and Brazil (180 million). On a per capita basis, the United States is a dynamo of production, raising about 1.53 metric ton of crops per person, compared with a mere 0.343 metric ton in China and a truly measly 0.18 metric ton for India. No wonder Americans are so fat.[3]

In a world of rising food consumption, the United States is nicely situated to be hog butcher to the world. With just 15 percent of the typical household's budget devoted to food, the country has a much better capacity to absorb price increases that may result from rising global demand. Americans have long experience of producing massive quantities of agricultural staples, run a highly industrialized production system, and have the infrastructure that allows for the transport of massive quantities of goods. Despite the prevalence of all-you-can-eat buffets, Americans cannot in fact consume all the chow they produce. And so exports of food have boomed. According to the U.S. Department of Agriculture, agricultural exports leaped from $61.4 billion in 2004 to $114.8 billion in 2008, fell to $98.5 billion in 2009, and then bounced back smartly to a record $115.8 in 2010. In the first ten months of 2011, agricultural exports were $112 billion, up 24 percent from the first ten months of 2010. The country ran a $33.9 billion trade surplus in agricultural products in 2010 and a $33 billion surplus in the first ten months of 2011. In a modern-day analogue of carrying coals to Newcastle, the United States ships beef to Brazil, rice to Japan, and soybeans to China. According to James T. Areddy of the *Wall Street Journal*, "Soybeans represent the U.S.'s single-biggest export to China: $9.19 billion in 2009, topping the combined value of semiconductors and plastic materials." All these exports are making farmers richer. Farm income, which rose 27 percent in 2010, was expected to rise another 20 percent in 2011, to $94.7 billion. As the U.S. Department of Agriculture noted, "The top five earnings years for the past three decades have occurred since 2004."[4]

The United States has also been showing signs in recent years of becoming a significant exporter of the other vital resource: fuel.

America's energy obesity, and its need to import energy, inspire self-loathing as well as a sense of victimhood. Spend a few minutes at your local food co-op, and you'll hear the lament that with just 4 percent of the globe's population, Americans account for about 22 percent of its daily oil consumption. Petroleum-related imports accounted for a whopping 44 percent of the trade deficit in 2011. But a funny thing has happened to the globe's Jabba the Hutt of energy: it's slimming down and becoming an exporter. Thanks to a greater focus on efficiency, utilities' output in May 2011 was at the same level as in 2007. Vehicle miles driven in the United States in October 2011 were at the same level as in October 2003. As the U.S. car fleet grows steadily more efficient and less reliant on petroleum, the rest of the world is bringing huge fleets of cars and airplanes online and plugging more and more appliances and gadgets into the grid. If only the United States could produce a lot of fossil fuels — or fossil fuel substitutes — and export them. In fact, that's happening, in increasingly large numbers.

Like Saudi Arabia, the United States sits atop a massive supply of a fossil fuel that everyone on the planet loves to burn. Estimated reserves are 261 billion short tons, enough for 249 years of consumption at current levels. But coal is going out of style. In 2010 coal accounted for 45 percent of U.S. electricity generation, down from 52 percent in the first quarter of 2008. The Energy Department reported that in the first quarter of 2011, coal's share of electricity generation was its lowest "in more than 30 years." In 2010 U.S. coal consumption was 1.048 billion short tons, down 6.5 percent from 1.12 billion in 2008.

Coal is getting less popular at home, thanks to a variety of factors. Vast new discoveries of domestic, cleaner-burning natural gas are keeping prices of natural gas low and spurring more utilities to use this fuel to generate power. Here too standards have played an important role. State mandates are encouraging greater use of renewable energy, and regulators have signaled to American power producers that they should use fuels other than coal. Environmental Protection Agency regulations issued in late 2011 on mercury emissions for power plants are likely to lead to more closures of coal-fired plants.

Yet anthracite still has global appeal. China, along with plenty of other emerging economies, keeps the lights on largely by burning lumps of coal. So U.S. exports are up. From a recent low of 39.6 million short tons in 2002, U.S. coal exports more than doubled, to 81.5 million short tons in 2008, fell in 2009, and rebounded in 2010 to 60.85 million short tons, less than 6 percent of total U.S. production. The biggest customers include South Korea, Brazil, and China. America even sent some coal to Newcastle; about 2.14 million short tons were shipped to Britain in the first half of 2010. In the first three quarters of 2011 exports of coal were 79.6 million short tons, up 30 percent from the first quarter of 2010. With the average price of coal exports rising from $67 per ton in 2005 to $155 in the third quarter of 2011, the value of America's coal crop rose sharply. The country exported about $7.3 billion worth of coal in 2010. In the first three quarters of 2011, exports were about $11.9 billion.[5]

There's much more where that came from. Most of the coal for export is mined in Kentucky and West Virginia and floated down the Ohio and Mississippi Rivers or to eastern points of departure like the DTA terminal in Newport News, Virginia. The vast supplies in the western states are effectively landlocked. China, which takes in about 6 percent of U.S. coal exports, or about 4 million short tons, would undoubtedly take much more if it could be shipped from the West Coast. That may be happening soon. In February 2011 the *Wall Street Journal* reported that the Australian firm Millennium Bulk Terminals was seeking to build a coal export terminal on the Columbia River, near Longview, Washington. Peabody Coal, which in 2010 estimated that coal exports to Asia could rise to 220 or even 250 million short tons per year in 2015, is seeking to locate a depot in the same area. "The first two such projects are seeking permits for infrastructure that would allow close to 110 million tons of coal export annually," the economist Thomas M. Power wrote in a white paper. That would represent a tripling of export capacity.[6]

Like all fossil fuels, coal is problematic. But here's some straight talk, my friends: China, India, Europe, South America, Africa, and the United States are going to be burning coal for the foreseeable future, especially in the absence of a more rapid embrace of climate change legislation. Even under an emissions trading or carbon tax regime, coal will still have a significant role to play. If the U.S. coal industry were smart, it would take some of the big profits it is minting and, in addition to building new coal export facilities, it would fund efforts to make scrubbers that remove carbon dioxide from coal emissions more affordable and work on carbon sequestration technology. That way, if in 2015 elites on China's east coast suddenly get as concerned about the quality of air entering their children's lungs as are elites on America's East Coast, the industry will have solutions.

Rising foreign demand and shrinking domestic demand are also enabling the United States to export liquid fuels. Many of the emerging markets in which car sales and gasoline use are growing most rapidly lack the expensive infrastructure—refineries, pipelines, and distribution systems—to produce their own fuel. But the United States has plenty of refining capacity, a relic of the period when its crude production was much higher. And so, as the American Petroleum Institute reported, thanks to sharply rising exports and falling imports, in the first quarter of 2011 the United States exported more refined petroleum products that it imported (2.49 million barrels per day versus 2.16 million). Customers include Mexico, a major oil producer, and OPEC member Ecuador.[7]

What's next, selling ethanol to Brazil? Why, yes. In 2010 U.S. ethanol production was 13.23 billion gallons, more than double the 6.5 billion gallons produced in 2007. But the domestic market is essentially saturated, since the EPA doesn't permit blending of more than 10 percent ethanol into gasoline. E85, which is 85 percent ethanol, can be used only by certain vehicles and requires the installation of separate pumps. Just as China needs to import soybeans, Brazil, the major producer and consumer of sugar-based ethanol, often suffers disappointing sugar harvests and needs to import ethanol. "Brazil imported 70 million liters of U.S. ethanol in 2010, up from just 1 million in 2009, according to the U.S. commerce department," the *Financial Times* reported. Overall, exports spiked from about 160 million gallons in 2008 to a record 397 million gallons in 2010, and through the first eleven months of 2011, 1.02 billion gallons were exported. There's room for much more. Given the weak dollar, Chuck Woodside, chairman of the Renewable Fuels Association, the ethanol trade group, and general manager of KAAPA Ethanol of Nebraska, told the *Financial Times* in May 2011, "As we sit here, ethanol produced in Minden, Nebraska, is the cheapest motor fuel out there." In 2010 just 3 percent of ethanol production was exported.[8]

In 2004 and 2005, when U.S. companies were building facilities to allow for the importation of liquefied natural gas (LNG), it was a sign of America's energy desperation. The thirst for fuel led to a Bad Idea for the Ages: a proposal to set up a floating LNG terminal smack in the middle of Long Island Sound, equidistant between the North Shore of Long Island and the South Shore of Fairfield County, two of the most expensive real estate markets in the nation. It was ultimately abandoned due to environmental concerns. Natural gas signifies vast export potential, and thanks to the advent of hydraulic fracking, U.S. reserves have risen dramatically. But production hasn't kept pace, in part because the discovery of new supplies has brought the price down and because the natural gas market is still comparatively local. Natural gas is used to generate electricity, a market that is essentially stagnant. "Shale gas has brought in a flood of supply, and the question is now, what do you do with it?" said Bill Cooper, president of the Center for Liquefied Natural Gas in Washington, D.C.

Strides are being made in using natural gas as a transport fuel. According to CNG Now, a coalition pushing for greater use of natural gas, some 110,000 vehicles in the United States run on compressed liquefied gas or natural gas. But that's just scraping the surface. Here again, the answer may lie in exports. Producers in Alaska have been exporting LNG to Asia for a few decades, largely because they had no way to ship the gas to the continental United States via pipeline. In the space of about thirty-six months, the United States has shifted quickly from being a country that needed to import large quantities of liquefied natural gas into one that can begin exporting. Still, exporting natural gas is more difficult than loading coal onto cargo ships or ethanol onto tankers. Companies have to build plants to liquefy natural gas, an expensive process that requires permits, capital, and customers who will commit to long-term purchases. When plants were built, their owners never contemplated having to turn the gas into a liquid. As the energy analyst Daniel Yergin told the *Wall Street Journal*, "It never occurred to anyone we may be integrated into it [the global market] as a seller."[9]

The hard work of turning one-way processing centers into import-export centers has already begun. Cheniere Energy Partners, which got an LNG incoming terminal up and running in April 2008 in Sabine Pass, Louisiana, a few miles from the Gulf of Mexico, is aiming to add liquefaction capabilities so it can become an export hub. In the fall of 2010 it signed a memorandum of understanding with a Chinese firm, ENN Energy Trading, in which ENN, which serves eighty cities in China, "intends to contract 1.5 million tonnes per annum . . . of bi-directional LNG processing capacity." Translation: if Cheniere gets the necessary approvals and installs the necessary equipment, ENN will consider importing natural gas. In rapid succession, over the next year companies in Spain, France, Japan, Italy, the Dominican Republic, and India signed similar memorandums of understanding for more than 10 million metric tons per year. In May 2011 Cheniere received an order from the U.S. Department of Energy authorizing it to export up to 16 million metric tons per year. In a bit of corporate-speak that happens also to be true, Charif Souki, chairman and CEO of Cheniere, described the transformation of the facility as a win-win-win: "The ability to export natural gas will further stabilize production for U.S. consumers, stimulate the economies through job creation and provide a boost to American global competitiveness. Exports will promote domestic production of U.S. energy and help reduce our country's reliance on foreign sources." He also noted that a bidirectional gas facility will help the balance of trade and put more cleaner-burning fuel into the world. Construction is expected to start in 2012. Natural gas exports have been on the rise, from 723,957 million cubic feet per day in 2006 to 1,136,789 in 2010, an increase of 57 percent. But nearly as much was exported in the first five months of 2011 (664,500 million cubic feet) as in all of 2007, and exports rose 50 percent for the full year. Projects in the works by Cheniere and the Australian infrastructure firm Macquarie would more than triple exports. As the *Wall Street Journal*'s Russell Gold wrote, "The two proposed Gulf Coast terminals could export 3.4 billion cubic feet of gas daily aboard tankers, about 5 percent of current U.S. consumption." [10]

In the vast energy sector, focusing on efficiency has meant freeing up resources for export markets. More broadly, the desire to tap into internal resources to boost productivity and growth is setting the stage for more exports. Chinese factory bosses' demand for junk—which they recycle to make all the junk Americans buy from China—creates jobs, tamps down the growth of the trade deficit, and might help save the planet. It is pushing people to invest more in systems that go deeper into the waste stream.

Take paper, for example. In 2010 recyclers recovered 51.55 million tons of paper, or 63.5 percent of the total consumed, up from 53 percent in 2006 and 46 percent in 2000. The industry now believes it can recycle some 70 percent of paper by 2020. Part of this is due to better equipment and systems, like BigBelly Solar compactors. But there's simply more money in recycling these days, thanks to China's relentless demand. According to Stan Lancey, the chief economist at the American Forest & Paper Association, U.S. exports of recovered paper soared from 10.5 million metric tons worth $866 million in 2001 to 20.7 million tons worth $3.26 billion in 2010.

Have you noticed all the guys with pickup trucks (and, yes, a few thieves) running around scooping up metal and broken parts, scouring construction sites and junkyards in search of material that can be reused? They're exporters too. Exports of ferrous scrap (it sounds like a Scottish breakfast dish but means waste iron and steel) rose from 166,000 metric tons in 1998 to 2 million metric tons in 2006, and up to a whopping 19 million metric tons in 2010, worth about $8 billion. That's a tenfold increase in four years. In 2010 the U.S. scrap industry recycled more than 74 million metric tons of ferrous metal, accounting for an amount equal to nearly 60 percent of the total raw steel produced in the United States. [11]

The image of scrap metal and coal loaded on containers bound for the Orient may not be particularly inspiring. But the United States also excels at exporting expensive, value-added, life-enhancing equipment. One of the most uplifting stories of 2010 was the saga of the thirty-three Chilean miners who had been propelled underground by China's demand for metals. Their liberation after sixty-nine days of captivity came at the hands of U.S. exports. As James Hagerty reported in the *Wall Street Journal*, "The drilling rig that blasted through more than 2,000 feet of rock was made by Schramm Inc., of West Chester, Pa., and the drilling bits [were] from Center Rock Inc., of Berlin, Pa." These relatively small companies export a great deal of value-added and lifesaving technology. Schramm, with 165 employees, has sales of $50 million per year, of which 74 percent are outside the United States, while Center Rock derived about 90 percent of its $30 million in annual sales outside the United States.[12]

Exports can emanate from anywhere. Center Rock is based in a town of 15,000 people seventy-five miles southeast of Pittsburgh. And orders for exports can come from anywhere. In March 2011 the industrial conglomerate Pratt & Whitney received its largest single order in the past half century: three hundred new geared turbofan engines from IndiGo, the Indian discount airline, worth $1 billion.

In April 2011, I attended the Qatar Business & Investment Forum at the Waldorf-Astoria Hotel in Midtown Manhattan. The main attractions for visitors: tins of dates, CNBC's anchor Maria Bartiromo, and a chance to witness the signing of a big export deal. In a grand conference room Akbar Al Baker, CEO of Qatar Airways, ceremoniously signed a transaction to purchase five 777Fs and two 777-300ERs worth $1.3 billion, and reminded his Boeing counterpart that there would be more to come. As Martha C. White noted in *Slate*, "With exports of just under $29 billion in 2009, Boeing made up 1.8 percent of our country's exports all by itself."[13]

In a less life-affirming turn of events, the Arab spring of 2011 is likely to lead to a massive increase in arms purchases in the countries of the Persian Gulf—up to $123 billion in new spending over the next several years, according to the *Financial Times*. The importers will be led by Saudi Arabia ($67 billion), the United Arab Emirates ($35 to $40 billion), and Oman ($12 billion). Guess who the world's biggest exporter of arms is? In fiscal 2010 the U.S. government, which is responsible for 43 percent of the world's total arms spending, exported $37.8 billion worth of weapons. It turns out all this instability is good for business. The Pentagon projected that exports for fiscal 2011 would rise to $46.1 billion, up 45 percent. Oh, and the Defense Department has a backlog of $327 billion in arms exports. As Vice Admiral Bill Landay, head of the agency responsible for weapons exports, told *Bloomberg*, "We have in excess of 13,000 active cases with more than 165 countries and institutions."[14]

Spend half a day with Jeff Immelt, the CEO of General Electric, and you'll come away with a greater appreciation of how rising global wealth is fueling demand for some really expensive machines made in the United States. At fifty-six, Immelt is youthful and energetic, though his hair has been whitened by a decade of low stock returns, managing through 9/11 and the financial crisis, and pushing back against accusations that the company pays nowhere near its fair share in taxes. Jeff—that's what everybody calls him—wears his authority lightly. When I met him in the lobby of the Westin Poinsett in the quaint downtown of Greenville, South Carolina, he was tieless and pulling his own wheeled carry-on suitcase. Just another business traveler dressed for the summer heat—except this one just arrived on his own plane and runs a $100 billion company.

I tagged along with Immelt to GE's plant in Greenville, the world's largest heavy-duty gas turbine manufacturing facility. First he told employees assembled in a large conference hall, all of whom were wearing light blue shirts, how he had been running around the world ginning up orders. "In the last month, I've been in China and the Middle East, and business is good," he said. "We sold more aircraft and services at the Paris Air Show than [at any other time in the company's] history." The company and its partners racked up $27 billion in orders for jet engines and service contracts, much more than they had expected.

Immelt gave a brief *tour d'horizon*. The world is thirsty for energy. Brazil, India, China, and Saudi Arabia have serious power deficits (i.e., they don't have sufficient generating capacity to meet demand), while Japan and Germany are moving away from nuclear power. "Every unit that gets manufactured in this site this year is going to be exported," Immelt told employees. The 2011 production schedule called for ninety units to leave that building for foreign shores. And that's likely to be the case for the next several years. The components and the nearly assembled turbines look like base-rocket launchers and retail for as much as $25 million apiece. One of them, a 375,000-pound model, was sitting on the floor, waiting to be trundled aboard a railcar that would ride into the plant. From Greenville it's a three-day crawl to the Port of Charleston, where it will board a ship bound for Iraq. The turbine is being sold as part of a $3 billion deal with Iraq's state electricity company.

The plant is a conduit for exports. Immelt and his team travel the world, wangling large deals from big companies and state-backed institutions, and then funnel the money from overseas to suppliers on the eastern seaboard, in the Midwest, and on the West Coast. Each year the Greenville plant spends $700 million with suppliers. The plant relies on sixteen so-called U.S. Tier 1 suppliers, from Corry Manufacturing in Erie, Pennsylvania, to Precision Castparts in Portland, Oregon. "For every person that is in the facility, there are eight jobs in the supply chain," Immelt told me, as we admired the gleaming turbine. "As we grow, our supply chain grows with us."

While there will be more pressure from customers abroad to have GE assemble and manufacture its turbines overseas, it's a lot harder to offshore a turbine plant than a shoe factory. Here in Greenville, labor makes up just 10 to 20 percent of the total cost. Though it employs 3,300 people, the cavernous plant is so mechanized and automated that it often seems as if everybody must be on break. But more orders mean more jobs here and, more significantly, in GE's large network of suppliers. "As night follows day, if we're going to double exports, we'll create manufacturing jobs," said Immelt.

Well, of course GE can easily substitute foreign demand for vanishing domestic business. It's a giant company with a century of operating history, huge existing global operations, the ear of the president, a massive captive financing unit, and its own fleet of jets. But, as I learned when visiting a family-owned wallpaper company in suburban Philadelphia, small businesses can pull off the same feat.

Wallquest was founded in 1985, when John Collins, who had run the U.S. wallpaper division of the British chemical company ICI in the 1970s, bought a French-owned wallpaper company. Joined by Carl Robinson, a third-generation wallpaper designer from the United Kingdom, he began making his own high-end designs. With brands like Sandpiper Studios, Fairwinds Studio, and Society Hill prints, some of which retail for $100 for a 21-inch-by-33-foot roll, Wallquest enjoyed some success. The classy prints are the types you'd find in the home of a lawyer or prosperous small business-person whose mother-in-law is a part-time decorator. In the 1990s Collins brought his sons, Jack and Brian, into the business; Jack runs the legal and financial operations, and Brian handles operations and sales. The headquarters is in a commercial district of Wayne, Pennsylvania, with offices attached to a 90,000-square-foot production facility. The company also has smaller production shops in Middletown, New York; Hawthorne, New Jersey; and King of Prussia, Pennsylvania. In 2006 it had revenues of about $15 million, about 90 percent of them in the United States. The company's approach to the market was simple: it sold through two large distributors, mostly to Main Street decorating stores and paint shops.

But starting in 2006 things started to go bad slowly, and then all at once. Small-time retailers were systematically killed off by big-box retailers like Lowe's and Home Depot, where the staffers weren't much interested in spending time poring over design books with customers. Meanwhile the rising cadre of home flippers preferred slapping down layers of paint to plotting expensive wallpaper schemes. And in the areas of hottest growth for the housing market, like Phoenix and Las Vegas, wallpaper wasn't widely used. "Between 2005 and 2007 domestic margins fell about 10 percent each year," Jack Collins said. "The traditional way we did business was disappearing." In 2008 the consumer economy tanked, and Blonder Home Accents, a Cleveland-based distributor that accounted for 35 percent of Wallquest's revenues, went bankrupt. In May 2008 Wallquest let several factory workers go and reduced pay by 15 percent for those left behind. The pay cuts lasted nine months for line workers and eighteen months for management.

Salvation came from an unexpected source: overseas. Wallquest's international marketing efforts had been desultory. The Collinses attended the massive Heimtextil home furnishings trade show in

Frankfurt each January. Early efforts to get into China had faltered. "We had an importer who started with $10,000 a month in purchases in Beijing. He got the product out on the market and opened his own factory and started copying our product, so we parted ways with him," said Brian Collins. But things picked up quickly. An email inquiry came through the company's website from a Taiwanese manufacturer who wanted to take Wallquest collections into China. Strong orders came in from Russia, the largest wallpaper market in the world. A Dubai distributor, a company run by Indian emigrants, signed on in 2008 and made inroads into the Persian Gulf, peddling classic American patterns with bright colors and little flowers. Said Brian Collins, "What has surprised us most is that in a market like Saudi Arabia, American country would sell, and sell well."

Wallquest was quickly transformed from a company focused on domestic demand to an exporter. The company has shifted from selling to two U.S. customers to selling to dozens of customers in more than fifty countries. In 2009 exports accounted for 35 percent of sales, and in 2010 they accounted for 65 percent. On the heels of these orders, sales rose to about $30 million in 2010, and payroll has nearly doubled since 2008, from about 80 employees to 150. When we met in the spring of 2011, Wallquest was poised to add another 30 workers at its plant in King of Prussia, Pennsylvania. In the production facility, its mostly Hispanic workforce was pouring paints and inks onto screens, testing products, and fiddling with the giant presses, some of which had been purchased for pennies on the dollar from busted printing companies. Rolls of product were marked for their final destination: Greece, Thailand, Kazakhstan. In mid-2011 China accounted for about 25 to 30 percent of the company's business.

Unlike GE, Wallquest doesn't participate in trade delegations. Its sales force consists of Brian and John Collins. They do get a little help from the government. The U.S. Export-Import Bank guarantees a portion of the company's line of credit with PNC Bank. That guarantee allows Wallquest to receive 90 cents on every dollar of foreign sales advanced to it as credit from the bank, instead of the 80 cents advanced under typical bank credit lines. "It just makes cash flow much easier," said Jack Collins. "Without them, we wouldn't be able to grow." But once the Collinses began to focus on foreign markets, they realized they were pretty good at it. "We started traveling and pushing more and learning more about product development for different export markets," said Brian Collins. "Last year we decided we were going to drive our business in Scandinavia. We worked closely with people there and have almost tripled the business in a year's time."

Going global has led to a series of adventures and lessons not available at the Frankfurt trade show. Clients helped them sneak into a Saudi holy city to check out a hotel where their products were being used. When we met, Brian Collins had traveled to China, now Wallquest's largest market, ten times in the prior eighteen months. On one visit he and his father dined with two Chinese counterparts in Beijing at a massive banquet table where they sat about fifteen feet apart. When a bowl of duck hearts was placed before him, he mused over the more than seventy ducks that had been sacrificed to make the dish and scooped some into a soup bowl when the host wasn't looking.

Wallquest has also learned to tweak its product offerings for local tastes. Many of the sample books look like high-concept fashion layouts, often featuring models. "You get to the Middle East, people don't necessarily want to see women without a lot of their clothes on," said Brian Collins. Chinese customers don't like birds or dead tree branches. "It is common for fabrics or wall covering to have birds or insects or butterflies. That's not home decor in China. That's food."

In the way it operates, sells, and perceives itself, Wallquest has undergone a near-complete transformation in three years—without the benefit of consultants, reengineering, or massive layoffs. "We'll always be an international company," said Jack Collins. "That's what we are now."

To avoid decline, all American companies have to embrace their inner exporter, as Wallquest did. The United States has the resources, the products, and the infrastructure to export on a significantly larger scale than it does now. In its 2011 fiscal year, the Port of Los Angeles handled 4.2 million loaded inbound shipping containers. It sent out 1.93 million containers filled with goods and products, but also sent 1.82 million containers, about 48 percent, back onto cargo ships filled with nothing but air. To fill up many more of them, American businesses need to adjust their mind-set. Brian Collins is matter-of-fact about how an international wall-flower became an exporter. "The key to our export growth is the mind-set. You've got to travel, you have to learn, cut timelines to be effective. If we have a deal in Beijing, you hop on a flight, have your meeting, and turn around and come home. You can't think, 'Well, it's a long way.'"

CHAPTER 8

The World of New Exports

In May 2010, in exchange for delivering a twenty-minute commencement address to the Lake Forest College Class of 2010, I received an honorary doctorate. I thought I had the better of the deal until I showed up at Ravinia, the summer home of the Chicago Symphony. This being the Midwest, temperatures were in the forties, snow flurries threatened, and the concrete and steel shed conducted the cold very effectively. President Stephen Schutt had asked me to "give them something to be optimistic about." So I did. Appearing after the student speaker, who started with a snippet from a *Dreamgirls* song (which put the kibosh on my plan to open with a rendition of "And I Am Telling You I'm Not Going"), I compared 2010 to 1933 and described how, given enough time, America had always been able to drag itself out of the ditch. I sat down next to the playwright Rebecca Gilman, a fellow honoree, and shivered as the 333 undergraduates walked by, the young women teetering on insanely high heels, the guys either sheepishly acknowledging applause or strutting by. At this small liberal arts college that doesn't have much of an international profile, the student body was a parade of ethnicities and surnames that would make the United Nations proud. Twenty-three members of the graduating class hailed from fifteen countries. The region once known as the hog butcher to the world is now exporting $200,000 sheepskins.

Higher education is a large component of America's vast service sector. Services account for about 75 percent of U.S. economic activity. But historically the country has been less prolific—or less interested—in exporting services like education than it has in exporting goods like missiles or cows. In 2010 U.S. exports were divided between goods, at $1.5 trillion, and services, at $605 billion, a 70–30 split. The United States can't reach its full potential as an exporter, and hence as a full participant in the global economy, unless it can become a prodigious exporter of services as well as goods. But here again, amid the cries of decline, there's good news. You wouldn't know it from listening to the doomsayers, but the United States *already* leads the world in service exports, and by a very large margin. In 2010 America exported more than twice as many services as China and Germany did. Even though the United States doesn't try very hard, and imposes needless barriers on itself, between 2005 and 2011 service exports rose more rapidly than goods exports did. And there's room for much more. Rising wealth around the world means greater demand for services.

Developing countries build exports—goods or services—by taking the low road: set up a factory to make cheap lightbulbs or build a low-wage call center, and you're off. But it's not all about a race to the bottom. The United States exports a lot of very expensive services—money management, education, health care, tourism—that have previously been unaffordable for the vast majority of humanity and that are getting more affordable. Like the Collinses of Wallquest before 2008, most American businesses were content to sell to their friends and neighbors and never gave much thought to selling overseas. But the math and the logic are inescapable. On one side: a home market of 320 million chastened consumers struggling to make ends meet in a slow-growth economy, shorn of the debt and rising home values that fueled so much consumption. On the other: an international market of 6.6 billion people with (Europe aside) generally rising living standards and a willingness to pay through the nose for what Americans are selling. Service exports are somewhat oxymoronic, because they often involve working with customers who come from abroad. Just as foreigners are helping to recapitalize America through foreign direct investment, they're replenishing American coffers by coming here and spending money on service exports.

Universities and colleges have long acted as magnets for foreign students: the Islamist Sayyid Qutb, who studied at Colorado State Teachers College in 1949; Barack Obama Sr., who attended the University of Hawaii in the 1950s; the aristocratic Greek in my freshman dorm at Cornell who muttered darkly about the "bloody Turks" and "the bloody socialists." That year, 1985, there were 343,777 foreign students at colleges and universities in the United States, about 2.8 percent of the total student body. Universities historically brought in international students for two reasons: graduate students to work as cheap teaching assistants, and rich undergrads as development prospects. Bring in the children of foreign plutocrats and aristocrats, the theory went, and they'll become big contributors after they take their place in the family conglomerates. And the theory has worked. In 2008 Ranan Tata, the Indian industrialist, a 1962 graduate of Cornell University, donated $50 million to his alma mater, half of which went to fund scholarships for Indian students.

But today the export of higher education promises more immediate paybacks to universities and to the economy at large. Each year America's business and engineering schools import thousands of people who go on to found and lead companies. Silicon Valley is full of foreign-born, U.S.-educated executives who stayed on after their education. The National Foundation for American Policy released a report in December 2011 that found twenty-three of the top fifty venture-backed companies in the United States had at least one immigrant founder.[1] Consider the career arc of Indra Nooyi. Born in Chennai (then known as Madras) in 1955, she graduated from Madras Christian College and the elite Indian Institute of Management in Calcutta and then worked at Johnson & Johnson in India before coming to the Yale School of Management for an MBA. Leaving Yale in 1980, she did stints at the Boston Consulting Group and Motorola before joining Pepsi in 1994. At Pepsi she rose to chief financial officer in 2001 and was promoted to CEO in 2007. Had she stayed in India, Nooyi would likely have succeeded, but only to a point. Given the prevalence of family-controlled companies and sexism in India's corporate world, it's hardly likely that she would have come to helm a global branded giant with 300,000 employees and sales of $58 billion. In twenty-nine years she went from first-year foreign grad student to highly compensated pillar of the U.S. business establishment.

Since 1972 the number of foreign students in the United States has risen every year, with the exception of the three years after 9/11. From a nadir of 564,766 in 2005–2006, the number bounced back to a record 690,923 in 2009–2010, up 22 percent in four years, according to the Institute of International Education. That's still only about 3.6 percent of the total number of students. Growth in recent years has been driven by China; in the 2009–2010 academic year, the number of Chinese students in the United States soared by 30 percent, bringing the total to 128,000, or 18 percent of the international student population. India is second, with 105,000, or 15 percent. Guess who is seventh? Saudi Arabia. "The United States continues to host more international students than any other country in the world," said Allan Goodman, president and chief executive officer of the Institute of International Education. Students from abroad often come to the coasts. There were 60,791 foreign students in the New York metropolitan area, and the University of Southern California is the nation's leading host institution, with about 8,000 international students. But they also come to the heartland. The University of Illinois at Urbana-Champaign (second overall), Purdue, the University of Michigan, Michigan State, and the University of Texas each have more than 5,000 foreign students.[2]

At many institutions graduate students make cheap teachers. "Our median economics PhD student is a Chinese woman," said Vance Roley, dean of the University of Hawaii's Shidler College of Business, where I spent a week in early 2011. But there's more to the story than low-paid teaching assistants, stipends, and incomprehensible dissertations. These days private schools charge up to $50,000 a year for tuition and fees, while state schools, sapped by perennial budget cuts, are pushing up tuition to $15,000, or $20,000 for out-of-staters. The deep recession of 2008–2009 has rendered many American families unable to foot steep tuition bills. The great desideratum for universities is to find paying customers, qualified students who don't need too much financial aid. The more students who pay full freight, the more colleges and universities can offer aid to athletes, minorities, and high-achieving students from less affluent backgrounds. The rise of a massive class of global affluents has significantly expanded the potential customer base. At Harvard 12 percent of the Class of 2015 are citizens of other countries. As Jacques Steinberg reported in the *New York Times,* one of every ten applicants for the Class of 2015 at Grinnell College in the heart of Iowa hailed from China.[3]

In its 2009–2010 "Open Doors" report, the Institute of International Education found that "more than 60% of all international students receive the majority of their funds from personal and family sources." Add in other sources, like scholarships from foreign governments and schools, and about 70 percent of foreign students are primarily funded through nonuniversity sources. And foreign students' economic contribution to U.S. coffers extends far beyond the tuition they pay. It's the money they spend on rent, food, airfare, and other outlays by their families. NAFSA, the Association of International Educators, estimates that the total economic impact of foreign students and their dependents rose from $14.5 billion in 2006–2007 to $18.8 billion in 2009–2010. That's a 30 percent jump in a three-year period in which consumer demand was slack, and a sum equal to the sales of Nike. In many areas foreign students are anchors of the economy. Michigan is a depressed state, with an 11.2 percent unemployment rate, a shrinking population, and a rotting city at its core. The University of Michigan and Michigan State University are home to around 11,300 foreign students.

Harvard doesn't have much of a problem recruiting applicants, just as General Electric can easily drum up foreign orders. But like Wallquest, smaller institutions such as Lake Forest College, which lack lucrative professional schools and prestigious graduate programs, have to work hard at it. Lake Forest is expensive: in the 2011–2012 academic year tuition was $36,920, plus $8,660 for room and board. That $45,580 price tag makes international recruitment all the more important. "In the countries that are thriving, there's increasing interest from families who want access to the American higher education system and are in a position to pay for it," said Lake Forest's president, Stephen Schutt. "U.S. education is a brand that travels well."

Lake Forest officials spend several weeks each year recruiting students in Eastern Europe, Asia, and India. The college employs an admissions officer who focuses exclusively on international students. Schutt, a lawyer and former University of Pennsylvania administrator who became president in 2001, views drumming up educational exports as an important part of his job. He spent the ten-day 2011 spring break in China, visiting two or three secondary schools in cities such as Hong Kong, Shanghai, Xi'an, and Beijing, with which the school has forged relationships. In addition to recruiting from the local powerhouse, New Trier High School, Lake Forest looks to Shanghai Datong High School, Xi'an Hua Foreign Language School, and Beijing No. 4 High School. The work pays off. Of the 410 students who matriculated in the fall of 2011, 63 (or 15 percent) hailed from thirty-three different countries. That's a significant increase from the 23 kids from fifteen countries who graduated in the class of 2010. In 2011–2012 international students provided somewhere between 12 and 15 percent of the net tuition dollars the freshman class brought. And it's not just the six kids from China. Several students from Swaziland, recipients of assistance from Shelby Davis Scholarship funds, are studying at Lake Forest. Schutt believes he's also doing a service to the domestic students. "I think it's just critical that in all ways possible, we prepare American students to live in and work in an international world," he told me. "At a place like ours that is small by design, the more we can internationalize the population and get kids comfortable with that on campus, the better they're going to be prepared."

The steady increase in foreign students willing to pay the full cost of attendance is especially impressive given the policy barriers that are in place. Vic Johnson, a senior policy advisor at NAFSA, notes that federal policy is not exactly designed to maximize this type of export. A State Department bureau charged with attracting international students doesn't collaborate much with the Commerce Department's trade missions for universities. And because one of the 9/11 terrorists, Hani Hasan Hanjour, came to the United States on a student visa without ever intending to go to school, the Department of Homeland Security rides herd on potential applicants. Foreign students admitted to American universities have to

go to local consular affairs bureaus, which make on-the-spot decisions about whether they can enter the United States based on
financial resources, criminal background checks, and an assessment
of whether they intend to immigrate. (Here's a bizarre wrinkle in
the law: The Immigration and Naturalization Act says students are
eligible for temporary student visas only if they declare their intention *not* to immigrate to the United States.) Johnson believes about
20 percent of admitted students are rejected. "We've got a reputa-
tion as an unwelcoming country," he says. If international student
enrollment had continued to grow at pre-9/11 rates, Johnson notes,
there would be more than 850,000 foreign students in the United
States, and they would create an additional $4.6 billion in economic
activity. A national goal of 1 million international students by the
end of this decade would produce a recurring revenue stream of
$28.8 billion per year.

As the United States was apparently pitching into decline and
growing fitfully, another measure of market interest in the country
grew stronger: tourism. In the bewildering months after the fall of
2008, tourism to the United States fell sharply, along with the volume of global trade. But as the world's economy perked up, so too
did the world's interest in visiting the United States. Call it the Neil
Diamond economy: on the boats and on the planes, they're coming
to America. In 2005 New York City welcomed — or didn't welcome,
as the case may be — 42.7 million visitors, of which 6.8 million, or
16 percent, came from abroad. In 2010 the number rose to 48.8
million, with 9.7 million, or 20 percent, of them international visitors. Both figures were records, and that's a 46 percent increase in
foreign visitors in five years. On December 21, 2011, New York
City chose Craig and Lucy Johnson, a couple from England, as the
honorary fifty-millionth visitors to the city. They had come to get
married at the observation deck atop the General Electric building
in Rockefeller Center. Walk the length of the High Line, the once-
derelict elevated railroad track turned chichi promenade in Manhattan's Meatpacking District, and you'll scarcely hear a word of
English spoken.[4]

When an Indian technology executive visits New York and
spends money at the Gap and the Marriott, that's calculated in the

national accounts as an export. When an American spends money at the Uffizi Gallery in Florence, that's an import. But Americans' lack of curiosity about the rest of the world is counteracted by the rest of the world's curiosity about America. In 2009, 30.3 million Americans traveled outside the country. In 2010, according to the Commerce Department, a record 59.8 million international visitors came to the United States, up 8.7 percent from 2009. Those lines of people talking funny, the ones swinging Gap bags or clogging up the line for Space Mountain at Disneyworld or posing for photos on Fishermans Wharf in San Francisco are exports just as valuable as the bushels of grain being loaded onto container ships at the port of Los Angeles. In 2010 tourism was a $134.5 billion export industry, rivaling agriculture, up more than 10 percent, from $120.3 billion in 2010. Thanks to Americans' general desire to stay put, the United States has reported a trade surplus in tourism every year since 1989. The surplus was $31.2 billion in 2010, a 48 percent gain from 2009. Each year international travelers support some 1.1 million jobs in the United States. According to the Commerce Department, the United States has an 11.2 percent share of world traveler spending, which leads the market.

As is the case generally with trade, Canada and Mexico are the largest sources of inbound tourism, with 20 million and 13.5 million visits in 2010, respectively. But the physical borders aren't where the action is. The global surge in growth is pushing more people around the world to visit the United States. Overseas visitors—tourists who come from countries that don't share a border with the United States—rose from 23.9 million in 2007 to 26.3 million in 2010. "In 2010, 14 of the top 15 countries posted increases in visitation to the United States," the government reported. (The United Kingdom, which is putting itself through a period of austerity, was the lone leading source of tourism to decline in 2010.) Nine of the top fifteen points of origin notched records, including Australia, India, and China. Brazil came in seventh, with 1.05 million visitors, up 35 percent from 2009. Some 743,000 tourists from the People's Republic of China came to the United States in 2010, an increase of 54 percent.[5]

These figures help explain some of the strange phenomena that pop up in America's great cities. For example, Eataly, Mario Batali's food emporium devoted to Italian imports, is full of imported Italian people. It may seem strange to schlep 4,000 miles just to eat a panini and lean against a counter to have a pitch-perfect espresso. But it's no different from Americans eating at a KFC in Beijing or a McDonald's in Israel or having coffee at a Starbucks in Turkey. (Your humble writer has done all three.) At the beachfront Loews hotel in Santa Monica in August 2011 around 80 percent of the guests were foreign: Spanish, French, German, and Italian. Never mind the meltdown back home. The euro was strong, and well-heeled Europeans still get the month off. The beauty of exporting tourism is that it uses a lot of resources and infrastructure that we already have in place. Hotels almost never have full occupancy rates. For the same reason we want to make sure that more containers leave U.S. ports full of goods, we should endeavor to ensure that hotel rooms and restaurants remain full year-round.

Imagine how much better U.S. tourism numbers would be if the United States wasn't so aggressively unfriendly to foreigners. Our security bureaucracy expresses widespread suspicion of foreigners from the south (they're all drug dealers), the Middle East (they're all terrorists), the Asian subcontinent (ditto), and East Asia (they're all prospective immigrants, here to steal trade secrets and jobs). And still they come in the millions. What if John F. Kennedy Airport, the principal entry point to the East Coast, weren't a dingy dump where foreigners are consigned to lengthy lines and surly officers? What if the United States could shuck its regrettable tendency to occasionally arrest, humiliate, and deport well-meaning tourists? Sure, the overwhelming majority of the world's population will never have the capital to pay for a flight to Los Angeles and five nights at a Holiday Inn. Far too many people live on $2 a day. But the number of people willing and able to spend $200—or $2,000—a day on a vacation is rising.

On the morning of Sunday, January 30, 2011, when a China Eastern Airlines A-340 touched down at Honolulu International Airport, the 263 passengers were greeted with the usual ceremony: leis, hula dancers, and Hawaiian music. But they were also greeted with the type of giddy enthusiasm that local officials don't usually express for dental conventions. This was the first direct flight from China to Hawaii, and in difficult times for the state's vital tourism industry such milestones offer a ray of hope. Hawaii depends on two principal areas for the bulk of its 7.1 million annual visitors: Japan and the West Coast of the United States. Twenty-five years ago massive luxury-goods temples were erected on Kalakaua Avenue, dedicated to Chanel, Tiffany, and Hugo Boss, to appeal to flush Japanese honeymooners. Lush golf courses were carved out of volcanic soil to appeal to Japanese and American tourists. But both core markets have been depressed for several years. Hawaii attracted 1.2 million visitors from Japan in 2010, down 12 percent from 2006, and the figures cratered in the wake of the March 2011 tsunami. Meanwhile domestic arrivals in Hawaii were down 10 percent between 2007 and 2010.[6]

Hawaii's great hope is that Chinese tourists will start to fill in the gaps. "There are more millionaires produced in China every year than any other country in the world," Juergen T. Steinmetz, president of the Hawaii Tourism Association, told *Maui Now*. "They can afford to spend $2,000 a day while vacationing, and they want to travel in style and comfort to a destination that understands their cultural desires and language." Even for a booster, that might be a little boosterish. Still, the ground is being prepared. In 2010 Bank of Hawaii signed a deal with China UnionPay that would permit the 2.1 billion cards (*2.1 billion cards!*) that UnionPay's member banks have issued to work in ATMs in Hawaii; Bank of Hawaii pledged to reprogram ATMs to provide Chinese-language options. By the summer of 2011 China Eastern was running two direct 287-seat flights per week. Many Chinese visitors also come via Korean Air or JAL, or as part of longer U.S. tours that originate on the mainland. For now, Chinese tourists are a small percentage of overall visitors; only 62,000 arrived in 2010, and another 37,000 through the first half of 2011. But their numbers are growing, and citizens of a country that was mired in desperate poverty thirty-five years ago are already known as the new big spenders. "Right now they are the highest per-person per-day spender," according to Daniel Nahoopii, research director at the Hawaii Tourism Authority.

"They beat out the Japanese." In 2010 the average Chinese visitor to Hawaii spent $350 per person per day, compared with $261 per Japanese tourist and a mere $140 for West Coast U.S. visitors.[7]

You've heard of the Chinese tiger mother. Now meet the Chinese tiger shopper. Several years ago the last thing the CEO of a big luxury department store was concerned about was the staffing levels at U.S. consulates in China. But retailers are beginning to see tourists as a significant chunk of potential spending. As Elizabeth Holmes reported in the Wall Street Journal, "Chinese visitors spend on average more than $6,000 apiece when they are in the U.S., more than twice their counterparts from the U.K." Tour groups construct itineraries that include the Mall of America. (Maybe they want to see where all the stuff their compatriots make winds up.) "The Commerce Department says Chinese tourists spent $5 billion in the U.S. last year, up 39 percent from the prior year," Holmes reported. But it can take a Chinese Carrie Bradshaw two months to get a U.S. tourist visa. As a result, Holmes wrote, "luxury companies including Polo and Saks Inc. are working through industry groups to press Congress for funding that would let the State Department process visas more quickly." Saks CEO Steve Sadove told the Journal that increased international tourism "could have an enormous impact on business." Bring me your tired, your well-heeled masses, yearning to spend freely.[8]

Of course, there are big spenders, and then there are really big spenders. Around Thanksgiving 2010 several dozen people who had reserved extremely expensive rooms at the Waldorf Astoria in New York were unceremoniously kicked out and rehoused in other hotels. The reason? King Abdullah, the eighty-six-year-old Saudi monarch, had come with a vast entourage to have back surgery at New York Presbyterian Hospital. His Majesty, no doubt willing to pay top dollar, took over a large chunk of the hotel, as well as a wing on the hospital complex's VIP floor.[9] A Saudi king blowing several million dollars on hotel and hospital rooms is an extreme version of a larger trend. When we hear the phrase "medical tourism," we think of Americans going to Thailand for a cheap face-lift, or to India for a cost-effective hip replacement. But the business also flows the other way. Moguls, politicians, and plain old rich folks from around the world come to the United States for six- and seven-figure treatments. The Cleveland Clinic, the cardiac surgery factory by the shores of Lake Erie, pipes Turkish- and Arabic-language channels into its TV system.

The changes in the U.S. economy make it difficult for many service industries to prosper. College tuition is rising out of reach for more and more Americans. Universities have to cut their prices, find new reservoirs of aid, or find a new source of customers willing and able to pay—and to help subsidize less wealthy students. Resorts and hotels that don't have a plan to appeal to the growing numbers of Chinese people with the ability and desire to travel to the United States are similarly missing out. Across the board, U.S. businesses and the U.S. government have to become more welcoming, more hospitable, and more comfortable with the notion that many of the best customers coming into our stores, restaurants, and hotels may not look, speak, or think like us.

Rising global wealth is also offering new opportunities for American individuals to export the services they provide. Major League Soccer, the still-fledgling U.S. professional league, has evolved to the point where it can shell out big bucks to import aging international superstars like David Beckham and Thierry Henry. But the young Americans who fill out the field receive peanuts; many of Beckham's teammates on the Los Angeles Galaxy make mid-five-figure salaries. For the past two decades ambitious American players have sought greener pastures abroad. Players like Tim Howard, a goalie at Everton, or Clint Dempsey, a striker at middling English Premier League side Fulham, easily rake in seven-figure salaries, much more than they could earn at home. According to Greg Seltzer, proprietor of the blog Noshortcorners.com, between sixty and seventy U.S. soccer players, enough to fill several Major League Soccer rosters, play in top leagues overseas. During the 2011 National Basketball Association lockout, Deron Williams of the New Jersey Nets signed a $5 million one-year deal with Istanbul-based Besiktas Milangaz. (Williams returned to the United States after fifteen games once the lockout ended, with no hard feelings.) The schoolyard phenom point guard Stephon Marbury frequently found that his NBA coaches wanted to export him to other teams. After washing out of the NBA, Marbury exported himself to China. First he signed with Shanxi Zhongyu Brave Dragons, in Taiyuan, a Nowheresville industrial city. He did so, as Wells Tower reported in *GQ*, in part because the team's owner had pledged to help him develop his dormant shoe business in China. After several months Ma Bu Li (Marbury's Chinese moniker) was shipped off to another Chinese team, in Foshan, and then moved to the Beijing Ducks.[10]

Or take publishing. Amid the morass of misery that is the New York City publishing world, at least one guy seems to be unruffled. I visited the superagent Andrew Wylie in his faculty lounge–like office in the Fisk Building, at the corner of Fifty-seventh Street and Broadway. Wylie's agency represents some 750 clients, including literary lions like Philip Roth, Salman Rushdie, and the estate of John Updike. And he's busy exporting them. At the Wylie agency, foreign rights, historically an afterthought, are now the main show. "As a general rule, we find that while the strongest market is usually the writer's home market, it's roughly equivalent to the rest of the world, and, increasingly, what's important is getting the rest of the world right," he said. "Fifty percent of American writers' sales should be outside the U.S." Wylie chooses his clients well. But in an era when Borders has disappeared and millions of Indians are joining the middle class, the book industry's center of gravity is shifting. "Philip Roth travels well, Salman Rushdie travels well. Henry Kissinger and Al Gore sold all over the place."

At the Frankfurt Book Fair in 2010 Wylie had three books that received multiple six-figure offers for English-language rights in India. "Two years earlier, the highest advance we had received from India was less than $10,000." When Henry Kissinger finished his book *On China,* Wylie staged a dinner with Kissinger and foreign publishers in Frankfurt. "The Chinese were the first to buy, and they took a very significant position in the book." (I didn't have the heart to ask how Cambodian rights did.) A half-dozen years ago the prospect of exporting literary works to China was a pipe dream; publishers would offer a token number of manuscripts. That's changing. "We first noticed a surge in China, I think, three years ago, when we had three Chinese publishers bidding six figures for a five-year license for Jorge Luis Borges," Wylie said. "That would have been inconceivable five years ago." The Chinese book market has matured very rapidly. In Beijing in the fall of 2011 bus stops were plastered with ads for the brand-new Walter Isaacson biography of Steve Jobs. Published in Mandarin on the same day it was published in the United States, in October 2011, the biography's first run of 250,000 sold out instantly. Several press reports cited the book's Chinese publisher, Citic Press, as noting that the book had garnered one million preorders.[11] The biggest kick I got after my previous book was published was going on *The Colbert Report* to talk about it. The second-biggest kick was meeting with my Chinese publishers in the restaurant of the Grand Beijing Hotel. They paid more for the publication rights than did their Japanese counterparts.

In fact, look around the world and you'll find that audiences and customers overseas gobble up all sorts of stuff when we make it available to them. In the fall of 2007 I visited a high school in Ho Chi Minh City, Vietnam, with some colleagues. We chatted in English with several girls who were wearing the school uniform of plaid skirt, white shirt, and red beret about what music they liked to listen to and the shows they liked to watch on television. Their accents were thick, but the parent of a grade-schooler can recognize the names "Hannah Montana" and "Miley Cyrus" in pretty much any patois. Having just toured the graphic Vietnam War Museum, I first thought: Haven't we done enough to these people for one century? My second thought was: Wow, there are 87 million people in this country who want to consume really bad American entertainment.

Hollywood is figuring this out. At home the revenues from box office ticket sales have been stagnant over the past few years. In 2011 U.S. movie attendance fell to 1.28 billion, a sixteen-year low. Overseas, however, business is booming. According to the Motion Picture Association of America, in 2010 international box office revenues were $21.2 billion, or 67 percent of the global box office of $31.8 billion, compared with $16.6 billion, or 63 percent, in 2007. Now consider how the launches of two installments of a highly profitable franchise have played out. In the first five days of its release in 2009, *Transformers: Revenge of the Fallen* did an impressive $200.1 million domestically and $129.6 million internationally, a 61–39 split. But the ratio was reversed for the opening week of 2011's *Transformers: Dark of the Moon.* At home *Dark of the Moon* took in $181.1 million in its first five days, while raking in a record $217 million by airing on 9,075 screens in fifty-eight foreign markets. In two years the domestic opening fell about 10 percent, while the international opening box office rose more than 80 percent, leaving a 46–54 split.[12] The fact that Paramount replaced a pneumatic American female lead, Megan Fox, with a pneumatic British one, Rosie Huntington-Whitely, might account for some of the difference. However, the writing is on the wall. In an age of fractured viewership and parsimonious spenders, actors have to get on more screens and stages around the world.

And for those who can no longer land A-list, *Transformers*-esque Hollywood roles, the global appetite for U.S. box office stars offers new export opportunities. When all else fails, export yourself, your face, and your charisma. In 2008 I sat in a hotel in Istanbul, overlooking the Bosporus, imagining myself in an Alan Furst novel, watching tankers float by. My reverie was interrupted by a high-concept commercial for Turkish Airlines starring . . . Kevin Costner. The spot showed Costner being treated like a big-shot movie star: he's asked for an autograph, hit on by a hot woman, fawned over by flight attendants. At the end Costner transforms into a Turkish everyman. See, the average Mehmet gets the same great treatment on Turkish Airlines as a Hollywood star. Costner isn't alone. Visit a European city and you're likely to see a turtlenecked George Clooney hawking Nespresso. In late 2010 Russia's Trust Bank signed up Bruce Willis, who reached his advertising apogee when doing blues-infused Seagram's wine cooler ads in the 1980s, to be its representative.[13] My Russian isn't so good, but I think the slogan on the billboard is something like "Bank Hard!" For 1990s-era box office draws, the new mantra might be "Go East, Not-So-Young Man."

Even for companies and commercial enterprises for which the United States is tapped out, there are great opportunities abroad. And if Kevin Costner, Bruce Willis, and their commercial analogues can find new financial life overseas, so can many more viable companies. To do so, however, they can't simply wait for customers to come to them. They must become more integrated directly into foreign markets and take a larger share of consumption in domestic markets around the globe. And it's possible to do so without exporting.

CHAPTER 9

Inports

Companies big and small can participate in global growth in lots of different ways. They can export the old way: put stuff produced in America onto ships and send it abroad. They can export the new way: sell services, things, and experiences produced in America to people who come from overseas to consume them on American soil. But there are limits. Exports rely on *pull:* somebody in the target market must decide to order a roll of wallpaper from a distant vendor; universities based in the United States have to reel in students willing to trek 6,000 miles for a college education. Because of the costs and barriers involved, and because of the still-huge gap between living standards in the United States and in much of the rest of the world, exports quickly bump into a ceiling. Increasingly, however, companies must figure out how to *push* products overseas. The far larger and more promising opportunity is to sell goods and services that are sourced locally to people who can consume them without having to leave home. American companies can—and frequently do—sell products made somewhere else to people who live somewhere else.

It's easy and tempting to view the great developments of our age—the bourgeoisification of Colombia and Brazil, the rise of consuming societies in Southeast Asia, the shift from subsistence to working class in sub-Saharan Africa, mass driving in India—as threats: there is now more competition for resources. But in large measure they represent a triumph for the United States. They represent a return on the huge investments made during the cold war.

131

But the shape of the world's economy now impels companies to go out and meet consumers where they are, on their own terms, and frequently in their own language. As the typical world citizen moves closer in wealth to the typical American, more people around the world will consume more like Americans. That means they'll be willing and able to buy a lot of American goods and services, even ones that don't necessarily bear a "Made in the U.S.A." stamp. Here, as in many other areas, the United States already has a huge advantage over its global competitors. Whether it is Starbucks in Turkey, Mary Kay in China, Euro Disney, Taco Bell in India, or an American medical school in the Persian Gulf, U.S. business concepts travel remarkably well and continue to gain popularity.

Sitting at home, stewing over slack demand and high unemployment, it's easy to think that the world is leaving the United States behind. In fact, the world is taking the United States with it through what I call "inports."

Inports are a more sophisticated and nuanced version of exports. Companies don't just export a commodity or a finished product; rather, they export the brand or consumer experience and then integrate it into burgeoning local consuming cultures. Such developments may not directly boost exports or lead to significant direct employment, but they can be hugely beneficial to American companies, and to the economy at large.

First and foremost, inports are good for shareholders, whose numbers include the tens of millions of Americans with pension funds or index funds. Standard & Poor's measures the percentage of revenues that companies in the S&P 500 index say they derive from overseas. In 2010, for the firms that broke out such results separately, 46.3 percent of revenues came from outside the United States, up from 43.5 percent in 2006. The biggest growth in overseas sales has come from sectors that have tapped into the global growth boom. Companies that make consumer discretionary goods, like clothing and toys, saw their shares of overseas sales rise from 35 percent in 2004 to 43 percent in 2010, while consumer staples firms reported a rise from 38.9 percent in 2004 to 45.6 percent in 2010. For some of the largest companies, the veteran globalists, overseas sales account for an overwhelming majority of sales. Intel reaps 85 percent of its revenues from non-U.S. markets. At PepsiCo, which operates in two hundred countries, international sales are 31 percent of the total. At IBM, which operates in 170 countries, the proportion is 64 percent.[1] As a general rule these companies' global sales are not exports. Think of Intel selling computer chips made in Manila, Philippines, to customers in Indonesia; or IBM consultants in Milan, Italy, servicing clients in Slovenia; or Coca-Cola bottled in South Africa sold to customers in Namibia. More and more, when investors buy U.S. companies on the New York Stock Exchange they're placing bets on the ability of U.S.-based companies to participate in the offshore economy. The stock market is famously a futures market, not a "presents" market. And future earnings are coming from abroad. This is one of the reasons the U.S. stock market bounced back so rapidly from the bottom of March 2009 and nearly doubled by the end of 2011. Stocks prices are driven in large measure by profit growth and hope for future profit growth. And for the big companies that populate indexes such as the S&P 500, rapidly rising global sales boosted profits.

Inports are also potentially good news for taxpayers. Aside from the insurer AIG, General Motors is likely to be the bailout recipient that will have the most difficulty paying back the taxpayer. The government got stuck with a 60 percent stake in the company after extending $51 billion in loans in 2009. In the first two years of its federal dependency, GM managed to pay back $23.2 billion. The initial public offering of GM in November 2010 created a currency that could, in time, make the taxpayers whole. But Treasury still owns 500 million shares, about one-third of the company, which was worth about $11 billion in the summer of 2011. For taxpayers to break even, the stock will have to rise to $56 from its late 2011 level of $23, and stay there long enough to absorb the government's share sales. That remains a long shot.

U.S. car sales, at about 13 million for 2011, have clearly bounced back from their 2009 nadir of 10.4 million. But they're still a long way from the 2006 peak of 16.5 million units. Holding down a 20 percent market share of the slowly growing U.S. car market can take GM only so far, because the United States is rapidly becoming something of a rump car market. As U.S. auto sales slumped after the crisis, global vehicle production ramped up from 73 million in 2007 to 78 million in 2010. The United States now accounts for less than 20 percent of the global market and has been a detractor from global auto growth in recent years. By 2015, J.D. Power projects, the world's drivers will purchase 103 million light vehicles per year, and 84 percent of those sales will take place outside U.S. borders.[2]

American carmakers can't really export in volume to many of the most rapidly growing markets. The dollar is too strong, and domestic quality standards and labor and shipping costs are simply too high to make large-scale exports economically viable. This was driven home to me by a visit in the fall of 2009 to the Chang'an-Ford joint venture plant outside Chongqing, China. Having visited some of the most modern plants, including the Prius plant in Toyota City, Japan, where rotating, flexing robotic arms call to mind *The Terminator*, I felt as if I had gone back in time thirty years. Hundreds of workers labored in the plant, which was air-conditioned by the chilly Chongqing fall fog, turning steel, light metals, and plastic into highly utilitarian minivans. The Chang'an minivans are a modern version of the Model T, machines in which peasants can move their families, equipment, and livestock around. With seating for eight, they can—and frequently do—hold as many as fifteen people. They retail for the local equivalent of $4,000.

Chang'an is an enabler of inports. It's a partner with Ford, as well as Suzuki and Mazda, and has an annual production capacity of 1.5 million vehicles. Virtually all the vehicles it produces remain in China. Chang'an makes the Chinese version of the Ford Focus, an entry-level car in the United States but a midmarket vehicle in China. It sells for about 110,000 renminbi (about $15,000 at the time of my visit) and is pitched at office workers. "Focus has the largest market segment, if you break it down," said Chang'an executive Cai Yong. "Although you may think the purchasing power is low, the Chinese people prefer the 100,000 to 120,000 price, instead of the 50,000 to 60,000 renminbi car."

But increasingly Chinese consumers like Buicks. In the fall of 2011 I visited a much more modern auto plant. As body frames moved slowly along the automated assembly line, teams of workers bolted on parts in an intricate choreography. Electric notes rang out every so often, a characteristic of the widely adapted Japanese Andon system. When the tones of "Old McDonald" or "London Bridge" rang out, they signified that a particular section needed help. Overhead, electric displays showed how many cars had been completed and the quality rate. When the lunch hour rolled around, hundreds of workers wearing blue and green uniforms filed into a lunchroom. It could have been Michigan, or Germany, or Japan. But this assembly line was in the Jingqiao district of Shanghai, an area of office parks, corporate headquarters, and sophisticated manufacturing plants. It belongs to GM Shanghai, a joint venture of General Motors and the Chinese car company SAIC. Here the revived car company is reviving a brand that has been left for dead in the United States.

Buick has a second life in China as an upscale brand. If you get picked up and taken to the airport by a car service, it's likely to be in a black, four-door Buick Regal sedan. The Excelle, a small vehicle modeled on the Chevrolet Cruze, is a high-volume product: 200,000 are made each year in China. The GL-8 SUV retails for 288,000 to 388,000 renminbi ($45,000 to $60,000). Buick is tapping into a long legacy in China; it is commonly noted that the last emperor owned one nearly a century ago. GM, which also makes various Chevrolet models for domestic sales at two other plants in China, has a network of about a thousand dealers. All in all, GM has the capacity to produce 1.2 million cars in China—600,000 in the two assembly lines at the Shanghai plant.

"We have standard processes through the world," notes David Gibbons, executive director of manufacturing at GM Shanghai. As Gibbons took me and a group of visitors on a buggy ride through the plant, he described how GM implemented its standards on ergonomics, productivity, and lean manufacturing here. Each station maintains just one or two hours' worth of inventory. Welding is 60 percent automated. In the final stages of the line, employees wear white gloves to protect the finishes. Turnover is about 1 percent. "These are permanent jobs," Gibbons said.

GM Shanghai has two plants elsewhere in China, where it makes Buicks and Chevrolets. While it employs about 8,000 people in China, only a few are Americans, mostly top managers in manufacturing, finance, logistics, and marketing. But the Chinese market provides important ballast for the car company and benefits all its stakeholders: investors who own its bonds and stock (including U.S. taxpayers) and workers who hope to collect pensions and receive health care during their retirement. In the third quarter of 2011 GM noted that sales in China rose to 620,000, up 9.3 percent from 567,000 in the third quarter of 2010. In the United States, by contrast, GM sold 555,000 vehicles in the 2011 third quarter. Having been deprived of so much for so long, China's consumers accept clogged roads and bumper-to-bumper traffic as a sign of progress. And that's keeping the assembly lines in Shanghai busy turning out Buicks. The plant runs two 10.5-hour shifts per day nearly seven days a week and can produce nearly ninety cars per hour. Said Gibbons, "We're fully loaded here."

The revenues and profits earned at factories like this, and at the hundreds of facilities owned by GM, Ford, and Chrysler around the world, get streamed back to Michigan and into the hands of bondholders to fund retirement and health care benefits. GM and Ford are in a position to hire and add staff at home, in part because of the successful domestic turnaround and restructuring efforts they have led. But they stayed afloat in large measure because of the ballast that the overseas operations provide. GM stakeholders—union members hoping to collect their pensions, stockholders expecting dividends, taxpayers hoping for a return of the bailout funds—are relying on cars produced outside the United States to satisfy local taste. In the 1970s advertisements identified the Chevy, the car driven to the levee in "American Pie," as a member of the nation's holy quartet of consumer goods: baseball, hot dogs, apple pie, and Chevrolet. In 2010 fewer than 40 percent of Chevrolets were sold in the United States.

Inports affect taxpayers in a different way. America's population of older companies is struggling to keep up with promises made to employees regarding retirement benefits and health care. GM and Chrysler filed for bankruptcy in large measure because of their inability to do so. Poor market returns, low interest rates, and management's refusal to set aside adequate resources have led to persistent shortfalls in corporate pensions. According to a fall 2011 report by Credit Suisse, America's largest companies, the constituents of the S&P 500, have a collective $388 billion in unfunded liabilities, with pensions only 77 percent funded in the aggregate.[3] Many of those are at large industrial companies where U.S. operations may be relatively stagnant or shrinking. Ford has a $17.8 billion gap, and Lockheed Martin is short by $14.3 billion. Without massive quantities of goods produced overseas being sold to overseas customers, these firms don't have a prayer of funding their pension obligations. And these represent immense potential liabilities for taxpayers. Through the Pension Benefit Guaranty Corporation, the taxpayers insure pensions of private companies. The PBGC itself has long been underfunded, and this means that a large-scale failure of pension funds would create pressure for a bailout of the PBGC. By helping companies bolster their balance sheet, inports are yet another means by which foreigners help to recapitalize the United States.

The United States has a competitive advantage when it comes to inports. One of the distinguishing characteristics of the U.S. economy is its ability to come up with things that are universally popular: constitutional democracy, Coca-Cola, McDonald's, Elvis Presley, Google, and all things Disney.

Disney has long been a shrewd and meaningful exporter. Its U.S. theme parks attract hordes of foreign visitors each year. But the Mouse is also proving to be a decent inporter. In October 2009 it released *Book of Masters*, a film for the Russian market, made in Russia, in Russian, with Russian actors, based on Russian fairy tales, on eight hundred screens. *Kniga Masterov* was the top-grossing movie in Russia in the first two weeks after its release, and the $8 million picture brought in $10.8 million in ticket sales. Elsewhere Disney has invested in infrastructure that attracts local consumers. Driving from Paris east on the E-50, you'll find the city and its suburbs give way to rolling countryside, picturesque villages, recognizable names of World War I battles, and billboards for the Davy Crockett Ranch. Euro Disney, which was founded in 1992, and of which Disney owns 40 percent, draws 15 million visitors each year. In some of the world's most populous markets, where hundreds of millions of people can't yet afford to travel to the United States, they can

afford to spend a day waiting in long lines for rides and interact-
ing with freakishly large humanoid stuffed animals. Tokyo Disney,
which is nearly thirty years old, pulls in 14.5 million visitors each
year; it is operated by a Japanese company under a license from
Disney. In April 2011 Disney and a Chinese partner said they'd
invest $4.4 billion to build a Shanghai Disney Resort. Hong Kong
Disneyland, in which the parent company owns a 47 percent stake,
offers a mix of the old and the new. Strolling through Tomorrow-
land, visitors can snack on Korean squid and fish balls, and while
they stand in interminable lines for the Tinker Bell Castle, they can
wash down their squid with a nice inported soft drink.[4]

In the United States the economy, concerned parents, and the
increasingly aggressive health police are conspiring against the sale
of fizzy drinks. But many overseas markets remain virgin territory
for the likes of Coca-Cola, which uses local products and local bot-
tlers. Between 1999 and 2009 per capita sales of Coca-Cola products rose 400 percent in Russia, 300 percent in China, 270 percent
in Pakistan, and 200 percent in India. In February 2011 Coca-Cola
trumpeted the arrival of its latest billion-dollar brand. The fourteenth billion-dollar baby is one that a college student in Minnesota
has probably never seen in a vending machine: Pulpy. A knockoff
of Orangina, with fruit juice and fruit pulp, which comes in a range
of flavors, Pulpy was developed and launched in China in 2005. It
has spread throughout Asia, and in 2010 pushed into North Africa,
Mexico, and Kazakhstan.[5]

Many brands that have lost cachet in the United States are finding
new life in new markets. Consider the experience of Yum Brands,
the parent company of Pizza Hut, KFC, and Taco Bell. As Janney
Montgomery Scott's restaurant industry analyst Mark Kalinowski
put it, "We tell our investors to think of Yum as a Chinese restaurant company that happens to be headquartered in Kentucky." KFC
has long been on the decline in the United States, thanks to rising
official disapproval of fried food and the growing influence of the
calorie, sodium, and fat policy. A down-market brand, it's offering
the Famous Bowl, a combination of side dishes and chicken in a
single high-calorie portion, which seems designed to lower the customer's self-esteem. In the United States, KFCs are closing down;

many are in tired locations, and the culinary zeitgeist is heading in the opposite direction. The number of American KFCs has fallen from 5,525 in 2004 to 4,804 in the middle of 2011. But in China, KFC is something of an aspirational brand. When I toured China in 2009, I learned that our handler from the Chinese Foreign Ministry had celebrated his wedding at a KFC. In 2011 the company's China unit, which covers mainland China, Thailand, and KFC Taiwan, opened 656 new restaurants. With 2,980 restaurants and a new outlet opening almost every day, KFC boasts that it is the "largest and fastest growing restaurant chain in mainland China today." In 2011 Yum derived 41 percent of its operating income from China and less than one third from the United States. I accounted for about $3 of those sales. On a side street around the corner from the Beijing Grand Hotel, I passed row upon row of vendors hawking chicken kebabs and lamb shawarmas, and then I ducked into a KFC joint. On an early Saturday evening it was packed. The two-piece with biscuit? Not bad. At the end of the third quarter of 2011, 3,448 of the 7,351 restaurants that Yum owned outright were in China, and only 2,355 were in the United States.[6]

The Turkish people know from coffee. Istanbul is believed to be the location of one of the world's first coffeehouses. Kiva Han was founded in the late fifteenth century in Istanbul. Yet when I roamed around the city in the fall of 2008, I saw Starbucks everywhere: off the bustling Istiqlal promenade on the Asian side, in Kadikoy, in the *haut bourgeois* neighborhoods of Bebek along the Bosporus, and in teeming Besiktas. There are now ninety Starbucks outlets in Istanbul alone. In mid-2011 Starbucks had about 32 percent of its stores and earned 25 percent of its revenues overseas. But the company, which has introduced Americans to exotic foreign locales through imports, is increasingly staking its future on getting more integrated into local markets overseas. Starbucks' expansion plans for 2011 and 2012 call for 1,400 net new stores, with 1,100 outside the United States. In the summer of 2011 I stood at a Starbucks counter at the Prague Ruzyne International Airport. Here, where a large mocha Frappuccino went for the equivalent of $8, it struck me that it would be relatively easy to divest myself of my last Czech koruna. Stepping up to the counter and hearing the baristas call out my order in the same singsong chorus they use back home in West-port, Connecticut, I felt as if I were inhabiting an exported experi-ence. But the coffee beans, the tea, and the milk weren't made in the United States. Neither were the scones, the cup, the cash register, or the barista. Rather it was the customer experience that was made in America and inported to Prague. And while commodities and labor are cheap around the world, brands remain expensive.

Until recently the huge markup on U.S.-branded products and experiences was a hindrance to the global growth of American com-panies. At a model Nike plant outside Ho Chi Minh City, Vietnam, I watched as workers laced together a few dollars' worth of leather, plastic, and twine into $80 and $120 pairs of sneaker. These labor-ers, and the overwhelming majority of Vietnamese, could never hope to afford a pair of authentic Nikes. But that model is chang-ing. In the new world of inports, rising chunks of the population of emerging markets can now afford to pay the premium prices for the objects made by U.S. companies in their own backyard.

Electronics has become a cutthroat industry in which European, Japanese, and American companies—and their Asian suppliers—struggle to wring profits from commoditized products. Here, as in so many areas, Apple stands the conventional wisdom on its head. It uses the same type of cheap Asian parts that go into HP com-puters or Zune music devices, whose prices only seem to fall, but manages to charge a premium through design, branding, and cul-ture. A study by Kenneth Kraemer of the University of California at Irvine, Greg Linden of the University of California at Berke-ley, and Jason Dedrick of Syracuse University found that making Apple electronic products isn't that profitable for anybody except the owner of the brand. "In the case of the iPad, Apple keeps about 30% of the sales price of its low-end $499 16GB, Wi-Fi only model (and more if the unit is sold through Apple's retail outlets or online store)," they wrote. "We estimate that Apple keeps a healthier 58% of the sales price of the iPhone 4." Now Apple is *in*porting that same mystique. As of summer 2011 about 113 of Apple's 300 high-volume retail stores were located outside the United States.[7]

On July 10, 2011, Apple opened a new store in Shanghai, one of twenty-five it plans to launch in China before the end of 2012. Like many things in China, the store design is a knockoff: the entrance is a glass cylinder that looks just like the entrance to the Apple Store in Midtown Manhattan. It is clearly aimed at locals in one of China's wealthiest cities. When Stephen Green, the chief economist at Standard Chartered Bank, first came to Shanghai in 2000, the foreigners were rich. "Now the Shanghainese are rich, and the foreigners are poor by comparison," he told me. But wealth is spreading throughout China's cities, and American brands and consumer experiences are following them. A sizable portion of the world's toys are made in China, but Toys"R"Us now has twenty-seven stores—small ones, not big boxes—there too.

Here again, American companies are just scratching the surface. "Of America's 100 biggest retailers by revenue, only about a dozen operate independent stores in China," David Barboza wrote in the *New York Times.*[8] Let's assume China becomes the world's largest economy and largest retail market. Assume further that Chinese consumers begin to save a little less of their income and spend a little more. The local base of American retailers, dominated by fast-food joints like KFC and McDonald's, will increasingly be joined by Walmart, which is a midlevel retailer in China; by Starbucks; and by Apple. Around the world, with each passing month, there are more places where upscale U.S. brands can thrive.

It turns out, in fact, that American companies have much to teach the world about marketing. In his book *Outrageous Fortunes: The Twelve Surprising Trends That Will Reshape the Global Economy*, Daniel Altman notes that one of America's competitive advantages lies in its ability to sell. America's commercial culture was forged hundreds of years ago when people from all over the world came together and were forced to figure out how to sell to one another. "We're very good at coming up with products and services that appeal to people no matter where they're from," Altman said. "We can sell our own products, sell other people's products, and we'll be able to teach other people to sell."

The experience of Mary Kay, the direct-sales firm, shows the potential to inport an entire culture of selling. Mary Kay was the brainchild of Mary Kay Ash, a Texas housewife who started her own business in the 1960s and built an empire of sales by and for women at a time when women had few outlets for entrepreneurship or management. Mary Kay–ism is part down-home faith (service to God is one of the firm's key tenets); part New Agey, Oprah-esque self-realization; and part good old American hucksterism. Associates move up the ladder by recruiting other sellers and aim for totems of performance recognition, such as diamond bumblebee pins and pink Cadillacs.

It all seems a little passé and retro at a time when women run Fortune 500 companies and universities, serve as secretary of state, and run for president. But in China, Mary Kay is quite au courant. Mary Kay China's headquarters occupy four stories in Tower 2 in Plaza 66, Shanghai's fancy mixed-use complex that houses high-end stores such as Fendi. The high-gloss offices are filled with images of the bejeweled, heavily made-up Ash and her many maxims in both English and Mandarin, as well as information about the company and its history, beliefs, and values. (A reference to God is changed in Chinese to a more anodyne statement about faith.)

Mary Kay was not an easy transplant to China when it arrived in the mid-1990s. Direct selling didn't catch on in a country where knocks on the door could signal something far less benign than the offer of a new moisturizer. When direct selling was banned in 1998, the company changed its model. It set up showrooms around the country, paid agents to represent the products, and maintained corporate control of the inventory. In 2006, however, a new law permitted direct selling, though sales directors must have fixed locations and licenses and selling in homes is still frowned upon. The company maintains thirty-five showrooms around the country.

Mary Kay China has 700,000 salespeople, and sales have been rising sharply. "This year, even with the economic situation, we're about 20 percent above last year," Paul Mak, president of Mary Kay China, told me when I visited the offices at the end of 2009. That year China accounted for 25 percent of overall sales. With great pride, Mak showed a group of visiting journalists around the four floors of offices, two of them connected by a curving pink staircase. There's a break room with a foosball table and a pool table, and a room where female employees—70 percent of the corporate arm's employees are women—can bring their small children. In the spirit of Mary Kay, who viewed her efforts as equal parts business and social work, the company makes interest-free loans to business-women. Mak points to photos of top-producing sellers, women whose ages range from twenty-seven to sixty-two. Women whose accounts bring in 100,000 renminbi per month for a year (about $170,000 in sales per annum) have the right to use a company pink Volkswagen. Chinese women aren't big users of makeup; consequently the Chinese product line is heavier on skin care and anti-aging and whitening creams, some of which can be quite expensive. A four-week supply of one cream that Mak showed us goes for about $120.

When you look out the window onto the broad expanse of Shanghai's traffic-clogged skyline, you can clearly make out a huge sign in the distance. It flashes "Mary Kay" in English and in Chinese characters. Mak notes that it looks over an elevated express-way that is frequently jammed with traffic. "When people drive, they have to look at it for two or three minutes." As a brand Mary Kay has found new life in China and throughout the world. It has 2.4 million sellers in thirty-five countries and racks up total annual wholesale sales of $3 billion. In 2011 it entered Armenia.

Mary Kay's experience provides further evidence for the argument against decline. If the United States were losing economic influence, we'd expect the value of its top companies to be declining on both an absolute and a relative basis. But that's not happening. In its annual ranking of the most valuable brands, the advertising research firm Millward Brown found that the world's top eight brands were American: Apple, Google, IBM, McDonald's, Microsoft, Coca-Cola, AT&T, and Marlboro. U.S. firms occupied sixteen of the top twenty slots.[9] Of course, these brands are valuable because of their dominant position in the world's largest economy. But their value continues to grow only because of their ability to export and inport their way to becoming universal brands.

As much as they deliver goods or services, brands impart an experience and instill and arouse a set of feelings in consumers. American companies are still able to tap into a legacy of decades in which American brands stood for a type of freedom—think of how Levi's and Pepsi had iconic status behind the old Iron Curtain. One of the first things the Russians did after kicking the communists out was to bring McDonald's in. Writing in the *New Republic* in 1990, Hendrik Hertzberg famously tabbed the McDonald's in Red Square as "a *real* Lenin's tomb." Disney exemplifies American-style fun and fantasy. Can you imagine a German amusement park company setting up shop in Malaysia? The Russian guy who popped open a Pilsner Urquell at 10 A.M. on a tourist boat circling lazily in Prague's Vltava River last summer was wearing a T-shirt that read "Surfing Is Freedom." When we got off and began wading through the throngs of tourists at the foot of the Charles Bridge, was it any surprise that, even in this town, with its centuries-long history of beer halls, there was a large crowd at the T.G.I. Friday's?

Inports have a lot of room for growth. As people in emerging markets become middle class, and even rich, they decide they want more of what the United States has to offer, not less. Given the trends in international tourism, with each passing year there are more people living in foreign countries who have had direct exposure to American-style consumption. Each year nearly 60 million people visit the United States and then return home. They become carrier pigeons for commerce. They attend the University of Nebraska, shop at the Mall of America, hang out in Miami, and return to Thailand, or Brazil, or Nigeria with consumption and brand habits they picked up here. Sure, European and Asian brands can travel well too. Uniqlo's stores in Paris and New York are popular, but they simply don't have the same degree of leverage as U.S. brands because comparatively few people have experience with them.

Today's global retailing climate, with its growing receptivity to inports, changes the strategy for American companies large and small. The old-school thinking was that if something succeeded in New York, it would expand to Boston or maybe Los Angeles. Then, only after having saturated the United States would a brand start to look overseas. That's why exports and inports have generally been the exclusive province of very large companies. But in a flatter world, smaller companies can think of Abu Dhabi, London, or Shanghai right out of the box. *Sex and the City* made the Magnolia Bakery in the West Village a required stop on the pilgrimage tour. The too-sweet cupcake shop parlayed TV exposure into some local growth, with four stores in New York and one in Los Angeles. In February 2011 Magnolia Bakery opened a new shop inside the Bloomingdale's store in the Dubai Mall—a case of an inporter piggybacking on an inporter. With only five locations in the United States, Magnolia is pushing to get into Brazil, Portugal, Mexico, and Japan. And why not? The pre-meltdown shenanigans of Carrie, Samantha, Miranda, and Charlotte now seem de trop at home, but *Sex and the City* resonates with the rising class of nouveaux riches around the world.

Health care and higher education, two sectors that are big purveyors of luxury goods, are taking baby steps toward inports. The Cleveland Clinic has branched out from its lakeside base to balmier climes populated by rich old Semitic people in need of heart-related health care, namely Florida. Now it's going to another hot zone populated by rich old Semitic people in need of heart-related health care. Visitors from the Middle East have long supplied a steady stream of customers for America's top hospitals. But in the months after the 9/11 attacks, when visas became more difficult to get, there was a sharp drop-off in the number of medical tourists from the Persian Gulf. In 2006 the Cleveland Clinic and Mubadala Healthcare, based in Abu Dhabi, agreed to construct a new hospital in a vast new development on Sowwah Island. When it opens in 2012, the 364-bed clinic-hospital will deliver locally sourced services to local clients, with a mixed American and local staff.[10]

A generation ago universities offered junior-year-abroad programs to give tuition-paying American students exposure to life overseas. Now they offer degree-granting programs in which tuition-paying foreign students can have an American-style university education without ever having to leave home. In 2002 Weill Cornell Medical College teamed up with the Qatar Foundation to create a six-year program that will grant graduates the same MD degree awarded to students who grind through the program on New York's Upper East Side. On May 4, 2011, the fourth graduating class received its degrees: thirty-one in all, eighteen women and thirteen men, from Qatar and a dozen or so other countries. Taught in part by a U.S.-based faculty, the students in the desert pay the same tuition for the six-year combined undergrad and graduate program as their counterparts in Manhattan: $41,325 for the undergraduate years and $46,000 for the graduate years. Armed with Cornell medical degrees, twenty-three of them obtained residencies in the United States.[11]

The employment implications of inports aren't huge. But the rise of inports does have implications for careers. At General Electric the path to the top office in Fairfield, Connecticut, historically ran through different posts in the United States. Jack Welch started as a chemical engineer at a facility in Pittsfield, Massachusetts, and moved up the ranks without ever working abroad. His successor, Jeff Immelt, rose through the ranks at the U.S. plastics, health care, and appliances division. The next CEO of General Electric, whose industrial units generate 60 percent of their sales overseas, will almost certainly need to make a stop in Brazil or China. It's no surprise that the current CEOs of iconic American brands like Coca-Cola not only have significant foreign experience but hold passports from other countries. The path to the top now goes through Asia and South America, not through the Midwest and the South.

The prevalence and rise of inports also shed new light on a recurring policy question: What should be done about the profits that U.S. companies rack up in overseas operations or in units that are domiciled in other countries? Thus far the response has been to hold profits hostage until Congress agrees to let companies bring the money home without paying significant corporate income taxes on it. A 2004 amnesty permitted companies to bring back about $300 billion at the low rate of 5.25 percent, instead of the usual 35 percent rate. While the amnesty didn't do much to encourage economic growth, it did encourage American companies to repeat the exercise. As the world has grown, and as U.S. companies have become more integrated into booming local markets, the cash has piled up. By mid-2011 companies were sitting on more than $1.2 trillion in unrepatriated earnings and were asking for another free pass. The United States should respond by ransoming the hostage, but should take another hostage on behalf of taxpayers in return. Ask the Business Roundtable and the U.S. Chamber of Commerce what rate they'd be willing to pay on foreign earnings—on the ones they've racked up in the past seven years and the ones they'll reap in the coming decades. Increase their offer by 50 percent. That becomes the new rate, payable each year. Let's assume that this new rate is 20 percent. It would bring in $240 billion immediately and about $60 billion annually, presuming companies make $300 billion per year in offshore profits. Here's the hostage: companies that repatriate must use the cash they bring home to fully fund their pension and retirement health plans before they pay out dividends or buy back stock. Ultimately the question of what to do about rising overseas profits is a high-class dilemma; the real problem would be if they didn't have overseas profits in the first place.

The ways the U.S. economy has become more engaged with the world since the Great Recession should give hope to those concerned about decline. For many industries, the answer to difficult, persistent problems came from abroad: attract new capital through foreign direct investment and find new customers through exports and inports. This model for thriving in the new economy certainly imposes new burdens and obligations on companies, businesspeople, and workers: they have to travel more, reach out, and be willing to spend more time away from home. However, the example of one state that reversed decline shows that tapping into these forces can encourage people who have left to come back home.

CHAPTER 10

More Like North Dakota

The economic gloom that pervades the Washington, D.C.–New York corridor, where I spend most of my time, has been so thick since 2008 that I've found it necessary to travel to some rather exotic locales in my search for economic optimism. In Xi'an, deep inside China, I marveled at dioramas depicting massive new industrial parks that were already under construction. In Bogotá, Colombia, the spirit of a country liberated from fear and relishing rising prosperity is palpable. I got the same feeling when I got off the plane in Bismarck, North Dakota.

Those who believe that the United States no longer has the ability to compete and that it lacks the potential to reverse seemingly inevitable decline should really visit North Dakota. If the rest of the country were a little more like the thinly populated Peace Garden State, we'd all be more sanguine about the future.

North Dakota is easily overlooked by the political, financial, and media establishment. It's very hard to check off the bucket list of states to visit, because it isn't really on the way to anywhere. The few airlines that fly there charge an arm and a leg. Delta charges more for a New York–to-Bismarck round trip (about $1,300) than it does for a jaunt to Europe. So go ahead, make your *Fargo* and Coen brothers jokes, and then go visit Fargo, or Bismarck, or the booming oil fields around Williston in the western part of the state. What you'll find is an upside-down mirror image of the United States.

The U.S. economy's growth may have resumed in July 2009.

But two years later, in the summer of 2011, the nation's hotbeds of innovation, lifestyle, and population growth still suffered double-digit unemployment: in California the rate was 12.1 percent; in Florida it was 10.7 percent; and in Nevada it was 13.4 percent. But the Plains states, bypassed by population growth, urbanism, and Whole Foods outlets, had extremely low rates. North Dakota enjoyed the lowest unemployment rate in the nation, at 3.5 percent in August 2011. In several counties the rate was below 1 percent. In August 2011 the state boasted 395,000 payroll jobs, up 18,900, or 5 percent, from the year before. If the other forty-nine states had been able to match this pace, the country would have created 6.5 million jobs in a year.

North Dakota is one of the smallest states by population (about 670,000) and one of the largest geographically, with 70,000 square miles. It had 0.7 unemployed persons for every job opening, compared with 4.25 for the United States at large. In May 2011 the state jobs office had 15,205 listings, up 64 percent from May 2010. In the entire United States the labor force participation rate—the proportion of able-bodied adults between the ages of eighteen and sixty-five who are working or seeking work—was an anemic 64.2 percent. In North Dakota it stood at a high-octane 74 percent.[1] But while its citizens are more hardy, friendly, and prone to using the word "shucks" and fishing for walleye than their fellow Americans, North Dakotans aren't superhuman. Rather, the state enjoys some built-in advantages that have allowed it to prosper in the emerging global economy.

While it may seem obvious, the tale of North Dakota's prosperity was unexpected and unforeseen. For in the lonely, cold steppes of the northern United States there was serious talk of decline long before it became fashionable elsewhere. The state's population peaked in 1930 and then began to dwindle inexorably. All the most powerful trends seemed to run against the state: the decline of agriculture, the rise of the service economy, the natural flow of population to the coasts and the sunbelt. In 1987 the sociologists Deborah Epstein Popper and Frank J. Popper published a famous article, "The Great Plains: From Dust to Dust," in *Planning*, in which they advised states like North Dakota how to manage their inevitable decline. "It is hard to predict the future of the Plains ordeal. The most likely possibility is a continuation of the gradual impoverishment and depopulation that in many places go back to the 1920s," they wrote. The Poppers were proponents of the Buffalo Commons theory, the notion that people would eventually leave and the lumbering mammals would reassert their dominion over the windswept prairies.[2]

Oops. Another wrongheaded vision of decline created by sketching existing trend lines endlessly into the future. In fact, visiting North Dakota today is like entering a bizarro economic world: everything is reversed. Here housing prices go up every year, budgets are in surplus, and public investments are rising. Far from being left behind, this landlocked, largely vacant state that borders other landlocked, largely vacant states has benefited enormously from the interconnections and trends in the global economy. North Dakota is a producing rather than a consuming state, and it is exporting with abandon. Public finances are sufficiently robust to support tax cuts and infrastructure investments. Other states may be caught in a death spiral of job cuts, lower taxes, public disinvestment, and decreased demand, but in North Dakota there's a virtuous circle. More economic activity leads to more investment, which leads to more employment, which in turn creates more demand for all sorts of goods and services, which creates more tax revenues, which leads to more investment and the creation of a large rainy-day fund.

In many ways North Dakota doesn't look or feel like the America most Americans know. The Missouri River meanders through vast empty spaces. The population is scattered among a series of small towns and cities, many of which are spread a hundred miles from one another along I-94. It's not at all diverse. The state is home to only two-tenths of 1 percent of the U.S. population. If you like warm weather, population density, exotic sushi, or walkable neighborhoods, North Dakota may not be the place for you. If you like wide-open spaces, cheap housing, and attractions like the largest buffalo in the world—the twenty-six-foot tall, forty-six-foot-long, sixty-ton sculpture on a hillside overlooking I-94 in Jamestown—it might be.

The United States doesn't have to become North Dakota, with

its austere landscape, abstemious habits, small houses, and lack of choices. (Although in Bismarck I did see a Mongolian stir-fry, which is an amenity that has yet to arrive in Fairfield County, Connecticut.) But perhaps the rest of the country should strive to become a little more like North Dakota, in its ability to tap internal resources, to produce as well as consume, to engage with the world, and to reverse decline.

The North Dakota miracle starts with some very good geological fortune and the application of a new technology to make much more of an existing internal resource. The boom in the state, whose economy grew a BRIC-esque 7 percent in 2010, is being led by oil.[3] First discovered in the 1950s, the oil fields in western North Dakota declined in the 1980s and 1990s. Oil production peaked at about 150,000 barrels per day in the late 1970s, and in 2001 it fell to a relative trickle of 85,000 barrels per day. But starting in the middle of the 2000s, new techniques were brought to bear in the Bakken Shale, the stratum of rock that lies under about 15,000 square miles of scrubland in the western part of the state. It turned out that hydraulic fracturing, or fracking—the technique first developed in the Barnett Shale in Texas, in which massive water pressure is applied to liberate natural gas from rock—can also be used to liberate liquid oil. In recent years drillers have also perfected horizontal drilling techniques, delving up to two miles deep and then two miles across—an efficient means of exploring vast stretches of territory. Once the two techniques were married in the Bakken Shale in 2007, oil rigs and workers came rushing in. Oil production rose sharply, from 45.9 million barrels in 2007 to 113 million in 2010 and more than 150 million in 2011, making North Dakota the fourth-largest oil-producing state in the United States and a larger force in the market than Ecuador, an OPEC member. With more investment in the Bakken Shale, which covers a swath of North Dakota that is larger than the state of Maryland, locals believe production can double from the current level of 418,000 barrels per day. In 2010 the United States as a whole produced about 2 million barrels per day.

The $12 billion-a-year industry is producing a lot of employment. At the end of 2011, 201 oil-drilling rigs were at work in the state, about one-quarter of the rigs in the country, said Ron Ness, the soft-spoken president of the North Dakota Petroleum Council. Each rig brings along about eighty suppliers in transportation, engineering, wholesale trade, and construction. Even though it takes only half a dozen people to run an oil well, it takes about a hundred people to build a new one and to get it up and running. Ness projected up to $5 billion of spending on oil- and gas-related infrastructure over the next three to five years. "We are now looking at an economic boom in that part of the state—it's the largest construction project in the U.S.," he said. The workforce directly employed in North Dakota's oil sector has risen from 4,500 in 2005 to 35,000 in mid-2011. "On any given Monday, we've got 1,700 job openings directly related to the oil industry," Ness continued. "And we've shown that if you have jobs, people will repopulate these areas." The average wage in the North Dakota oil and gas extraction industry was more than $90,000. The boom has created demand for truckers, accountants, cooks, and HR managers, in addition to roughnecks. Even low-skilled jobs can command high wages. In tiny Williston, population 14,716, gas stations, convenience stores, and McDonald's are offering $12.50 to $15 an hour for entry-level jobs. "Man camps"—temporary housing structures carted in from out of state—were seeking to hire cooks and cleaners making $1,500 and $1,000 per week, respectively.

The boom is rippling back across the state. Tax collections related to oil and gas production and extraction soared from $251 million in 2007 to $750 million in 2010. Many North Dakotans are finding that the mineral rights left to them by their rustic grandparents have turned into windfall annuities. Bismarck, the state capital, is home to MDU Resources, a miniconglomerate with units that specialize in construction, infrastructure, and electricity. One of the few publicly held companies based in the state, MDU was until recently North Dakota's only member of the Fortune 500. Like many locals, it spent much of the past few decades prospecting in balmier climes. During the height of the construction boom, Las Vegas provided the biggest chunk of its business, with around 1,500 employees engaged in casino-hotel projects like the Wynn, the Encore, and the Fontainebleau. Post-bust, employment in Sin

City fell to about 500, and in 2011 the company employed twice as many people in North Dakota as it did in Vegas. "All our businesses are impacted—in construction, energy, and the utility," said CEO Terry Hildestad, sitting in a corner office of his Bismarck headquarters, which offers fifty-mile views across the Plains. "It's a good place to live, a good place to do business. If we need to work out a problem, we know where everybody is at." The company's utility unit, which provides electricity to the oil fields, saw its business rise 5 percent in the past year—which is hypergrowth for a utility. MDU's natural gas pipeline in the west is operating at capacity. In oil country MDU is leasing land and drilling, building roads, and making asphalt.

The sprawling Tesoro refinery in nearby Mandan, across the swollen Missouri River from Bismarck, is likewise benefiting. "So far this year we've hired twenty-five people," raising the employee head count to 245, John Berger told me in June 2011. A Bismarck native who interned at the refinery in his junior year at the University of North Dakota, Berger is now the refinery's manager. In 2001, with oil production down, BP Amoco essentially gave up on the refinery, which was built in the 1950s. "BP declared that we were materially insignificant, put us up for sale," Berger said. The refinery covers a thousand acres, with one-third reserved for the refinery, one-third for water storage ponds, and one-third for a wildlife management area. (The plant's slogan: "Industry in Harmony with Nature.") A $120 million upgrade under way will boost its capacity to 2.5 million gallons (60,000 barrels) of gasoline, diesel, and jet fuel per day. In the first half of 2011, with local demand high, Tesoro notched five of the six highest production days in its history. In the summer of 2011 it was poised to kick off another $35 million expansion, which would boost capacity by 10,000 barrels per day by the middle of 2012, to 70,000.

Local demand may be keeping the Tesoro Mandan facility busy, but external forces are keeping the price of oil high. While U.S. oil consumption has been decreasing even as domestic production has risen, global demand for this fungible commodity is working wonders in North Dakota's oil fields. The story is similar in the eastern and central parts of the state, which are dominated by agriculture. They're not prone to boasting, but North Dakotans have justifiable pride in their ability to raise crops. The state is the largest U.S. producer of fourteen crops, including barley, canola, durum wheat, navy beans, flaxseed, sunflower seeds, and a few grains and seeds I hadn't heard of before. Pinto beans may be a staple of Mexican food, but the ones you're eating in that Taco Bell chalupa were likely grown by a gringo of Scandinavian extraction in North Dakota. Despite the parade of plus-size citizens you'll see at Disney World, Americans aren't eating much more than they were in 2007. But the rest of the world sure is—and it's eating much better. As a result North Dakota's farmers are finding new markets—and selling into commodity markets kept buoyant by global demand— and plowing funds into equipment and processing capabilities. "We've seen phenomenal growth in our export markets, triple-digit growth in the last few years," said John Mittleider, manager of agriculture and energy development at the North Dakota Department of Commerce. Mittleider was my guide for a day's tour of Brobdingnagian food production, which included my first ride in an air taxi, a rattling Cessna Skymaster that was held together by roughly the same amount of duct tape as you'd find in a battered New York City taxi. "We're not a consumption state," he said.

In one way or another North Dakota's healthy agriculture economy is all about exports and global demand. And it perfectly highlights the state's combination of provincialism and global reach. The ground floor of the state's unassuming capitol features portraits of locals who have made it big elsewhere: Roger Maris, Lawrence Welk. There I met Doug Goehring, the state agricultural commissioner, who farms two thousand acres twenty miles southeast of Bismarck. Goehring, who used to work in international marketing for the U.S. Soybean Board, described how North Dakota farmers and ranchers have become more aggressive about exporting directly to customers overseas rather than simply selling to wholesalers and brokers: "We started [to make] more and more trade trips, trying to explore what options existed for our commodities in other countries. We started talking about all our commodities, and buyers were surprised and perplexed. Spring wheat, durum wheat, barley,

barley hops, black beans, navy beans, canola, flax—all of a sudden they're finding out that this stuff comes from here."

These days North Dakota farmers are making direct links to new markets in ways that were simply unthinkable ten or even five years ago. Goehring whipped out his phone to show me a picture of some nervous-looking cows in a pen on a 747 bound for Kazakhstan. After the fall of the Soviet Union, the cattle herds in the region thinned out. First, North Dakota ranchers looked into whether they could export sturdy bull semen to the steppes and -stans of Central Asia. "But the real key was to make some sales of high-quality northern-type cattle into the region and let them start a cross-breeding program," Goehring told me. In the fall of 2010 Global Beef Consultants, a firm based in Prince, North Dakota, brokered a deal to ship 1,600 heifers to Kazakhstan at a cost of about $1,600 per animal. For the first flight, about 160 heifers were prodded onto a Korean Air 747 in Fargo, packed four or five to a crate, netted down, and sent on their thirteen-hour journey to Borat's homeland. Steerage class indeed.

The high prices for grain and meat are floating local boats. "You put money in a farmer's hand, and he services his debt and makes capital expenditures," said Goehring. When I visited in June 2011 a good chunk of the real estate in the Bismarck region was underwater, due to the flooding of the Missouri River. But the mortgages on them weren't. Modest housing is the norm. The governor's residence is a little ranch house. In 2009 the median price of a North Dakota home was $137,000; the national median was $172,000. But the gap is closing. The price of a typical North Dakota home rose to $144,000 in 2010 and $155,600 in 2011, while home prices continued to fall in the rest of the United States. (At the end of 2011, the median sales price of an existing home in the United States was $165,000.) In some parts of the state they have literally run out of homes. "I was in Williston, where we have forty-five Realtor members, and they usually had a hundred homes on the inventory," said Jill Beck, executive vice president of the state's National Association of Realtors chapter. "When I was there in December, they had nine." Building has been on the upswing. In 2011 building permits for 3,245 housing units were issued in the state, up 1,707 from 2009, according to the North Dakota Association of Home Builders. In the first quarter of 2011 North Dakota was last among the fifty states in loan-delinquency rates, with just 1.62 percent of loans thirty days late, and it boasted the lowest foreclosure rate in the country. Beck attributed this performance to the state's conservative culture. "We didn't experience what the other states did, because our real estate people and bankers are conservative. They didn't make those crazy loans. People didn't go into homes knowing they couldn't afford them," she said. "People in the state are too proud to default on the loan. They're going to work hard to keep that loan from defaulting."

Well, perhaps. But other factors unique to North Dakota may help account for this performance. Due to the lack of appreciation, the small size of the market, and low housing prices, the mortgage industry largely left North Dakota alone during the housing boom. North Dakotans aren't rubes when it comes to finance. Farmers are plenty conversant with futures, options, and hedging. But the concept of debt as a product made, produced, and distributed for its own sake is as foreign here as arugula is. There's another important factor: in the rest of the United States bad money pushed out good money; in North Dakota good money kept out bad money.

North Dakota had a source of good money. The state-owned Bank of North Dakota was established in 1919, a reaction by prairie agriculturalists to the malign influence of eastern bankers. With assets of $4.03 billion, about the size of a middling New York hedge fund, it is the leading financial institution in the state. State agencies and entities deposit funds in the bank, and it deploys capital in the state. Community banks set the rate for home mortgages, and then the Bank of North Dakota purchases them. Think of it as a state-level Fannie Mae, except without the huge executive salaries and lobbying budget.[4]

In September 2011 the Bank of North Dakota accepted a new deposit from a new customer: the state's Legacy Fund. In the fall of 2010 the state's voters easily approved a constitutional ballot initiative that created a sort of state-level sovereign wealth fund. Agricultural states suffer consistently from droughts and floods, and recognize that the weather may not always be favorable and that crop prices may not always be high. So it makes sense to set aside funds for lean years. The new legislation stipulates that each year 30 percent of the gusher of corporate oil and gas revenues is to be siphoned off into the Legacy Fund and locked away from lawmakers until 2017. At that point the legislature will need a two-thirds majority to use the funds, and even then it will be able to withdraw a maximum of 15 percent per year. In 2012 and 2013 about $613 million is projected to roll into the fund, a figure equal to about 7 percent of the state's budget. The first monthly deposit, of $34.3 million, was made in September 2011.[5]

The Legacy Fund isn't the only way North Dakota is turning the good fortune of its oil production into a common resource. When it comes to state finances, the state is a mirror image of most U.S. states. Revenues from oil and gas, sales, and income taxes have been strong. That's what happens when lots of people are working and investing in a state. For the 2011–2013 two-year budgeting cycle, or biennium, North Dakota projects oil extraction and gross production tax collections of $2.04 billion, with chunks distributed to local government, the general fund, the $613 million for the Legacy Fund, and $341.8 million for a fund that supports reductions in property taxes. In addition to socking funds away for lean years, North Dakota has been able to cut taxes while increasing spending on education, health care, and infrastructure. Like every other low-population state, North Dakota relies disproportionately on the federal government for funds. When the Tax Foundation published studies ranking states by how much money they sent to Washington compared with how much they received between 1981 and 2005, North Dakota frequently came in second or third, receiving up to $1.70 for every dollar in taxes it paid. But if the Great Father in Washington decides to adopt an austerity regime, North Dakota will be able to weather the storm. While Washington hems and haws about infrastructure, the state's 2011–2013 budget pledges $958 million in infrastructure investments building roads and water systems to support the oil and gas industry.[6]

The state's self-reliance in finance is a by-product of geographic isolation and (well-deserved) mistrust of out-of-state banking interests. Spend a few days in the state and you get a sense of how self-reliance on nonfinancial resources breeds a focus on efficiency, conservation, and scale. We tend to conflate efficiency with density—it's impossible to have public transit in rural areas, and long distances make everything from personal travel to school bus routes less efficient. But there's more to efficient living than small apartments and light-rail systems. In North Dakota the relationship between efficiency and self-sufficiency is evident. With few people around, farmers and companies have to be efficient with labor. I visited the home of Terry Wanzek, a state senator, who farms 10,000 acres outside Jamestown. He grows corn, soybeans, barley, and wheat and cleans and processes dry edible beans with a labor force that consists of himself, his son, a few family members, and occasional seasonal workers.

In nearby Spiritwood a giant concrete and steel complex rose up that neatly encapsulates the combination and potential of industrial-scale agriculture and energy efficiency. Spiritwood is an appropriate location for a malting house owned by Cargill, the giant agricultural conglomerate. Here natural products are processed into the base for alcoholic spirits. A set of 210-foot-tall concrete towers built in the early 1970s, Cargill Malt is the world's largest malting facility under one roof. Barley soaks in giant, 160-foot-long beds, is germinated and heated in kilns at 180 to 200 degrees Fahrenheit, and is then dried and processed into malt, the essential ingredient in beer. The facility can process up to 420,000 metric tons of malt (from 22 million to 25 million bushels of barley) per year.

Cargill exports huge quantities of material from the state. Each year its wet corn mill in Wahpeton spends about $200 million on corn and processes about 5 million tons into corn sugar and corn gluten feed. Historically the Cargill malting house in Spiritwood has been a local business, supplying the two major players in the highly consolidated U.S. beer business: Anheuser-Busch and SABMiller. But the U.S. beer business, now largely in the hands of foreign owners, seems to be in a slow-growth mode. "Americans are drinking less beer. It's down in total one or two percent," said Doug Eden, president of Cargill Malt. "The category shift from mainstream brands to the budget brands has an impact on our business. And so does shifting from full-bodied to light. Light beers have less of our ingredients than a craft beer." Yet Spiritwood was operating at about 80 percent capacity, in part because rising foreign demand is making up for slack domestic demand. About 35 percent of the malt is shipped overseas. Customers include Mexico's two major brewers, Grupo Model and Femsa, and the largest brewer in the Dominican Republic, Cervecería Nacional Dominicana. Those markets are growing at about 5 percent per year. Less beer, *más cerveza*.

Of course, productivity, efficiency, and natural resources can do only so much. North Dakota suffers from a shortage in one vital resource: people. Companies like Cargill are finding it difficult to keep up with the opportunities provided by rising global demand. Eden noted, "With unemployment rates as low as they are, and specifically for this facility, many of the people have been there for thirty-five or forty years. We have a population that will soon be retiring, and replacing those people will be hard. We oftentimes have to post jobs for a significant amount of time—biochemistry people, maintenance, supervisors with engineering degrees." I visited Cavendish Farms' frozen french fry factory in Jamestown, a town of 15,000 about a hundred miles east of Bismarck. To get there, you turn off the highway and follow the smell of cooking oil that wafts over the farmland. A marvelous set of machines transforms 340 million pounds of dirt-covered potatoes into neatly bagged, flash-fried, flash-frozen potato products, with little human intervention. Director of Operations Andrew MacLeod says the plant, with 220 employees running three shifts around the clock, faces two major challenges to keep up with growing demand: a lack of raw potatoes (supply is down this year) and a lack of people. The company would like to expand its capacity by 15 percent. "But attracting employees is probably our biggest challenge today," he told me. The plant is looking to add about fifteen people, mostly to operate the line and test the product. (Yes, you can get paid to eat french fries. But not much.) "When we hire people, we're pretty careful about who we hire. We screen for drugs. We're not getting a lot of applicants. If we want to grow and expand, we have to attract people here."

The challenge isn't simply a matter of demographics. Many of the positions open in North Dakota—in the oil fields, at Cavendish Farms—are jobs, not careers. And they're hard ones that, in many instances, don't pay all that well. The positions Cavendish is trying to fill are shift work: three twelve-hour days on, followed by two days off, paying anywhere from $12 to $17 per hour.

Across the state employers are casting their rods more deeply into the labor pool, and older and disabled workers are able to find opportunities in North Dakota that may be unavailable to them in other states. The labor force participation rate is 74 percent, compared with 62 percent in the country at large. Even at that rate, you can still get good, friendly service at Starbucks. And North Dakota, which exports so much food and energy, is dealing with its labor shortage by importing people. Oil field workers come from out of state for a few weeks at a time, and foreign students have been brought in for fast-food jobs as part of work-exchange programs sanctioned by the government.

In the eastern, more urbanized part of the state—where the economy is anchored by the university towns of Fargo, home to North Dakota State; and Grand Forks, home to the University of North Dakota—service employers like hospitals and technology firms attract commuters from across the Red River in more densely populated Minnesota. From an economic perspective, the Red River Valley looks more like the United States at large. Growth is driven by population centers and anchored by education, health care, and services. North Dakota has a small technology cluster and a larger health care sector. Microsoft's campus in Fargo is the technology giant's second-largest outside its home base in Redmond, Washington. It was originally the headquarters of Great Plains Software, which Microsoft acquired in 2000.

Here too North Dakota has shown an ability to use existing resources and sound investments to turn what should have been a declining sector into a booming one, and one that helps import the most valuable renewable resource into the state. As we've seen, higher education is one of the best ways to export services and import new citizens, from abroad and from other states. In recent years the price of public education has risen rapidly as states have lost their ability to support it. In a national and international market, public institutions that are able to hold down costs while investing in quality have an immense competitive advantage for public university systems. Simply holding the line on tuition and investment has been a major achievement in recent years. As Kevin Helliker reported in the *Wall Street Journal*, North Dakota's public education system has become a magnet for human capital.

As the state's population aged and dwindled, North Dakota began to hemorrhage teenagers. The number of high school graduates fell from 9,058 in 2000 to 7,400 in 2010, off 18 percent in the decade. But rather than cut aid to education, as California and other states have done, North Dakota maintained investments in its network of eleven public colleges. In the 2009–2011 biennium, the state appropriated $2.49 billion for higher education. In the 2011–2013 budget, the total investment was $2.629 billion, up 5.6 percent. "As others raised tuition, North Dakota held its price down," Helliker wrote. In the 2011–2012 school year, tuition and fees for out-of-state students were $17,000.

These measures have helped stave off what seemed to be an inevitable decline. Enrollment in the state's public colleges rose 38 percent from 2000 to 2010, to 48,120, with a 56 percent jump in nonresident students. Many of them came across the border from Minnesota. In the 2009–2010 school year 8,381 Minnesotans studied in North Dakota. But the system is also importing students from more exotic locales. From 2000 to 2010 international enrollment rose to 1,600 from 1,125, up more than 40 percent. "My roommates are from Mongolia and South Korea," Delaney McCormack, a Kansas resident studying technical theater and design at North Dakota State, told the *Journal*. The university system is showing signs of attracting students from areas even more alien than the steppes of Central Asia, like the preps of central Connecticut. Diva Malinowski, a graduate of the snooty Miss Porter's School in Farmington, Connecticut, is the first graduate of her school, the alma mater of Jacqueline Kennedy Onassis, to attend the university. "I won't be the last," she said. Call it the Little Sorority House on the Prairie.

Of course, students frequently leave college towns for big cities in other states. But some chunk of the foreigners flocking to North Dakota for higher education stay in the state. In Fargo, home to North Dakota State University, 39 percent of nonresidents remain in the state at least one year after graduation. That trend has pushed Fargo's population to 105,000, up 16 percent from 2000. As Helliker noted, many of the science graduates go on to work in the "array of defense, medical, computer science and other firms [that] have sprouted along the Red River."[7]

North Dakota's demographic profile is like Japan's: homogeneous, aging, and shrinking. And like Japan, it entered a period of demographic decline. But North Dakota shows that decline can be reversed. The state's population, which peaked at 681,000 in 1930 and slumped to 642,195 in 2000, rose back up to 672,591 in 2010. Growth doesn't just attract more people; it gives the existing population the optimism to stay put and expand. The Realtor Jill Beck, who lives in Mandan, noted with wonder that her daughter's second-grade class had twenty-eight children.

North Dakota has some great resources, particularly oil, coal, and fertile land, that other states lack. And it's easier to turn things around when you have a small population and a lot of oil. But North Dakota also has plenty of the disadvantages that afflict rural states. Yet it has thrived by doing more with less, tapping internal resources, investing in public infrastructure, and actively seeking new ways to participate in rapidly growing global industries and markets. The United States would be further on the road to recovery if the other forty-nine states were a little more like North Dakota.

CHAPTER 11

Reshoring and Insourcing

Unfortunately, not all Americans can simply pick up and move to North Dakota or remake their local economies in that state's image. The United States can't hope to avoid decline unless it starts to recoup some of the 8.78 million jobs obliterated in the Great Recession of 2008–2009. And so the persistent question remains: Where will the jobs come from?

It's likely that some jobs will come from the same place that is providing investment, orders, and a rising proportion of sales and production for American companies: abroad.

In the twenty-first century, regardless of where they were created, companies are essentially stateless, especially when it comes to paying taxes. In a fantastical super-flat world, many businesses can theoretically be located anywhere. The dispersion of production and service jobs throughout the world has been one of the factors weighing against the U.S. economy. A national economy no longer owns or hangs on to jobs by default. But there are still plenty of reasons—financial, economic, political, and logistic—for foreign and American companies to locate production, sales, and distribution in the United States. The trends in foreign direct investment show that non-U.S. companies have been onshoring jobs in the United States in recent years. But there's a new trend: An increasing number of U.S. companies are finding it makes sense to reshore and insource jobs to the United States, including some that have been active exporters of jobs.

The conventional wisdom holds that U.S. companies simply

can't afford to make things at home any longer. So large chunks of the U.S. manufacturing sector, having concluded they can't keep up with Asia's cheap labor, have packed up and moved. Worse, the trend is bound to accelerate, climbing the value chain from textiles and electronics to legal services and journalism. After all, as the rest rise, they're acquiring the skills and technology necessary to do a lot of the jobs Americans perform—but at much lower salaries. Educated Indian workers can answer phones, read mortgage documents, and rewrite corporate earnings releases just as well as their American counterparts. And that means more and more jobs, professions, and disciplines fall into the tradable category, so companies can choose to locate the positions in any of an increasing number of countries. Now that millions of manufacturing jobs have already been offshored, surely America's 91 million service jobs will be the next to go? The Princeton economist Alan Blinder ignited a near panic among the chattering classes with an article in the March–April 2006 issue of *Foreign Affairs*, in which he estimated that between 28 million and 42 million service jobs were in danger of being offshored in the coming years.[1] With one voice, pundits and economists have been singing the mournful line from the Bruce Springsteen song "My Hometown": "Foreman says these jobs are going, boys, and they ain't coming back."

There's a flip side to this trend, though. Let's take another look at China. When countries become more wealthy, employers pay higher wages. The average wage in China rose 150 percent from 1999 through 2006. Rising wages lead to higher levels of domestic consumption, which leads to more types of new businesses that don't have to rely solely on cheap labor to produce goods for exports, and these new businesses lead to more income. That's one of the ways poor countries become middle-income countries, and middle-income countries grow rich. This process provides some favorable results for the United States: it leads to more foreign direct investment from China, more exports to China, more tourists and college students coming from China, and more U.S. inports inside China. There's much more room for growth. Many typical Chinese workers can already afford to eat at a local KFC. There will come a day when Beijing's legions of Dilberts might be able to afford a trip to the real Disneyland. That day may come sooner rather than later.

Labor in China is likely to become more expensive for several reasons. Bizarre as it seems, the nation of 1.3 billion people is going to start to run out of workers pretty soon. Parents haven't totally adhered to the one-child policy that started in 1980, but they've come close enough. Between 2000 and 2010 the population grew by just 0.57 percent per year. Wang Feng, a specialist in demographics at the Brookings-Tsinghua Center for Public Policy in Beijing, told the *Wall Street Journal* that the decennial population census found a fertility rate of 1.5. That's below the replacement rate of 2.1. In 2010 people over sixty constituted 13.3 percent of China's population, up from 10.3 percent in 2000, while those under fourteen were just 16.6 percent of the population in 2010, down from 23 percent in 2000. The number of workers age twenty to twenty-four is already declining. Unless it starts to encourage large-scale immigration, China may find its labor force shrinking as soon as 2016.[2] More old people needing support, fewer people working—it sounds a lot like Japan. The tightening supply of labor should continue to push Chinese wages up.

And in the years since the Great Recession, Americans have effectively paid more for this labor, for reasons having nothing to do with wage inflation. In recent years China's economic mandarins have realized that the best way to fight inflation and improve the lot of your people isn't to pay them a little more to make cheap junk that they can send elsewhere. Rather it's a good idea to let your currency appreciate so that the cost of things people and companies need to import, like food and oil and coal, doesn't gobble up such a huge chunk of disposable income. Despite all the complaints about China's currency manipulation, the renminbi has appreciated in value against the dollar in recent years, rising from 8.27 per dollar in October 2005 to 6.38 per dollar in October 2011, a 23 percent increase. In 2011 a dollar simply bought much less of a Chinese worker's time than it did in 2006, but more than it will buy in 2016.

The per-hour cost of labor is just one component of labor costs to consider. When wages are high, companies invest in training and equipment that make better use of employees' time. In 2011, according to Boston Consulting Group, "fully loaded" factory wages—wages plus benefits and associated taxes—were $22.30 per hour in the United States, compared with $2 in China, more than eleven times higher. But since U.S. workers are far more productive than their Chinese counterparts, employers need to purchase less American labor to produce more stuff. It's not that factory workers in Mississippi work any harder than factory workers in Chongqing; rather, they work smarter, using machines, equipment, and software to greater effect. When taking higher U.S. productivity into account, BCG concluded that China's labor costs are only 55 percent lower than those in the low-cost U.S. states. Should wages in China continue to rise at a 15 to 20 percent clip, that difference will slip to 39 percent in 2015. These findings were published in an intriguing report titled *Made in America, Again: Why Manufacturing Will Return to the U.S.*[3]

The United States remains a high-wage market by global standards. But the equation has changed in recent years. Real wages fell during the recession, and continued to fall in the months after it ended. The near-bankruptcy and restructuring of some of America's largest industrial employers, the dominance of cost-cutting companies, continued population growth in the South and the sunbelt (areas of traditionally low wages and low union activity), and the ongoing decimation of the labor movement have altered the dynamic between labor and management. In 2010 only 6.9 percent of private sector workers were represented by unions, according to the Bureau of Labor Statistics. That's down from 9 percent in 2000. Some of the largest and most influential industrial employers, like General Motors, have successfully introduced two-tier wage systems, with entry-level workers getting paid about half what established employees make. There are epic levels of slack in the U.S. labor force. All this has given U.S. employers the upper hand. A report by the Bureau of Labor Statistics shows that U.S. manufacturing wages in 2011 were only the fourteenth highest in the world. "China's low-wage advantage will disappear over the next five years," Christian Murck, president of the American Chamber of Commerce in China, told the *Wall Street Journal*'s John Bussey in May 2011.[4]

But while it is frequently the most discussed item, the cost of labor is just one input that companies must consider. There are very real nuisances and downsides to working in China, where the supply of electricity is frequently erratic and the price of land is rising. It's not uncommon for government officials to show up and tell factory owners that they need to relocate to make room for a new development or a new highway. Shipping has grown more expensive due to high fuel prices. And time always equals money. Under normal circumstances it takes much longer for goods to reach a store in Denver from a factory in Guangzhou than it does from a factory in Pennsylvania. Long supply chains can easily be torn asunder by a tsunami in Japan, political unrest in Egypt, or a volcano erupting in Iceland. In hypercompetitive markets, in which businesses have a renewed focus on efficiency, considerations such as speed to market, the ability to customize, and quick inventory turns come to the fore. Taking these items into consideration, BCG declared in *Made in America* in August 2011, "Within five years, the total cost of production for many products will be only about 10 to 15 percent less in Chinese coastal cities than in some parts of the U.S. where factories are likely to be built," like South Carolina, Alabama, and Tennessee.

The economist Herbert Stein is remembered for coining the maxim "If something cannot go on forever, it will stop." That applies equally to foreign countries and the United States. In the coming years "a surprising amount of work that rushed to China over the past decade could soon start to come back—and the economic impact could be significant," said Harold L. Sirkin, a BCG senior partner and the coauthor of *Made in America*. As soon as 2015 the changing calculus "should prompt companies to rethink where they produce certain goods meant for sale in North America." Production of small, soft things—clothes, shoes, textiles—will remain largely offshore. But in areas where materials and logistics cost a lot, and when time to market is crucial, the calculus changes. BCG has identified several sectors, including cars and auto parts, appliances, furniture, and fabricated metal products, that together accounted for about 70 percent of the U.S. imports from China in 2009, and that are poised for reshoring. Should the shift take place, it would add $100 billion to U.S. output, help cut the trade deficit, and support between 2 million and 3 million jobs.

That sounds a bit optimistic, even for my tastes. After all, many of those jobs could migrate from China to cheaper pastures in Asia. In the 1960s electronics jobs first left the United States for Taiwan and Japan, which were then low-cost, low-quality production centers, and then migrated to China once Taiwan and Japan became higher-cost, higher-quality production centers. Visit China today and factory owners will describe how the lower end of the manufacturing market—T-shirts, shoes, low-quality minibikes— has already decamped to Vietnam. While visiting Vietnam, I heard repeated warnings from garment factory owners that local firms were already looking to Cambodia, where costs were even lower. Two days later, as I walked around Phnom Penh, Cambodia, still destitute, haunted, and depopulated thirty-five years after the Khmer Rouge's genocide, I figured this had to be the last link in the low-cost labor chain. But of course, there's always Laos or Burma. Sweatshops have a way of finding new sod.

But the remaining low-cost locations don't have what China has. The continual search for ever cheaper labor yields diminishing returns. It's not always cheap to conduct business in developing countries. Luanda, Angola, tops the Mercer Consulting survey of the most expensive cities and countries for business, followed by Tokyo, N'Djamena in Chad, and Moscow.[5] You can get all the cheap labor you like, but if there's no clean water, if office space is insanely expensive, if an Internet connection costs thousands of dollars per year, and if organized crime runs rampant, the costs can pile up. Driving around Vietnam is an adventure. The narrow streets of Ho Chi Minh City and its exurbs are clogged with traffic. Hordes of scooters carrying everything from four-person families to pigs jostle with semitrailers. Traffic lights are few and far between. Each electrical pole is festooned with an insane spaghetti of electrical wires. Sure, a Nike contractor can build a state-of-the-art factory to manufacture shoes outside Ho Chi Minh City, but it's difficult to get the Air Jordans out of the country. The same lack of transportation infrastructure plagues India, Bangladesh, and sub-Saharan Africa. With costs rising in China, executives feel their options are dwindling. "You can't do hard goods in Vietnam, and you can't get anything out of India," the CEO of one large consumer products company told me. That's why we hear much more about India's exports of services like tech support, which can be delivered over phone lines or fiber-optic cables, rather than India's exports of goods like textiles, which need to travel on trains, trucks, and ships.

Manufacturers continually monitor costs and calculate the relative value of locating production in China, Taiwan, Tennessee, or Michigan. And while the United States may not yet be cheaper, the ability of businesses to run better, stronger, and faster can make up for the wage difference.

In March 2009 US Block Windows, an acrylic block window manufacturer based in Pensacola, Florida, bought its competitor Hy-Lite, a division of Fortune Brands. Hy-Lite was outsourcing the molding of acrylic blocks to China. "It became very evident to us that we could do it cheaper in-house, because we had the facilities, and we were operating at less than capacity," said Roger Murphy, president of US Block Windows. But in a world where efficiency and speed matter more than ever, there were other advantages to be gained from reshoring. In a period of rising consumer expectations, US Block Windows aims to ship orders within four days of receipt. The lead time for production in China is twelve to sixteen weeks. In a period when it's difficult to forecast demand far out into the future, "it's very difficult to match those two things up," said Murphy. In September 2009 US Block Windows moved Hy-Lite's molding work from China to Florida.

US Block Windows products are once again being made in the United States. And so are some other bits of Americana. The baseballs used in the World Series are made in a factory in Costa Rica belonging to Rawlings, a unit of the consumer products company Jarden. Based in St. Louis, Rawlings also owns factories in Asia and in the United States, including one in tiny Caledonia, a speck of a town with a population of about 2,800 in the southeast corner of

Minnesota, across the river from La Crosse, Wisconsin. Caledonia is home to Dave Kunst, the first person to walk around the Earth. In a factory in the southwestern part of town, Rawlings makes Miken metal-composite softball bats, which retail for up to $300. In 2004 Rawlings sent production of another bat brand, Worth, to Asia. In April 2011, however, Rawlings reshored Worth production from Panyu City in Guangzhou back to Caledonia.

Why? Inflation has been pushing labor rates up by 10 to 15 percent a year in China, and workers are shifting to higher-tech jobs. "Our third-party suppliers have had to increase their wage rates to maintain a stable workforce, and that has passed through," said Robert Parish, president of Jarden Team Sports, the division that owns Rawlings. Other considerations play a role. Today firms don't like to hold more inventory than is absolutely necessary; it ties up cash and increases the chances of getting stuck with goods that can't be sold. "Softball and baseball are played in a relatively short period of time, so you're either in stock or not," Parish continued. "Retailers have a two-month window to make hay, and if you miss it, then you're dead for the year." In many parts of the United States baseball and softball equipment enjoy robust sales in the late spring and then go into hibernation for the winter. The lead time for producing bats in Asia and delivering them to the United States is six weeks. By comparison, bat models in high demand can be pushed out from the Caledonia factory in a week. What's more, when it comes to high-value items, manufacturers have to consider the carrying costs of material and inventory of expensive items, like $200 bats. Shipping expensive bats over long distances means tying up a lot of cash. So, yes, wages are higher in Caledonia than they are in China, but for Rawlings, manufacturing bats in Minnesota means a 68 percent reduction in inventory carrying costs and a 45 percent improvement in working capital compared with manufacturing bats in China.

An investment in efficiency helped tip the scale in favor of Minnesota. In China workers manually wound carbon around a mandrel to form the barrel and handle of the bats. In the United States, Miken "developed a new piece of equipment that would allow us to automate [that] portion of the production of composite bats," Parish said, helping to further reduce the cost advantage held by the Chinese factory. And when you're making a product that is used in America's national pastime, it helps to be able to put a big "U.S.A." tag across it, like the one Worth bats now boast. Miken has hired twenty new employees in Caledonia, where it now runs two shifts. "We shouldn't delude ourselves to think that all kinds of manufacturing is going to come back here," Martin Franklin, the chief executive officer of Jarden, told me. "But things that can be done with injection molding, things that are high value-added," are candidates for reshoring. In May 2011, Coleman, another Jarden unit, said it would bring back some production of large plastic coolers from China to Wichita, Kansas.

A similar, small-scale migration can be seen at the lower level of the services sector. Network television programmers have an uncanny ability to call the top in cultural and financial markets. They air shows just when the trends are about to end. *Bull*, a show about hot young twentysomethings doing stuff on Wall Street, aired on TNT in August 2000, just as the stock market was going to melt down, and *Hot Properties,* an ABC sitcom about hot young real estate brokers in Los Angeles, debuted in the fall of 2005, just as the housing market was about to peak. The NBC sitcom *Outsourced,* about the hilarity that ensues when a young American runs a call center in India, aired in the fall of 2010. At precisely that moment the smart money was beginning to move in the other direction.

Like manufacturers, some service companies have found that they may have taken outsourcing or offshoring one or two steps too far. The same set of factors that push executives to reconsider manufacturing in the United States are leading some to reconsider the location of service positions that had been offshored. Stagnant wages in the United States, combined with India's erratic power grid and rapid wage increases, means the differential in costs for service operations between the United States and developing countries is narrowing. As GE CEO Jeff Immelt noted in a March 2011 speech to the Economic Club of Washington, "We run call centers now in the U.S. that are only 10 percent more expensive than [in] India."[6] Just as with manufacturing, there are sound business reasons—beyond wages—to think about reshoring service jobs.

Many customers, it turns out, don't like the hiss on the customer service line that signifies a call is being answered in Manila. Some react negatively to the disembodied voice with the heavy accent and the fake English name. The drive for efficiency is leading companies to exert greater control over all their processes. Many companies want to keep their outsourcers closer to home, with locals handling the calls and work performed in existing facilities. Others are willing to pay a slight premium to avoid being stigmatized as a company that ships jobs overseas.

Somewhere in Hollywood it's quite possible that a young show-runner is working up a script called *Insourcing,* about the misadventures of an Indian manager sent to run a call center in the United States. Or he could just crib from the May 2011 *Washington Post* article by Paul Glader. Glader visited a call center in New York run by Aegis Communications, a unit of the Indian conglomerate Essar, where workers earn $12 to $14 per hour to "make or take calls for customers of prescription drug plans or Medicare contracts and enter and verify information." Like Sunil Godhwani, the Indian financial services executive I met in Davos, Indian outsourcing bosses see the United States as a prime area for growth. In 2010 Aegis employed about 5,000 people at nine U.S. call centers serving customers like American Express and the health insurer Humana. When it signs up big firms like Citibank and Hilton as clients, Tata Consultancy Services, another big Indian outsourcer, is now likely to keep that work in the United States. "It plans to hire more than 1,000 Americans in 2011 and to base 10,000 of its 185,000 global employees in the country," Glader wrote.[7]

Many large companies are onshoring and insourcing even as they continue to offshore and outsource. While its engineers are busy setting up industrial capacity around the world, General Electric's engineers have also been planting new flags in the United States. It's not as easy, or as cheap, to move stuff around the world with oil at $90 a barrel as it was when oil was $50 or $60. "Twenty years ago, we were in the process of moving every appliance manufacturing job to China or Mexico," Jeff Immelt said in 2010. "When I open up the safe under my desk I can't find the pennies that we have saved. . . . So the next generation of products are going to be made in the U.S." In 2010 GE said that by 2014 it would invest $432 million in factories that design and make refrigerators in Louisville, Kentucky; Decatur, Alabama; Selmer, Tennessee; and Bloomington, Indiana.[8]

Executives manage and assess opportunities by constructing matrices that help them sort priorities and costs. On certain matrices, including ones where efficiency is as important a factor as cheap labor, the United States comes out ahead. Whirlpool, the appliance manufacturer, has been reducing its footprint in the United States, shuttering plants in Oxford, Mississippi, and Evansville, Indiana, in 2009 and 2010. When it was casting about for a new plant to make built-in cooking ranges and ovens, it looked at Mexico, Central America, and Asia. But instead it settled on investing $300 million to build a new factory in Cleveland, Tennessee, where the existing plant was a hundred years old. Whirlpool added 130 staffers to the town's 1,300-person workforce.[9]

In the globalized world it has seemed for years that every U.S. plant is on the verge of closing, and in coming years many more will undoubtedly shut down. But now it appears that the same forces that drew jobs offshore are putting many plants on the cusp of regaining work. Because U.S. labor costs have long been comparatively high, companies tend to build and keep open only the most highly efficient plants. It's no surprise that Subaru's innovative zero-waste car plant is in Lafayette, Indiana, rather than China. In an age of rising costs and increased focus on efficiency, the logic of locating auto production closer to end users is more compelling. While U.S. companies have shipped plenty of automobile assembly jobs to Mexico, South America, and Asia in recent decades, there has been a corresponding growth in U.S. employment by Asian and German car companies. Global Automakers, the trade association of foreign automakers active in the United States (which doesn't include the German companies), says that in 2010 its members employed 80,000 people directly in the United States and accounted for 40 percent of U.S. production and sales for the year.

Restructuring has also played a role in setting the stage for reshoring. By 2011, having pushed through two-tier wage systems as part of their epic restructuring, the Big Three U.S. automakers were in a position to throw American unions some meaningful sops in negotiations. In the fall of 2011 the Big Three sealed new contracts with the United Auto Workers. Each agreed to invest more in assembly plants and to do some onshoring. Reuters reported that Ford agreed to move some of the work involved in assembling Ford Fusions from Mexico to Flat Rock, Michigan, where it planned to add a second shift. GM's deal, the *New York Times* reported in September 2011, "will create or preserve 6,400 jobs over the next four years, mostly by hiring new, entry-level employees but also by retaining work in the United States that was going to move to Mexico." Chrysler's agreement involved promises of a $1.3 billion investment in a factory in Kokomo, Indiana, and the retention of 3,500 jobs there, plus more work at Belvidere, Illinois, and Sterling Heights, Michigan. "If it was not for the UAW bargaining, all these jobs would be going to Korea and China and Mexico," UAW President Bob King said. King told the Associated Press that the deals "together would add 20,000 jobs by 2015."[10]

These numbers pale in comparison with the jobs lost over the past decade. But the reshoring and insourcing show that U.S. manufacturing has shifted rapidly from a very expensive labor model to a cheaper one. That may be a sign of decline. But it may also be a factor that helps inhibit further decline. When an economy has lost so many jobs, it has to start somewhere. Focusing solely on the number of people employed directly by the Big Three, or other manufacturers, largely misses the point. Just as every job in GE's Greenville, South Carolina, turbine plant represents eight jobs in the supply chain, other lean manufacturing operations tend to spur job growth outside the factory walls. A new factory in a town means jobs for local people, but also for people in other U.S. services: truckers and shippers, logistics experts, contractors, vendors, suppliers, security guards, and construction workers. A new law firm will buy some supplies and provide a stream of business to restaurants. But a new manufacturing plant helps reshape the geography of the local and regional economy.

NCR, the Atlanta-based company that has evolved from a manufacturer of cash registers to a producer of ATM machines and checkout kiosks, has followed the logic of offshoring and outsourcing. The company does business in 130 countries, and in 2011 rang up 65 percent of its sales outside the United States. It owns manufacturing operations in Beijing and Budapest and, until recently, outsourced production in the United States. "We're big believers in having a regional manufacturing model," said Peter Dorsman, senior vice president of global operations. "There's so much change occurring—political, economic, natural disasters. I think it's critical that you have a balanced approach to manufacturing and that you have a supply chain that is agile and nimble and capable of responding."

In 2009, in order to gain better control over its manufacturing process and to continue to expand globally, NCR decided to establish two new factories. The location of one was a no-brainer: Manaus, Brazil. But the decision to build a new factory in the United States went against the prevailing wisdom. "When I made my decision in June of 2009, a lot of people probably thought I should have got my head examined. It was the worst economic conditions we had faced in years," Dorsman said. But the logic was inescapable. ATMs are a low-volume, high-mix manufacturing business. Factories turn out a relatively small number of units, while offering a host of different options. A factory may make 100,000 ATMs a year, which is not a lot compared with, say, cell phones or T-shirts. But it doesn't simply stamp out 100,000 of the same product. Customers require many different features and configurations and tend to buy ATMs in small batches. So NCR places a premium on its ability to customize and to get products to the market quickly. ATMs are also heavy and expensive; a two-ton model starts at about $10,000. "From my perspective, when you look at total landed costs—material, labor, taxes, duties—you have to look at it all in. If you're shipping a two-ton ATM over a long distance, then freight costs and shipping times become more significant," Dorsman said. In addition, building state-of-the-art ATMs calls for more than cheap, unskilled labor. Lean manufacturing of machines with hundreds of components requires a strong network of suppliers and local universities that can supply engineers. Incentives that some U.S. states and local governments offer can also help tip the scale in favor of a U.S. location. Many developing countries simply don't provide such amenities and resources.

After looking at seventeen states, NCR settled on a 350,000-square-foot facility in Columbus, Georgia, where Panasonic used to make batteries. The plant had been vacant since early 2006 and stood as a depressing example of unwanted, unused industrial capacity. NCR took over the property in June 2009 and proceeded to install production lines and modernize the facility. The factory earned LEED certification, in part because NCR used concrete it had removed from the plant to make exterior walkways. When it posted a notice for 80 jobs in July 2009, it received 2,200 applicants, which state agencies helped it to screen. NCR, which had committed to hire 870 people within five years of opening, was up to 500 people on two shifts by the summer of 2011. In addition to making 60,000 ATMs each year, some of which are exported to Argentina, the Columbus factory makes entertainment kiosks and self-checkout retail terminals.

But the economic impact goes far beyond NCR's immediate payroll. As part of its strategy, NCR aims to use suppliers that are close to the factory. Dorsman says that about 35 percent of the components for its ATMs come from Asia, and that's not going to change: "They're electronics parts that will always come out of the Far East." But the other 65 percent comes from suppliers within a few hundred miles in all directions. And so Porter's Fabrication, a company in Bessemer City, North Carolina, that makes components for ATMs and safes, has added fifty workers to help feed the Columbus plant.

Every day, in less conspicuous ways, the United States brings in resources that contribute to job growth. About twenty years ago the United States onshored a married couple from China. Mei Xu and David Wang came to the country in 1992 when Mei enrolled in the University of Maryland's graduate journalism program. David was an engineer. After Mei graduated, she couldn't find a job in journalism. Instead of going into public relations, as most frustrated J-school graduates do, Mei and David, who lived in Annapolis, started making candles in their basement. They went to trade shows, networked, and quickly signed up Bloomingdale's as a customer. Chesapeake Bay Candle, like so many of its peers in the world of housewares, began producing in China in 1995. It opened a second factory in Vietnam in 2002, and a third factory there in 2007. The couple became American citizens in 1995. So far, so typical: immigrant family comes up with business idea, works hard, and manufactures in Asia.

Things began to change in 2008. Labor costs rose in Asia. The company bought key ingredients like fragrance oils in the United States and Europe, paid to ship them to Asia, and then paid to ship the finished goods back. The price of raw materials and the rising strength of the renminbi added another layer of costs. More significantly, Chesapeake's primary customers became much more demanding in the wake of a steep fall in retail sales. Most of the company's $84 million in sales were in the United States, but big clients like Target, Kohl's, Bed Bath & Beyond, and Hallmark were less willing to maintain high inventory levels and started to demand that suppliers deliver new products more quickly. That's no big deal if you make a product like birthday candles, the demand for which is steady throughout the year. But the higher-end candles that Chesapeake makes are seasonal products. It takes six to eight weeks to get candles from a factory in Vietnam to the Gold Crown Hallmark Store in Des Moines, Iowa. In the short fall retail season, a retailer that runs out of its first order of pumpkin spice candles can't restock.

In June 2011 Chesapeake Bay Candle opened its first U.S. factory, in a former warehouse in Glen Burnie, Maryland, about an hour away from the company's headquarters in Rockville. It employs fifty people in research and development and quality control and on a production line. The factory accounts for about 15 percent of the company's U.S. volume. But in the coming years Chesapeake Bay Candle expects that it will make about half of its total annual production in the United States.

The onshoring trend is real, even if the numbers are small—50 jobs here, 150 there, a few thousand here. And just as with exports, small companies are part of the trend. Taphandles, which makes handles for beer taps, was founded Seattle in 1999 and first started manufacturing in China in 2006. The company, which has annual revenues of $11 million, encountered the same type of problems that NCR did. "The lead time for orders coming from China is three weeks, and all of our brewery clients want our products faster," the founder and CEO Paul Fichter told the *New York Times*. "Right now, we're losing orders because of lead time." Meanwhile the company's labor costs have risen fourfold in the past five years. "I like to do business by the rules, but as an American operating in China, the rules are not always entirely clear," Fichter said. In the fall of 2011 he signed a lease on a factory in Woodinville, Washington, twelve miles east of Seattle. He hired a handful of workers, paying low wages of $9 to $16 per hour to start, with hopes of employing up to 150 people at the plant.[11]

For Peerless Industries, which makes mounts for flat-panel television screens ("audiovisual mounting solutions," in the parlance of the trade), reshoring production from Asia was a matter of control, speed, and differentiation. In March 2010 the company, which was founded in the early 1940s, announced that it would build new headquarters and a highly efficient factory on 22.5 acres in Aurora, Illinois. "We want to merge all operations to reduce operating expenses, and we are committed to being environmentally responsible as well as returning all manufacturing to the U.S. to shorten lead times and regain complete control," said Michael A. Campagna, the company's president and chief operating officer. Peerless installed solar panels and wind turbines and figured out a way to recycle heat generated by its processing equipment to help keep the plant warm in the cold winter months. As the company noted, reshoring production makes Peerless "the only major domestic mount producer with a 100 percent U.S.-based manufacturing operation."[12]

And so on. Even if it this type of activity takes place only on the margins, it helps contribute to a virtuous circle: more production leads to more purchases of locally sourced goods, services, and labor, which create more demand, which leads to more production. It's a safe bet that for the next several years a fast-growing Chinese economy will spur an increase in local wages, a rise in the renminbi, and a growing appetite for domestically produced goods. The same force is also likely to keep energy prices high. If current trends continue for just a few more years, the people making the decisions on where to locate production may increasingly decide to reshore. The jobs created won't be huge in number, and they won't pay the Cadillac wages and benefits that jobs did in the 1960s and 1970s. But they will be meaningful to the people who have them. And they will bring investment, capital, and suppliers back to many communities. The 3 million jobs that BCG projects can materialize on our shores in the next five years would go a long way toward clawing back the jobs lost in 2008 and 2009. But let's say only 25 percent of them, or 750,000 jobs, materialize. That's more than were created in the first half of 2011. And it also helps upend the myth that American companies and workers simply can't compete with global rivals. Many can right now. Many more will be able to do so in the near future.

CHAPTER 12

The Efficient Consumer

In previous periods of economic self-doubt, such as the post–cold war recession of 1991–1992 and the post–dot-com-bubble recession of 2001, the U.S. economy was rescued by powerful forces that touched many different parts of the economy and helped raise incomes—and not just for the top 1 percent. We can thank the Internet in the 1990s and housing in the 2000s. Without a new source of momentum, it's difficult to see how Americans can boost their collective income at a time when companies aren't willing to raise salaries. In 2010 the typical family earned $49,445, compared with $53,252 in 1999.

As we wait for a deus ex machina to appear, one source of salvation is already apparent: efficiency.

In the first phase of the recovery, the mania for efficiency was primarily a business phenomenon. Companies lowered their bottom line, boosted value, reflated assets, and put themselves in a better position to withstand shocks by strengthening their core. That was good news for the stock market, lenders, and shareholders. But in the United States consumers account for about 70 percent of economic activity. Gains from an increased focus on efficiency will be limited until people figure out how they can run their household and personal financial life better, stronger, and faster. The past decade has proven that we can't rely on the management of large corporations to raise our salaries. We've got to do it ourselves. The good news? Although most Americans with payroll jobs have little control over their top line (i.e., wages), they do have more control than they might think over their bottom line (i.e., costs). Economically speaking, reducing costs and increasing income produce the same salutary effect.

Year in, year out, the corporate sector increases its productivity by more than 2 percent. Executives know that every dollar saved is a dollar of income gained. But what if consumers could do just half as well as that? What if Americans could increase their own productivity 1 percent each year? What if they could reduce spending by 1 percent while maintaining the same quality of life? Personal consumption expenditures were $10.245 trillion in 2010, and they were running at a pace of $10.8 trillion in 2011. Improving the efficiency of this spending by 1 percent would free up $108 billion per year, a sum almost equal to the 2011 payroll tax cut. This money could be saved, or invested, or spent at the Olive Garden, or used to pay down debt. The payroll tax cut put a maximum of $2,000 in the pockets of people who earned $106,800 or more. For people in high tax brackets who live in high-tax states, cutting $1,300 from after-tax costs is like giving yourself a $2,000 raise.

Consumers have historically been at a significant disadvantage compared with businesses when it comes to seeking efficiencies. Most households don't have resident MBAs or consultants who spend every working day figuring out how to wrench pennies and seconds out of daily processes. At home rationality does battle with emotion and desire on a daily basis. As behavioral economists continually point out, Americans aren't efficiency-seeking machines. They don't take maximum advantage of 401(k)s and tax breaks, and they frequently ignore the long-term implications of short-term financial decisions.

The conversation about personal productivity and efficiency generally begins and ends with cost cuts: make spaghetti at home instead of dining at the Olive Garden (actually, that trade-off makes abundant sense for culinary reasons, not just financial ones); walk to work instead of driving; drink crappy home-brewed coffee instead of stopping at Starbucks. This approach requires relinquishing some of the goods and services that give us pleasure and make modern life worth living. Besides, personal cost-cutting initiatives are the province of weirdos, cranks, and personal finance writers.

It's possible to increase mileage and reduce the use of gasoline by up to 20 percent simply by accelerating slowly, gliding to a stop, and sticking to the speed limit. But that strategy is likely to make the motorist a pariah around town, not to mention late for appointments. Most people are not sufficiently anal or disciplined to devise maps that avoid left turns, as UPS does so assiduously. And while returnable cans lying on the side of the road represent free money, few people stop to pick them up. Besides, there's a degree to which doing more things for yourself can actually detract from efficiency. If Mitt Romney were to mow his own lawn instead of hiring a landscaping company that may (or may not) employ illegal immigrants, it would save him some money, but his time is likely more valuable than that of the landscapers. Growing your own carrots may be satisfying, but it's not necessarily cheaper than buying them at Stop & Shop. Finally, there are plenty of very large businesses that rely on consumer inefficiency. Having invested heavily to rope consumers into nonefficient spending, they expend a lot of money and effort to keep them there.

When I talk about efficient consumers, I'm not talking about self-denial or being a champion do-it-yourselfer. Living without splurging or paying others to do things you don't want to do isn't really living. No, I'm talking about spending more intelligently. If your income depends on businesses like magazines and books, as mine has, you tend to spend a fair amount of time thinking about decline and how you might do more with less. And so I embarked upon my own 1 percent solution. It was relatively easy for me to net out savings that maintained my quality of life—and in many ways enhanced it—while spending more efficiently. I did so by following a few simple steps: stop patronizing businesses that charge for things they should be giving away for free, or that they already give away for free; stop paying for things you don't use; make more intelligent trade-offs about spending a little more now in exchange for spending a lot less in the future; and look into money-saving devices, goods, and services that make positive contributions to quality of life.

One doesn't have to move to Portland, Oregon, become a Dumpster diver, and subsist on nettles and foraged mushrooms to become an efficient consumer. But the Freegans, who have resolved to spend as little as possible, are onto something. People throw out a lot of valuable stuff. One of the valuable things they throw out is money. We live in a world in which nobody needs to pay AOL $25 per month for an email account, and in which very few people need to pay AOL for Internet access. Since 2006 AOL, which started life selling dial-up Internet access, has been offering email accounts for free, and the overwhelming majority of Americans have Internet access through a cable modem, DSL line, Wi-Fi, or smartphone. And yet at the end of 2010 AOL reported that it had "3.9 million AOL-brand access subscribers in the United States." Sure, the number had fallen dramatically from 6.9 million at the end of 2008, but the access business, in which people pay AOL for the ability to get connected to the information superhighway, still throws off a lot of cash: $1.023 billion in 2010, or about $262 per paying subscriber. Many of those subscribing were doing so needlessly. In a profile on AOL's CEO Tim Armstrong in the *New Yorker,* Ken Auletta wrote, "The company still gets eighty percent of its profits from subscribers, many of whom are older people who have cable or DSL service but don't realize that they need not pay an additional twenty-five dollars a month to get online and check their e-mail." An AOL executive told Auletta that three-quarters of the people who pay every month don't have to. In other words, Americans are needlessly blowing $767 million for something they could be getting for free. To put it in perspective, AOL's total operating income, before its deductions for the falling value of its brands and properties, was $677 million.[1]

Not all those fools who effectively subsidized AOL's splashy purchase of the *Huffington Post* are shut-ins and victims of dementia. After reading Auletta's article, I checked out my American Express bill and realized that I was one of them. I signed on with AOL in 1996, when I got my first Gateway 2000 computer and the only way to connect was through a dial-up modem. My wife had opened an account before we got married. Over the years we stuck with the AOL addresses, even as we acquired free email accounts from Yahoo! and Gmail. And we kept on paying, even as we installed cable modems that provided Internet access. Every month, like clockwork, AOL charged $25, twice, to our credit card: $600 per year. Of course, AOL didn't loudly inform its customers that they shouldn't be paying, and it didn't make it particularly easy to opt out. But after reading the *New Yorker* article, I spent about ten minutes navigating the site, punched a few numbers and letters into the computer, and voilà: our annual household operating income rose $600. That's 1 percent of the typical household's total annual income.

AOL isn't alone in having a business model that relies on people not paying attention to automatic billing, so I figured there must be more surprises lurking in my bank and credit card statements. It turns out that automatic payments, which have been a great force for efficiency and cost saving, can be a countervailing force against both. It's quite easy to sign up for recurring monthly or annual payments for goods and services that you might not need after a few years due to changes in personal situations, technology, or paradigms. When I combed through bank and credit card statements, I found an annual Costco membership ($50), even though I hadn't been to a store since 2006, and a Napster subscription ($150) that has been rendered redundant by iTunes. Bam! Another few minutes online, another $200 in annual costs chopped.

Plenty of other business models rely on people's inertia. There's no reason for anybody with a computer or a smartphone to pay the $1.99 it costs to dial 411 anymore. Replacing five calls per month with Google searches, or by dialing 1-800-Bing411, as my employer has instructed me to do on my work phone, saves $120 per year. When I travel abroad, I often wind up calling home from hotel phones to ensure a good connection, or I have my family call me from home. Those minutes easily add up to another $40 per year. But in the fall I finally installed Skype on my laptop and on our computers at home; a twenty-minute investment yielded instant returns. Or consider bill paying. At Chase a sheaf of five hundred checks costs $75, or 15 cents each. If I add the stamp (45 cents) and envelope (14.3 cents), every monthly payment I mail instead of paying online costs an extra $8.80 per year. I quickly found four bills that fell into that category. Those three items add up to another $100 per year. And don't get me started on bottled water. Americans spend $21 billion per year on bottled water, which comes down to $67 per person and $270 per family. That's equal to the amount of credit card debt written off as unpayable in the first half of 2011. My New Year's resolution for 2011 was to stop patronizing Poland Spring.

Harvesting this low-hanging fruit resulted in nearly $1,000 in annual efficiencies—without my spending a single penny. As businesses know, just as it costs money to make real money, it costs money to save real money. And this axiom is a major obstacle to efficient consumption. It's tough to find new funds to invest in efficiency in an age of austerity. But it can be done if consumers simply start to think a little more like businesses. The *Wall Street Journal* and *Financial Times* are crucial tools of my trade, and I pay for them myself. After my subscriptions lapsed—these were two items I hadn't put on automatic renewal—I hesitated to renew. After all, it would require a commitment of $254 for the *Journal* and $348 for the *FT*, a total of $602. But I wound up buying copies at the newsstand or near my office nearly every day, at a combined cost of $4.50 per day, and then going out on the weekend for the excellent Saturday editions of both papers. It adds up: $27 per week, 50 weeks per year, comes to $1,350. And even with all the purchases, I still wasn't getting access to the papers' online content. So I bit the bullet and bought subscriptions. The result: a savings of $748 while I received the same product, plus the benefit of time-saving delivery and digital access. That's like buying a stock that doubles in a year and then pays a 124 percent annual dividend.

Investments in energy efficiency carry even better risk-return-reward profiles. Like many Americans whose homes are blessed (or cursed) with a swimming pool, I've come to look forward to the summers with a certain amount of dread. A wave of ecoguilt washes over me each time the hiss of the propane-fueled water heater pierces the air. It is then replaced by nausea when the propane bill arrives. Our ancient pool is a veritable Hummer; it's shaded by pine trees and has a ten-foot deep end and creaky circulation. In a typical summer we'd buy between three and four three-hundred-gallon deliveries of propane, an average of about 1,050 gallons for the season. The easy way out—not heating the pool at all—would have saved a couple of thousand dollars per year, but it would also have inspired a domestic insurrection that would make the Civil War look like a slap fight by comparison. The way to avert a decline in living standards isn't self-abnegation, but efficiency. So I looked into solar pool covers.

Solar pool covers are plastic sheets with bubbles on one side that sit on the water's surface, absorb thermal energy, and trap heat in the pool. The Thermo-Tex Solar Cover I bought made extravagant promises: it could cut heating costs up to 70 percent and reduce water evaporation by up to 95 percent. All together, the cover, the reel it takes to operate it, and the guy who helped drill a few holes in it cost about $450 and a couple of hours of assembly time. Though it didn't work exactly as advertised, the cover worked phenomenally well. The first year we used it, our propane use fell by 43 percent, or about 450 gallons. According to the Energy Information Administration, propane releases 12.67 pounds of carbon dioxide per gallon burned, compared with 19.56 pounds per gallon of gasoline. Cutting annual propane use by 450 gallons thus prevented the release of 5,701 pounds of carbon dioxide into the atmosphere. That's the same amount of emissions produced by driving 5,500 miles in a car that gets twenty miles per gallon.

The real payback came in reduced fuel use. Thanks to the fuel savings, my upfront investment was paid back in several weeks and returned 144 percent in three months. And the savings have risen as the price of propane has risen, from $2.40 per gallon in 2008 to about $3 per gallon in 2011. In 2011, avoiding 450 gallons of propane use translated into savings of $1,400. The cover also delivers less easily quantifiable enhancements to quality of life. In addition to helping to keep the surface temperature warmer, the pool cover, by trapping heat, makes the temperature more uniform and saves a lot of water by stopping evaporation. In summers past I spent countless hours engaged in the Sisyphean task of fishing pine needles and leaves out of the water. No more. There are a few downsides, of course. The reel has slowly fallen apart, and holes began to appear in the plastic, so it's likely to need a replacement after its fifth season. The pool cover eliminates (or at least makes less comfortable) spontaneous dives. And a twenty-foot-wide spool of blue plastic bubble wrap doesn't really fit into any outdoor decorating scheme. Yes, the truly green alternative to an uncovered pool would be to disconnect the heater, drain the giant concrete bathtub, replace it with a massive compost heap, and seek summertime recreation in rivers, lakes, or the ocean. But the whole point of living in a bourgeois suburban society is to engage in bourgeois suburban activity. What's better than floating around an 88-degree pool, lounging on a made-in-China floatie, while blasting Lee Greenwood's "God Bless the U.S.A."?

There were more dollar bills lying around the household energy budget. Americans spend $241 billion a year on home energy use. When calculating the Consumer Price Index, the Bureau of Labor Statistics presumes the typical household devotes 4 percent of its budget to energy use.[2] If the typical household could cut its energy bill by 25 percent, that would result in a 1 percent increase in resources for spending on other items, or about $96 billion per year. But weatherization and other efforts to spruce up the house so that it is more energy efficient are classic examples of having to spend a lot for uncertain and tough-to-calculate future returns. Ripping up walls and installing expensive new insulation can't be done quickly or on the cheap. And it's very difficult to measure the precise savings on the different energy bills that arrive throughout the year.

But here again, my own experience suggests there's room for improvement. My utility company, Connecticut Light & Power, has a difficult time keeping the lights on when storms hit the state. But it has an excellent program to encourage greater efficiency. In May 2010 I signed up for a home energy assessment. A couple of days later New England Smart Energy, a local company, contacted me to schedule a home visit for $75. From the minute Val and Vitaly Siretsanou, brothers from Moldova, showed up at my front door, I was ahead of the game. The $75 fee is essentially a copay. The (much larger) cost of their supplies and labor is paid for by the Connecticut Energy Efficiency Fund, which is in turn paid for by a small per-kilowatt-hour fee levied on Connecticut electricity users' bills. In other words, I've been paying for neighbors to have access to the same service.

The Siretsanou brothers handed me a box of merchandise that

comes with every assessment: a Kill-A-Watt electricity monitor, ten General Electric dimmable compact fluorescent bulbs, four basic compact fluorescent lamps, and a couple of low-flow showerheads. The retail value: well over $100. Next Val and Vitaly did a "blower door test." They set up a canvas with a fan embedded in it across the open front door and turned up the fan to depressurize the house. As I followed Val around, I was alarmed to feel wind being pulled through the door to the garage, through uninsulated electrical outlets, cracks in the wall, and holes where pipes and wires pierced walls. My house, it turns out, isn't so much a secure shelter against storms as a perforated wooden box. Val whistled under his breath and instructed Vitaly to take notes. Their task was to reduce the flow of air through the house by a number of cubic feet per minute, or CFM, equal to 25 percent of the square footage of the house—that is, to cut the flow by 625 CFM for a house of 2,500 square feet. Over the next three hours they put insulated pads behind electrical outlets, attached stripping to doors, put aluminum foil tape around an exhaust duct above the stove, and shot foam insulation into gaps in the ceiling and walls surrounding pipes and wires. They went up to the attic to test the air duct from the central air-conditioning unit and ironed out some kinks.

When they finished, Val and Vitaly reran the blower tests. The volume of air going out the front door fell by 1,300 CFM—twice the goal—and the duct's efficiency rose significantly. Stephanie Weiner, founder of New England Smart Energy, which conducts about thirty such assessments per week, ranging from condos to 9,000-square-foot homes, says these assessments typically result in customers reducing their energy bills by between 7 and 11 percent. With heating oil near $4 a gallon, a 10 percent reduction in heating oil use would save about $500 per year. And since Connecticut has some of the most expensive electricity costs in the continental United States, with most customers paying 22 cents per kilowatt-hour, more efficient circulation of cooled air could save another couple of hundred dollars annually.

In the year after the work was done we monitored energy usage and programmed thermostats a little more intelligently. Even though we plugged more devices into our sockets—a new Mac, an elliptical machine, iPhone chargers—monthly electricity usage generally fell between 8 and 18 percent. That's a savings of about $420 per year on electricity. With heating oil, the story is a little more complicated because variations in the severity of the weather can have a big impact on usage. But despite a bitterly cold winter in 2011, our heating oil usage fell by about 120 gallons, for a savings of $480. Since we had spent $75, our recurring efficiencies were worth about $900 per year.

These efforts at personal consumer efficiency took very little time and very little investment and have paid enormous dividends. Every household can engage in similar exercises. But a significant challenge remains. For much of the past three decades, Americans haven't so much bought quality of life as borrowed it. And since the onset of the Great Recession, Americans have been rebuilding their balance sheets, deleveraging, and avoiding new financial encumbrances. In the post-bust age, consumers routinely experience what behavioral economists call "the pain of paying," the wince-inducing sensation that occurs when people remove bills from their wallets and pocketbooks. This seemingly unseverable connection between consumption and debt is one of the root causes of declinism. If Americans can't—or won't—borrow to purchase vital goods and services, how can they hope to maintain their standard of living?

Efficient consumers can break the link between debt and consumption. Again the solution isn't to stop consuming and buying; it is to consume and buy more intelligently. That means transitioning from an Ownership Society to what might be called a Rentership Society. Here the American aptitude for adapting, generating new business models, and marketing them effectively has served a useful purpose. From housing to clothes, from textbooks to cars, new businesses have sprung up that offer new pricing models for established goods and services. And as strapped consumers embrace these models, they help build a culture of efficient and intelligent consumption.

Housing is the biggest single component of consumption in the U.S. economy. The typical household spends about 32 percent of its expenditures on shelter. In general, that consumption has meant borrowing a lot of money to take ownership of a home. At its peak in 2006, the homeownership rate stood at 69 percent. At first blush, homeowners in the post-bust era don't seem to have much room for improvement. They can reduce operating costs by focusing on energy efficiency, and many people have been able to refinance at lower rates. But according to the real estate information firm Core-Logic, 22 percent of U.S. homes in the third quarter of 2011 were underwater, with the mortgage higher than the value of the home. And because banks have tightened their lending standards in the wake of the housing meltdown, even people with home equity are finding it tough to refinance.

Renting is a far more economically efficient way to pay for housing. A one-year lease represents a much less onerous financial obligation than a thirty-year mortgage. It's difficult to get into too much financial trouble as a renter. And in an era when regional job markets differ vastly, homeownership can serve to keep workers bound to areas where prospects are dim. Since the bust, renting has clearly gained market share, in part due to necessity, and in part because homebuilders and property owners have adjusted to the new climate. The homeownership rate has fallen from a peak of 69 percent in 2006 to 66.3 percent in 2011. The foreclosure crisis, which has caused millions of Americans to turn over homes to lenders, is responsible for much of this decline. Compared with the second quarter of 2008, there were 10.2 million fewer mortgages in the third quarter of 2011. What's more, given the weak labor markets and higher lending standards, today more Americans have a difficult time scraping together the required down payment. A lot of this is rational rather than just a matter of necessity. According to Moody's, by late 2011 it was cheaper to rent than to own in 72 percent of metropolitan areas, up from 54 percent a decade ago.[3]

The decline in the ownership rate means that today about 3 million more households rent than did so at the height of the housing bubble. As Derek Kravitz of the Associated Press reported in May 2011, "All told, nearly 38 million households are renters." Builders have slowly caught on. Homebuilding remains in a permanently depressed state. New home starts fell from 1.05 million in 2007 to 587,000 in 2010 and rose to 607,000 in 2011. But housing starts for

multifamily units have risen sharply. In 2011, single-family housing starts were off about 9 percent from 2010. But starts of structures with five or more units were up 60 percent in the same time
period, from 104,300 to 167,400. The sharp rise in apartment construction is more than compensating for the continuing decline in
house construction. In 2011, permits for freestanding houses were
off 7.6 percent from 2010, while permits for structures with five or
more units were up 31 percent. And increasingly the builders of
these structures intended to rent them out. In 2007 only 62 percent
of the housing units in buildings with two or more units were built
for rent; the rate rose to 84 percent in 2009 and 87 percent in 2010.
In the first three quarters of 2011, 90 percent of such units completed were built for rent.[4] If the housing market starts to turn up
and lenders begin to loosen their purse strings, it's probable that
Americans will begin extending themselves to buy homes. But the
housing bust has left deep scar tissue. The culture of house flipping,
of no-money-down mortgages, of new homeowners getting into
trouble after one or two payments—all that has been banished for
at least a decade.

Efficient consumption is a greater challenge with another big
expenditure: vehicles. Propelling a couple of tons of steel, plastic,
and rubber with expensive gasoline to move one person for a few
miles is remarkably inefficient. And financially it's not very efficient for many users. Owning or even leasing a car requires assuming a set of large financial obligations of which the car payment is
only the beginning. Factoring in finance costs, depreciation, repairs,
insurance, taxes, and gas, the American Automobile Association
calculates that an owner of a midsize sedan who drives 15,000 miles
per year spend $8,588 per year on his car.[5] The Bureau of Labor
Statistics says that private transportation—owning and running a
car—is the second largest cost for a typical American household,
accounting for 16 percent of expenditures. And while the experience of renting compared with owning isn't qualitatively different
when it comes to shelter, relying on rental agencies for daily use of
vehicles is time-consuming and expensive. People who don't own
cars lose mobility, especially in areas where mass transit isn't developed. For a large majority of the population, it's essential to have

a car available at all times. Over the twentieth century the promise of a car in every driveway and a chicken in every pot was expanded to include two cars in every driveway and a package of frozen fried chicken in every freezer. In 2010 there were 254 million vehicles in the United States.

A large and growing segment of the population wants to have use of a car without having to assume the financial burden of ownership. On an increasing number of college campuses students are strongly discouraged, and in some cases prohibited, from having a car. People who live in New York City, Boston, Washington, or San Francisco don't need a car, but they often like to have one. The problem is that it's very expensive. (I still lie awake at night thinking about the thousands of dollars I paid to park my rarely used car in New York between 1994 and 2002.) There are a growing number of cities, suburbs, and regions with light rail, bike lanes, and walkable, new urbanist developments. These efforts to encourage efficient living also encourage more efficient use of vehicles.

In the aftermath of the bust, new businesses that aimed to cash in on the growing market for efficient vehicle use were launched. Chief among them is Zipcar. Founded in 2000, it grew by focusing on cities and college campuses. It uses information technology to manage the fleet and control access; members get a card that lets them into garages where cars are housed and then into the cars. Users in New York pay a $60 annual fee and then $8.75 per hour on weekdays and $13.75 per hour on weekends; they do not pay for gas or insurance, and there is no charge per mile. As the U.S. economy contracted, Zipcar went into hypergrowth: 225,000 members in 2008 to 350,000 members in January 2010 to 650,000 members and 9,500 cars in November 2011. Zipcar has had predictable success in the big cities of Boston, New York, and San Francisco, but its vehicles can also be found on 350 college campuses. The company struck a deal with Ford to provide memberships to college students for as little as $25 and with rates as low as $7 per hour. As it has gained scale, Zipcar has moved from exclusively serving efficient consumers to providing solutions to efficiency-seeking businesses and institutions. It has signed deals with the New York City Department of Transportation, the city of Chicago, and the General Services Administration to offer cars to employees.[6]

Zipcar, which went public in April 2011, is making money; it scraped out a small profit in the third quarter of 2011. But the profit is beside the point. The value is what it saves consumers who get the full, or near-full, utility of ownership without the enormous associated costs, and how it benefits the economy at large. Zipcar saves people money, and then encourages its customers to drive less or more strategically. On its website, Zipcar touts a study that shows "each car shared takes 15 privately owned vehicles off the road, and that vehicle miles traveled per driver is reduced almost 50 percent when car owners switch to car sharing." Zipcar's financial success has also spurred competition and innovation from other components of the auto sector, the nation's largest retail market. Large rental agencies like Enterprise and Avis have rolled out similar services.

Other businesses have prospered by spreading the gospel of rentership. Of the students who graduated from college in 2010, nearly two-thirds had student loans. In that group the average debt load was $25,250. Most of the borrowed money went to pay for tuition, but a chunk went to pay for textbooks. College textbooks are, in effect, rental goods. Students buy them at retail, use them for four months, and then resell them to the campus store or a used-book dealer at a substantial discount. In 2010 the U.S. market for new college textbooks was worth about $4.5 billion, according to the American Association of Publishers. Now, however, digital technology enables the renting of textbooks. Chegg.com, which was cofounded by Aayush Phumbhra and Osman Rashid in 2001, has raised more than $200 million in funding and is aiming to displace the college bookstore. A Harvard undergrad enrolled in Professor Gregory Mankiw's EC 10 course can buy the sixth edition of Mankiw's *Principles of Economics* at the Harvard Coop for $263. At Chegg.com the student can rent a hard copy for 180 days for $94 or an electronic copy for $127.99 for the same period of time. As more students come to campus with Kindles, Nooks, iPads, and other e-readers, the efficient consumption of college textbooks is likely to grow rapidly.[7]

Spending less money on textbooks would leave students more money to spend on vital college supplies like beer and wings. But college students' discretionary budgets are always pinched. Which is why Rent the Runway, another efficient consumer business, has found such great traction on college campuses. Buying clothes for formal events is a little like buying textbooks; a student might need several items each year, and there's a tendency for people to sell them to others at steep discounts after one use. Why not rent them instead? In 2009 Jennifer Hyman and Jennifer Fleiss, Harvard Business School classmates, started Rent the Runway. "We call ourselves the Netflix for fashion," Hyman said. As with Netflix, customers open accounts and then pay for the temporary use of goods sent to them through the mail. A Thakoon Black Bustle Bombshell dress, which retails for $1,190, rents for $150. A Thread Social Poppy Sweetheart dress, retail $365, rents for $50 (perfect for that spring tea). Accessorize with Crislu Crystal Tear earrings (retail $96, rent for $20). Like so many other online businesses, it has tapped into the highly developed and integrated logistics, customer service, shipping, inventory management, and payments systems that serve as a competitive advantage for all U.S. companies. In business for less than two years, Rent the Runway has raised $31 million in venture capital, has attracted 1 million customers, and is turning a profit.

All these models involve more sharing than American consumers are typically accustomed to. But the culture is changing. Consider how quickly consumers' attitude to housing has changed. At the height of the boom, people believed their home generated cash by serving as a source of home equity credit or by returning a profit when it was sold. Both of those dynamics have faded. But thanks to another postrecession business, efficient homeowners have come to realize that their home can still generate cash. Airbnb, founded in August 2008, is dedicated to the premise that lots of people are willing to earn money by renting out a room in their house and that lots of other people are willing to save money by crashing at a stranger's place rather than a motel or hotel. As the company describes its mission, "We connect people who have space to spare with those who are looking for a place to stay. Guests can build real connections with their hosts [and] gain access to distinctive spaces." Only in America could entrepreneurs rapidly transform couch surfing into a high-tech business worth more than $1 billion in the space of thirty-six months.

With more than 100,000 listings available in more than 16,000 cities and 186 countries, it's a real business. It has booked over 5 million nights' accommodation. In July 2011 Airbnb raised $112 million from venture capital firms Andreessen Horowitz, DST Global, and General Catalyst. But the value of Airbnb isn't what it brings to investors. Rather it's the cash it puts into the hands of homeowners. The company says the average booking generates $80. Five million times $80 per night is $400 million.[8]

Even taken together, companies like Zipcar, Chegg.com, Rent the Runway, and Airbnb won't transform the U.S. economy. Many of today's consumer inefficiencies are habits acquired over decades, and they won't be broken easily. But these businesses all got off the ground and gained critical mass, customers, and, crucially, funding in the teeth of the downturn. Once the economy improves, it's possible the efficient consumption businesses will run out of steam as consumers return to their profligate ways. But that day seems a long way off. And over time, logic tends to trump emotion in economic affairs. It just makes more sense to rent textbooks than to own them, and to sign up for Zipcar rather than own a car in New York City. There will come a day when nobody needlessly pays AOL $25 per month for online access. A combination of increased vigilance and the rise of new business models can easily spur a rise in consumer productivity of 1 percent a year.

And there's much more to come. What if more businesses were able to translate to consumers the efficiency services they've been offering to corporate customers? Imagine the savings for municipalities and individuals if dumb home garbage cans could be replaced by BigBelly solar-powered trash compactors. EnerNOC writes software that controls complex corporate thermostats; now the Apple veterans who founded Nest Labs have created an affordable thermostat that performs a similar function for the home. The Nest Learning Thermostat learns energy use patterns and effectively controls and adjusts the temperature to save on heating and cooling costs. It sold out its first product run in 2011 And just as more stringent federal mileage standards will turn Americans into more efficient drivers, the new standards that consign the old-fashioned filament lightbulb to the dustbin of history will make every American home more energy-efficient.

The best part is that American consumers can encourage greater efficiency simply by doing what comes naturally: glomming onto hot new trends. Many of the efficient consumer business models are pitched at young consumers, who are likely to acquire habits and then stick with them as they become the driving force of consumption. They can have many of the same things—clothes and a car, shelter, entertainment, textbooks—without the debt and tying up of resources that it takes to own them. The generation coming of age financially today won't cotton to landlines or expensive cable packages. When it comes time for them to get married, people who were raised on Evites will likely forgo the four-figure costs of expensive wedding invitations. Just as U.S. companies found significant internal resources to help them weather the storm and strengthen their balance sheets, U.S. consumers are doing the same.

There's a final point worth noting. Aside from having a common impulse, the efficient consumer businesses that have grown up rapidly share several other characteristics that function as a competitive advantage for the United States. They have proven able to build ideas to scale and to plug into financial, trading, investing, and consumer systems that can supercharge growth.

CHAPTER 13

Supersize Nation:
Scale, Scope, and Systems

At the World Economic Forum in Davos, Switzerland, in January 2010, the world's good and great gathered to observe and meditate (yet again) on the demise of America as a vital economic force. But in the space of a couple of hours toward the end of the confab, I experienced a set of revelations that set me thinking that the Davos consensus was wrong yet again. First, I stopped by the annual Friday night Shabbat dinner, the trifecta of bad food: Swiss, institutional, and kosher. The crowd listened closely to words of wisdom from the Nobelist Elie Wiesel and President Shimon Peres of Israel and to a brief talk on the week's Torah portion by Israel's onetime Ashkenazi chief rabbi, Yisrael Meir Lau. But things really perked up when Randi Zuckerberg, the sister of Facebook's founder Mark Zuckerberg and a senior executive at the company, sang "Jerusalem of Gold" in a bright vibrato. In violation of both good taste and the laws of Shabbat, Zuckerberg, one of the emerging It Girls of the global economic scene, proceeded to post the clip on Facebook. Throughout the week at Davos, insiders swapped tales of glimpsing Mark Zuckerberg the way people on safari note the sighting of a cheetah. The social networking site had definitely arrived, and it was staking its claim as a hot new player.

After dinner the crowd scuttled down the icy Promenade, the street that runs the length of town, to the event that is frequently the hottest ticket of the conference: the Google party. Each year since 2005 Google has flown in deejays and bartenders and taken over several ground-floor rooms in the Steigenberger Grandhotel Belvédère. (Among the things I've seen at the Google party over the years: Goldman Sachs president Gary Cohn high-fiving a bartender after being served a whisky on the rocks ahead of other partygoers; the right-fielder on my 1990s-era softball team, now a senior YouTube executive, making a show of checking the identification of Blackstone Group's founder Steve Schwarzman to ensure he was on the list; and the veteran Washington pundit David Gergen engaging in some dancing that, even by Davos's extremely low standards, was quite embarrassing.)

The crowd at the Google party was entranced, and not because of the thumping house music or the high altitude. No, once past the velvet ropes, status-hungry attendees were alternately checking out the name tags that hung around people's necks and fondling, cradling, and looking lovingly . . . into their iPhones.

Then it struck me: high in the Alps, at a place where American decline is a perennial preoccupation and theme, where new models of success and dynamism are thought to emerge from everywhere *but* the United States, three of the most significant presences were U.S. companies. Apple and Google were the nation's second- and ninth-largest companies by market capitalization, respectively, with a combined value of nearly $600 billion. Facebook, not yet public, had been valued at more than $100 billion in the private market. Combined, they were worth nearly $800 billion in early 2012, close to the gross domestic product of the Netherlands.

Large U.S. companies have always been a mainstay at Davos, and they have been among the largest economic forces in the world for the past half century. But consider this: in 2002, in the wake of the previous meltdown and crisis in American confidence, none of these companies existed in anything like their current form. Their combined market capitalization was a few billion dollars, consisting mostly of Apple, an also-ran personal computer maker whose stock traded for less than the value of the cash on its balance sheet. Google was a piece of code, not one of the most profitable businesses known to man. Mark Zuckerberg was just entering Harvard. All three exploded from nothing, gained mass and scale during the long expansion of the 2000s, and boomed in the years after the Lehman Brothers crash. For these companies, the period of decline has been an era of triumph.

Eight hundred billion dollars in market capitalization can vanish rather quickly. But there's much more to these companies than the value investors ascribe to them at any given minute. Facebook, Google, and Apple are global brands, prolific exporters, iconic magnets of human capital. They represent American economic dynamism the way Chevrolet and McDonald's once did. They've added significantly to quality of life and to productivity, and they have made a lot of people rich. Most significantly, they've created platforms for other businesses, industries, and entrepreneurs to create new economic arrangements; they function as new economic systems that in turn invite innovation. All of which is to say they are perfect metaphors for the ability of the U.S. economy to innovate, regenerate, and lead—to run better, stronger, and faster.

The forces that made Google, Apple, and Facebook into juggernauts speak to another advantage the United States possesses: supersizing. It turns out the United States can still create brands, products, and services and turn them into global phenomena— almost overnight. As a result, new entrants can hit the domestic market, which remains the largest and wealthiest in the world, and participate in the amazing growth outside our borders. Over and over again in the period since 2008 U.S. companies have been able to plug into existing commercial networks, make them run better, and create new ones.

Some believe that America's most rapidly growing and valuable companies can't contribute much in the recovery. The United States needs 5 million new jobs to recover all those lost in the Great Recession. And unlike earlier titans such as Ford and IBM, the new champions simply don't employ that many people. In late 2011 Apple had 60,400 direct employees, Google had 31,353 employees around the world, and Facebook had a mere 3,000. Even Apple, a manufacturing company, hasn't done all that much to promote employment growth. As Timothy Noah wrote in the *New Republic* after the death of Steve Jobs, "His surname to the contrary, he did not create a lot of American jobs." Noah cited data from the

University of California Irvine Personal Computing Industry Center, which showed "the number of people *worldwide* involved in making and selling Apple's iPod (which includes Apple employees and non-Apple employees) totaled a mere 41,170. Of those, only 13,920 were employed *within the United States.*" The idea that massive value can be created for owners and investors without creating significant wages for workers helps contribute to the widespread pessimism.[1]

This line of reasoning is 90 percent right and 100 percent wrong. It misreads these companies' present-day impact and misapprehends U.S. economic history. Critics miss the boat by focusing on how many people Internet and social media companies employ directly, or even indirectly, just as they would have missed the true impact of the railroads in the 1870s and the telephone in the 1950s simply by noting how many people worked for the Union Pacific and AT&T. The beauty of the Internet, from an economic perspective, is not that it created jobs for those who built it, but that it functions as a powerful platform on which all sorts of new businesses, and ways of doing business, can be rolled out.

A lot of the value of these companies derives from what they allow other consumers and businesses to do. Apple's well-told story—the comeback of Steve Jobs, the iMac, and then the iterations of the iPod, the iPhone, and the iPad—is perhaps the best ever case study in corporate turnaround and reinvention. The ability to create new economic ecosystems lies at the root of the tale. Apple launched the iTunes Store in April 2003 with a single product: songs selling for 99 cents. In seven years the iTunes ecosystem has evolved into a business far larger than the 10 billion songs that have been downloaded and has extended to audiobooks, movies, ringtones, apps, and e-books. That has been coupled with tremendous innovation and expansion of the devices and services on which content can be accessed, stored, and manipulated: the iPod, the iPhone, the iPad, and the iCloud. Now consider all the other software, hardware, and content manufacturers that have found new life, or a reason for being in the first place, in Apple's world: retailers, movie studios, independent coders, game publishers, Jobs's biographer Walter Isaacson, the contributors to *Fortune*'s Apple 2.0 blog, mobile ad networks, analytics firms, and accessories makers. The market for cases, sleeves, and headphones, and other iDevices, is north of $1.5 billion annually. In March 2011 the venture capital firm Kleiner Perkins doubled the size of its two-year-old "iFund," which backs app makers, to $200 million. Clearly Apple spurs a huge amount of economic activity beyond the wages it pays and the supplies it purchases.

Similarly, Google's $29 billion in 2010 revenues is simply the start of its economic impact. Google's oft-told tale is impressive. The creation of two guys with absolutely no connections or standing in the marketplace went from being nothing to being a global standard in a few years. Google's rise is a story of superior engineering and execution meeting an existing, widely used commercial platform (the Internet), and making its use better and easier. Google tuned up a system that had already been constructed to work much better, and in so doing created an entirely new economic environment: the Googleplex. There was Internet search before Google; it just wasn't very good or as powerful as an economic force. Google's algorithms helped turn a network of rivers and lakes, plagued by uncertain tides and obstacles, into a highly functioning canal system. Google has changed the way people search for and access information, the way young people seek out careers, the way all sorts of firms market themselves. In the process it has created jobs and professions for others: companies and fields based on search engine optimization, for example.

Like Google, Facebook piggybacked on the existing infrastructure, but then proceeded to carve out an entirely new system and economic ecology within it. An environment for networking and hanging out, Facebook has also enabled the creation of large, highly scaled businesses that were not imagined during the creation of the system. Zynga, the social gaming business founded in 2007, was created essentially to exist within Facebook; in late 2011 its initial public offering endowed it with a $7 billion market value.

Creating entirely new ecosystems is another discipline at which the United States has excelled. "In a reset, we get great individual innovation," notes the sociologist Richard Florida, the author of *The Great Reset.* "More importantly, we get the rise of systems innovation," like Thomas Edison and George Westinghouse turning electricity from a science experiment into a utility. "That leads to new models of infrastructure and new kinds of consumption." The United States has demonstrated a unique ability to develop such working models. When you have a large installed user base, a product or service rolled out on it can gain scale more quickly, and its value can grow exponentially. The development of the U.S. economy over time highlights the power of network effects—the notion that the value of a network to its owner, and to each user, rises as more people join. When a country has the world's largest economy, with a large population spread over a large landmass and possessed of excellent connections to the global economy, network effects can work wonders. As a launching pad for products and services with global scale, the United States has certain advantages: the world's largest domestic market; the paths blazed overseas for decades by brands like Coca-Cola, Disney, and McDonald's; and the use of English as a commercial, financial, advertising, and consuming lingua franca. China has the ability to supersize, but in its case the process mostly involves laying down physical infrastructure over the largely vacant commercial space in its vast interior. Its supersizing efforts—whether constructing the Three Gorges Dam or bringing the equivalent of a coal-fired electricity plan online every day—extract a huge environmental and physical toll. Many of the world's most valuable supersized businesses remain uniquely American. Could we imagine a Steve Jobs thriving in France's hierarchical corporate sector? A Facebook originating in a class-based society like Britain or in terminally shy Japan? Or a company that aims to catalogue and dispassionately disburse all known information thriving in China?

Under the old supersized model, U.S. companies would take years or even decades to establish deep footprints at home, and only then would they attempt to establish themselves overseas. Walmart spent three decades planting big boxes in the United States before it turned its attention abroad in earnest, and then it was mostly to adjacent markets like Canada and Mexico. In a supersized world companies can tap into systems to go global first, not last. Hyperconnectivity and the rise of inporting mean companies can gain scale and go abroad before they finishing saturating the U.S. market. Amazon.com has only 0.5 percent of the vast U.S. retail sales market, a very small portion, and it still has plenty of room to grow in its home base. But in 2011 the seventeen-year-old company derived 45 percent of its revenues from overseas, with operations in eight foreign countries. Groupon and Living Social, the daily-deals sites born in the middle of the recession, grew from nothing to significant national and global presences almost instantly. Living Social's international growth reads like the itinerary of a backpacker on a gap year: in November 2010 it bought Jump On It, an Australian site; in early 2011, by buying a majority stake in Spain's LetsBonus, it entered Spain, Italy, Portugal, Argentina, and Mexico; in June 2011 came a majority position in the French site Dealissime. Next it headed to Asia, using acquisitions to enter markets in Thailand, the Philippines, Indonesia, and the Persian Gulf. HomeAway, the vacation rental site launched in 2005, has expanded internationally, making seventeen acquisitions in six years. In 2010, just five years after its founding, it reaped 38 percent of its revenue from outside the United States, mostly from Europe. By June 2011, as the *Wall Street Journal* reporter Lynn Cowan noted, it had "31 websites in 11 languages with rentals located in more than 145 countries."[2]

I spent much of the 2009 Davos conference searching for an optimistic CEO. And I did find one: Reid Hoffman, the founder of LinkedIn. Hoffman may seem atypical for a Silicon Valley player. Friendly and not intimidating, he has a shambling mien and a body type that suggests he doesn't spend his weekends winging around the Los Altos hills on a $6,500 road bike. Yet he exemplifies the Silicon Valley mentality, continually plugging into infrastructure to create new types of businesses. Hoffman was an early executive at PayPal, which piggybacked on the success of eBay, one of the Internet's new economic ecosystems. In 2002 he founded LinkedIn, a free networking site where people can post their résumés and work histories and figure out how they are connected to other professionals. When the meltdown came in 2008, U.S. companies began to shed hundreds of thousands of jobs each month. As they packed up their possessions in bankers' boxes and turned in their ID cards, white-collar workers signed on with LinkedIn.

"Networking is cycle-resistant," Hoffman said. "It was interesting to see all the people from Lehman Brothers join" in the fall of 2008. LinkedIn experienced hypergrowth as the job market cratered, growing from 32 million users in 2008 to 135 million members in more than two hundred countries in November 2011, with 59 percent of the total outside the United States. The site is available in sixteen languages. LinkedIn staged an initial public offering in May 2011. Eight years after its launch it turned a profit, and it occupies prominent office space in the Empire State Building. Its value, again, lies far beyond its market capitalization or the people who work for it. Rather, it lies in its ability to help people find jobs, make connections, and strike deals.

The ability to scale is one of the key enabling features of supersizing. In the current environment, when a great idea comes along, it rolls out very quickly and goes from being easily dismissed fantasy to being conventional wisdom in a matter of months. When American consumers latch onto something, they create new standards because the domestic market is so large and rich. Consider the number of new services that have zipped from zero to standard in a matter of months: Twitter, iPhones, eBay, Google, LinkedIn, Facebook. My previous book for this publisher, *Dumb Money*, which came out in February 2009, was an e-book exclusive for the first few months of its life. As such it was a curiosity, with very low expectations for sales, because at the time only a few hundred thousand people owned Kindles or other e-readers. Two years later, of course, e-books are standard. I would not be surprised to see rented textbooks, such as those Chegg.com offers, become the norm on college campuses within a few years.

When large institutions adapt new technologies and ideas, they too can instantly create scale. Imagine if the solar-powered trash compactor systems made by BigBelly, or an imitator or a competitor, were adopted by New York City, the National Park Service, or the military. When something better and faster comes along, the economic impact can be massive, swift, and transformative—at home and abroad.

The supersize tendency shows that there is much to be gained from tweaking and improving existing infrastructure. That highlights the importance of systems, of virtual, digital, and concrete infrastructure. Most observers would agree that the United States was pretty well wired together with complete transportation and communication systems a few decades ago. But there is still plenty of room—and need—to build new infrastructure and upgrade systems. In the years since the meltdown, America's shambolic infrastructure has been the subject of a lot of debate and argument. The prevalence of crumbling bridges, pothole-ridden streets, and idled construction equipment at home, combined with the rapid growth of gleaming new infrastructure abroad, has contributed to a sense of decline. The inability to do better makes people think that we've simply lost our mojo. As Larry Summers put it, "You can argue whether we need a new high-speed rail system or whether we don't need a new high-speed rail system. But I don't know what the argument is for letting bridges collapse."[3] Like so many other items, infrastructure investment has turned into a political football in recent years. President Obama and other Democrats have generally favored investment, citing the ability of "shovel-ready" projects to create jobs, put blue-collar workers back to work, and help businesses. Republicans have generally opposed these efforts, in large part because Obama supports them but also because they'd prefer keeping taxes at historically low levels to raising taxes to pay for better infrastructure.

The United States has a great deal to gain by building out infrastructure that in turn allows more growth and serves as a platform for new investment. The infrastructure we tap into is already very powerful. It could be made more powerful still if investment were deployed to create more effective systems that enable growth, innovation, and movement. Historically the United States has gained more than other countries from excellent internal and external wiring because it covers a very large territory and has much lower population density compared with other developed economies, and because there were big obstacles like the Appalachians and the Rocky Mountains. The Erie Canal, America's first grand infrastructure effort, was an expensive ditch to nowhere. A New York State agency floated the unheard-of sum of $7.9 million in debt to create a lot of miserable, low-paying jobs; immigrants got paid $12 per month and endured appalling conditions to create the canal. But the long-term economic impact was massive. Canal towns became seaports, the Midwest became a global breadbasket, and the Hudson Valley became a center of industrial innovation. New York City, in the words of Peter Bernstein, the author of an excellent history of the Erie Canal, *Wedding of the Waters*, became the central span in the "bridge between the inexhaustible supplies of grain from the Midwestern United States and the inexhaustible demand for food from Europe." Later in the nineteenth century the building out of national rail and telegraph networks created new platforms for innovation and growth. In *Scale and Scope: The Dynamics of Industrial Capitalism,* the business historian Alfred Chandler described how the telegraph's and railroad's creation of national markets in goods, services, and information allowed new businesses, from the Associated Press to national beer brands, to supersize quickly. Many of those industries help define the U.S. economy in the twenty-first century.

Entire economic ecosystems exist today because of infrastructure and public works built in the 1930s. In his first hundred days as president, Franklin D. Roosevelt said he wanted 250,000 young men working in the forests for $1 a day. Despite the howls of organized labor, a quarter of a million men were toiling in the Civilian Conservation Corps by the summer of 1933. They planted 3 billion trees, built eight hundred state parks, and saved the nation's topsoil. Larger public works programs like the Civil Works Administration swiftly put millions of people to work erecting bridges and building dams. Those efforts helped reduce unemployment and put demand into the economy. As Robert Caro documented in his biography of Lyndon B. Johnson, stringing electric wire across rural Texas did more for the region's economy than relief payments ever could have. It is probably impossible to calculate the value of the George Washington Bridge, which was completed eighty years ago and today allows 100 million vehicles per year to cross the Hudson. The construction of the Hoover Dam put 20,000 people to work during the Depression, but its value lies more in the gigantic electric generation station it hosts and its ability to help distribute water to a large portion of the western United States.

A host of regional economies exist today in large measure because of infrastructure investments made during the Depression. To get to Hawaii Volcanoes National Park on Hawaii Island, you drive up Highway 11 through mildly sulfuric volcanic fog. In February 2011 I spent the day with my family hiking the park's trails, from rainforest to moonscape, from mountain to sea level, clambering over a stony path to observe ancient petroglyphs. In the evening we watched the hills light up with molten lava. But in this universe of natural wonders, the most useful and interesting information was found on a small plaque at the visitor center that commemorated the members of the Civilian Conservation Corps who helped build it: "From the research offices to the hiking trails, the CCC laid the foundations for much of the infrastructure that we see and use today in the Park." The small sums spent on backbreaking, low-wage infrastructure jobs seventy-five years ago today help form the basis of a microeconomy: restaurants, gas stations, guesthouses and hotels, and the park itself.

The interstate highway system is one of the great, frequently overlooked pieces of the puzzle that helped the U.S. economy reach new levels in the second half of the twentieth century. And again, it was created not for the jobs or the economy but to help provide arteries by which missiles and other defense matériel could move about the country efficiently. "We invested in the interstate highway system in the 1950s for reasons of national security, but it had tremendous economic benefits that nobody could have antici-pated," says Mark Zandi of Moody's Analytics. Consider what it brought about economically and the forces it unleashed. It enabled Walmart, coming out of the highly isolated Ozarks, to conquer the country. "It has smoothed what was once rough country," as Earl Swift writes in *The Big Roads: The Untold Story of the Engineers, Visionaries, and Trailblazers Who Created the American Super-highways.* "It is a vast and powerful economic engine that provides millions of jobs, [and] gets goods to Dakota ranchers with the same speed they reach the big cities back east."

The United States doesn't have to invent new Googles to take advantage of scale, networks, and infrastructure. It has to improve the systems and infrastructure that exist and make the existing systems more efficient and effective. The investment is necessary because some bridges and roads are falling apart and because we need to make up for past neglect. But we need the investment more for the future. The new economy of online retailing and e-commerce, rising exports, and more tourism, goods, services, and people whizzing around the world, which has already done so much to spur growth, demands better infrastructure of all types. The Panama Canal is undergoing a $5.25 billion widening and expansion program that will allow for the passage of larger ships. That means U.S. ports will have to be upgraded. If the volume of trade continues to rise, if exports are to double, then rail, trucking, intermodal, and shipping infrastructure will have to expand as well. To attract and handle more tourists, American airports need a face-lift and major internal surgery; they have to become as efficient as their counterparts overseas.

These are signs that the United States is falling behind, especially when countries such as China are making splashy, highly visible infrastructure investment. In its 2009 Infrastructure Report Card, the American Society of Civil Engineers (ASCE) estimated that the United States needed to invest $2.2 trillion in infrastructure over five years, and that only $903 billion of that total had been budgeted. And Larry Summers said, "Compare Kennedy Airport with the airport where you land, and you ask yourself which is the airport of the greatest country, richest, most powerful country in the world?" The comparison can indeed be depressing and can easily send one down the path of decline. But remember, the failure to invest in infrastructure is a choice; it's not inevitable. The U.S. economy is capable of either generating or attracting the cash necessary to improve our transportation systems at a very low cost. The range of options includes public-private partnerships, an infrastructure bank, a higher gas tax to fund roads, and user fees. It's a question of will, not ability; desire, not capability.[4]

Even relatively small-scale investments in infrastructure can contribute to growth. Just as Google made an existing system work much better for all parties involved, investments in broadband infrastructure can have wide-ranging effects. The United States may have invented e-commerce and led in its adoption, but there is still much more room for improvement. Broadband allows for better connections, creates jobs, and brings more people into the system. A 2009 study by Professor Raul Katz of the Columbia University Business School estimated that as many as 128,000 jobs could be gained over four years in the construction of new broadband networks. But that would be just the beginning of the gains. I still remember trying to use Priceline.com's grocery-shopping matching system on a dial-up modem in the late 1990s; it took forever, so I tried it only once. In 2011 the United States ranked twenty-fourth in the world in the percentage of consumers with broadband access, with 54 percent, according to ITU, a UN agency. When it comes to speed, the country is twenty-sixth, behind Hungary, according to Pando Networks' August 2011 download speed report. Again, one can take these distressing metrics as further evidence of relative decline, or one can look at it this way: the United States manages to do an incredibly large volume of e-commerce with only half its population fully wired in, and with many Americans accessing the Internet more slowly than people in Gyor and Szeged. As hyperconnected and wired as the U.S. economy already is, there is a great deal of room for improvement.[5]

Recall the power of network effects. From the telegraph to the railroad, infrastructure has always served to rope people, especially in rural areas, into the wider, larger system, enriching both the lives of the individuals and the companies that ply their trade on the new medium. It's no different with the Internet. Faster connections mean more people are digital, doing transactions, watching content, able to take advantage of free things and become more efficient consumers themselves. The stimulus package allotted $7.2 billion for expanding the nation's broadband infrastructure into mostly rural areas. "Many people who got on the Internet in the midnineties had real progress in their lives in these remote rural areas, managing their health conditions or a home business," only to be left behind when broadband passed them by, said Wally Bowen, the founder and executive director of the Mountain Area Information Network, a nonprofit wireless-Internet provider in western North Carolina. He cites an octogenarian widow in the small town of Murphy who has been supplementing her income with eBay sales but was having difficulty with dial-up. MAIN is part of a consortium of local businesses and public-private partnerships that in 2010 sought $50 million in broadband stimulus money to lay new fiber and erect wireless towers.

The electricity network is another universal system that can be souped-up and serve as a platform for innovation and development. Transforming the nation's energy production and transmission system "will take an investment of trillions of dollars over decades," said Dan Arvizu, the director of the National Renewable Energy Laboratory. I met him in the summer of 2009 at the lab's brand-new, hyperefficient headquarters in Golden, Colorado. "The private sector has to make this happen." A November 2008 study by the Brattle Group found that by 2030 the electric industry "will need to make a total infrastructure investment of $1.5 trillion to $2.0 trillion."[6] Despite the widespread outages and the apparent dysfunctionality of the U.S. grid, however, there are investments being made in energy generation, transmission, distribution, and storage. Many of the efforts to make U.S. businesses and consumers more efficient rest on improvement in the energy infrastructure. The drive for efficiency leads to greater infrastructure investment, and a drive to make existing dumb infrastructure more intelligent, hospitable, and encouraging of new types of businesses. The innovation surrounding energy is leading to less centralized production, new sources and types of production, and even different uses for electricity, including as a fuel for transportation. Modernizing the grid will lead to new types of economic arrangements: systems under which utilities pay or credit homes for electricity generated by rooftop solar panels, and sophisticated electricity-demand management.

Skepticism about the potential for millions of green jobs to materialize overnight is warranted. But in some areas a process similar to the iTunes experience is developing. All-electric vehicles may be a distant dream, but fleets of buses and trucks powered by electricity are already on the roads. So too are plug-in hybrids. Henrik Fisker, CEO of the electric car manufacturer Fisker Automotive, said, "The development of this industry will influence how we make electricity in this country." The burgeoning electric car ecosphere includes battery manufacturers like A123 Systems, based in Watertown, Massachusetts; and Coulomb Technologies, a small company in Campbell, California, that makes software and hardware for electric-vehicle charging stations. Google has built parking structures with solar panels on their roofs so they can charge electric cars. Ford and the solar panel manufacturer SunPower joined forces in August 2011 to produce panels that can be installed on the roofs of plug-in hybrids. In December 2011, while visiting Israel, I drove a Renault Fluence electric vehicle to one of the battery-swapping stations being rolled out by A Better Place, an electric car systems and infrastructure company. Founded by the software executive Shai Agassi and headquartered jointly in Silicon Valley and Israel, A Better Place is aiming to turn automobile fueling into a system. It relies on information technology, demand management, and a network of battery-charging and -swapping stations and home-based charging stations to eliminate drivers' anxiety that their battery will run out of juice. A Better Place, which has raised $750 million in venture funding, is building networks in Hawaii and setting up charging stations for electric taxis in San Francisco.[7]

Supersized networks can also produce results when the resources they connect are human. The more people there are connected to a network, the more valuable the whole thing is, and the more valuable every component in it. That is why infrastructure investment can also help fix some of our other thorny economic problems, like housing, mobility, and unemployment. In 2010 Governor Chris Christie of New Jersey won plaudits for killing a proposed rail tunnel under the Hudson River. He argued that it wasn't worth spending $8.7 billion to create 6,000 construction jobs. True enough. But Christie fundamentally misconstrued the potential economic benefits of a piece of infrastructure that would speed rail travel from New Jersey to Manhattan. A study by the Regional Plan Association showed that by reducing commuting times, the tunnel would add $18 billion in value to the region's economy. In the New York area, as in many other population centers, home values (and frequently quality of life) rise in inverse proportion to the length of time it takes to get to the region's economic center. By shortening commutes, the tunnel would boost values for homes within two miles of train stations by an average of $19,000, thus creating a higher tax base.[8] As any real estate broker will tell you, homes in towns with train stations tend to command significantly higher prices, and real estate in towns that are closer to transportation hubs tends to be more expensive than homes that are farther from them. In New York, Washington, Boston, Chicago, and many other regions people pay for proximity and short commutes. There's not much that can be done to move houses closer to the core. But improving transportation systems can have the same effect.

Better transportation infrastructure isn't just about helping people get home more quickly after a day at the office; it's also about establishing new links and strengthening systems. The collapsing housing market has turned many Americans into prisoners in their own homes. With mortgages underwater, people in Southern California's Imperial Valley, where the unemployment rate was 30 percent in July 2011, can't easily sell their homes and move to North Dakota, where jobs are plentiful. The "superstar cities" thesis, advanced by Christopher Mayer of Columbia University and Joseph Gyourko and Todd Sinai of the University of Pennsylvania, explains why real estate values in certain cities around the world have held up well. Superstar cities have lots of people, big industries, and limited land and zoning regulations that help stop massive development. Crucially, they also have big transportation networks that bind residents together. It's not uncommon for people who live in New Jersey to work in Westchester, New York, or to commute from Brooklyn to Manhattan. Lose your job in Stamford, Connecticut, and look for a new one in Manhattan. As Dana Rubinstein reported in the *Wall Street Journal* in June 2011, the office vacancy rate in New Jersey cities with significant rail connections was about half that for other parts of the state, 14.7 percent compared with 29.7 percent, though rents were higher.[9]

Transportation infrastructure also functions as a form of stimulus. Proximity to Central Park matters in Manhattan real estate values, but so does proximity to the subway. The extension of the 7 line one station west in Manhattan, at a cost of $2.1 billion, is helping to encourage billions of dollars of investment in the Hudson Yards development zone, a warren of unused railroads. The

Second Avenue subway line, a $17 billion project several decades in the making and scheduled for completion in 2017, will be likely to have a similar effect. Even infrastructure that doesn't really go anywhere can pay dividends. Build something new, something interesting, something useful, and it invites others to do the same. Take the High Line. The elevated freight rail line on the West Side of Manhattan was unused and in disrepair until a group of arty visionaries had the idea of turning it into a park. It has become a platform for billions of dollars of investment in stores and restaurants, condominiums, offices, and hotels.

Not every place is New York, but many regions and many cities could benefit from the sort of network effects that New York enjoys. Many of the biggest metropolitan areas in the United States are remarkably unnetworked. Knitting physical space more tightly together in networks would help boost real estate values and encourage investment at a time when it is much needed. This process has already been happening, even as infrastructure enthusiasts wring their hands at the lack of investment. Contrary to the common view, significant investments and advancements have been made in recent years. In fact, many cities have successfully rolled out or expanded systems in the era of pinched resources and ambitions. Phoenix's Metrorail, a twenty-mile light-rail system that went into operation in December 2008, carries about a million passengers per month. Seattle's light-rail offering, which debuted in July 2009, attracts about 25,000 daily users. When Norfolk's small light-rail system opened in September 2011, officials thought it would attract about 2,900 riders per day, but in its opening months the Tide attracted about 5,000 daily riders. In these and other cities construction of light rail has spurred transit-oriented development and generally boosted the local interest in and appetite for expansion. Again, the payoff isn't in the jobs created to build the rail or to set up express bus systems. Rather, it's in the rent that landlords will get, the ability to attract more workers for employers, and the benefit to homeowners. But that means many afflicted areas have a great deal to gain from new transportation infrastructure.

Historically, and to this day, America's approach to infrastructure has been decentralized, underfunded, and halting. The canal system was a matter of great controversy in the early republic. The early growth of the telegraph was so chaotic that one historian dubbed the period of takeoff one of "methodless enthusiasm." The crazy-quilt rollout of broadband, in which companies laid down miles of superfast long-distance connections, saw speeds peter out as phone and cable companies botched the rollout of the "last mile" to homes. In the United States the creation of new commercial plat-forms is poorly coordinated and prone to bubbles and hucksterism. But it's difficult to argue with the long-term results. The United States has many excellent systems, and it routinely comes up with, funds, and implements plans to improve their functioning. Time and again in recent years the country has shown the ability—and desire—to create new economic infrastructure, improve existing systems, and take new ideas to scale.

The Myth of American Decline

So is the United States of America a nation in terminal economic decline?

If your private sector responded to a once-in-a-lifetime shock by paying down debt, becoming more efficient, boosting productivity, shoring up savings, and doubling profits, you may not be a nation in decline.

If you are a magnet for immigrants, tourists, and capital, and if record numbers of people come to visit, tour, study, work, and invest, you may not be a nation in decline.

If your population continues to grow, and you have a set of demographic conditions that supports growth rather than imperils it, you may not be a nation in decline.

If you have businesses, brands, and business models that can take the world by storm, grow from nothing to being extraordinarily profitable, and show a continual ability to break into new markets, you may not be a nation in decline.

If you are growing at a 3 percent annual rate from the highest base in the world, adding $160 billion in new economic activity every quarter, $1.33 billion every day, you may not be a nation in decline.

There's no question the United States has a very long way to go to make up for the lost ground in the economy at large, in housing, and in jobs. The scourge of underemployment and unemployment is a national crisis. And it won't do for economists and policymakers simply to note that modern recoveries tend to be jobless in their early stages and that it takes a long time to get out from under debt collapses. Half-completed financial sector reforms and recalcitrant bankers impeded progress. The fiscal outlook is grim, and there are serious questions about the sustainability of our collective health care and retirement systems. The future is uncertain. Other parts of the world exhibit more dynamism, spirit, and growth than America.

And yet.

Look at the distance the United States has traveled since the terrible fall of 2008. While the country was ostensibly entering a period of decline, it managed to pull off a swift policy and private sector reaction; deal with the twin crises of growth and a crippled financial sector much better than other countries did, if not with absolute competence; become more efficient and intelligent about tapping into internal resources; attract high levels of foreign investment; boost exports to record levels; become more integrated and involved in foreign markets; and create and develop new businesses and economic ecosystems, and then supersize them. In the months since the Lehman debacle the United States no more lost its ability to grow and innovate than reality television producers lost their ability to coax ever more skanky behavior out of New Jersey's youth.

By any measure the metrics testify to a huge comeback. It hasn't always been pretty to watch. The mechanics stink and the plays roll out in ungainly fashion, with herky-jerky motions and a lot of wasted energy. Our Bible-thumping piety and appeals to a higher power and faith are easily mocked. And yet the way we roll is strangely, predictably effective. The U.S. economy, it turns out, is a lot like the pious Denver Broncos quarterback Tim Tebow. But there are signs that the crucible of the Great Recession forged an economic structure that is more sturdy and resistant to shocks than the brittle vessel that shattered in 2008. Three years of balance sheet repair, focusing on efficiency, diversifying away from housing and domestic consumers, and tapping into new sources of growth and energy mean the U.S. economy now relies on a different set of muscles from those it used in 2006 and 2007. Throughout 2011, as a series of blows hit the global and U.S. economy, from high gas prices to debt ceiling brinksmanship, from Europe's meltdown to a Chinese growth scare, the U.S. economy strengthened. Even as fear of a second recession intensified, the pace of economic growth *escalated* each quarter: 0.4 percent in the first quarter, 1.3 percent in the second quarter, 1.7 in the third quarter, and 3 percent in the fourth quarter. Meanwhile Europe was sinking back into a self-imposed double-dip recession, and growth was slowing in developed and developing economies alike.

The triumphant, optimistic narrative I've laid out invites a chorus from what I call "the Yessbuts." The Yessbuts aren't a new band out of Portland; they're the people who, while conceding some of the positive points, relegate the accomplishments to the past, conclude that they're inadequate, and warn of the big obstacles still in our way. Yes, we avoided a second Great Depression, but at a great cost. Look at the deficit and the impact of the Fed's zero-interest policy. Yes, we've recovered some economic ground, but there's so much still to recover in housing and employment. Yes, the U.S. economy has entered its third year of expansion, but it's likely to conk out at any minute. Yes, but what about housing? Yes, but what about global warming, peak oil, the deficit? As the economy lights candles, the Yessbuts call for more darkness.

The usual response at the end of a book like this is to point a way forward by ticking off a host of sensible, sane policy prescriptions that will lead the United States back to the economic promised land. I'm going to resist the temptation of creating yet another goo-goo laundry list. First, it has been done better and more comprehensively by a host of center and center-left authors. I've read Matt Miller's *The Two Percent Solution*, Bill Clinton's *Back to Work*, and Thomas Friedman and Michael Mandelbaum's *That Used to Be Us*, and suggest you do the same. I heartily endorse their calls to get America's fiscal house in order, have the wealthy pay higher taxes, simplify the tax code, impose a tax on carbon emissions, create financing mechanisms such as an infrastructure bank to improve infrastructure, support alternative energy, invest in and reform public education, and make health care more efficient and affordable. Their proposals are eminently reasonable, technocratic, and logical—and will, of course, never happen, thanks to our constipated political system and the general unwillingness of the current Republican Party to engage in large-scale, forward-looking legislation that doesn't involve massive tax cuts for the rich. And, no, a technocratic third party will not emerge to enact the agenda that gets heads nodding in assent at events hosted by Washington think tanks.

But that doesn't mean we should despair. To a large degree the recovery has happened *in spite of* politics and policy, not because of them. Dysfunctional politics have always been with us and always will be. There was a time when the sitting vice president from one party (Aaron Burr) shot and killed the former treasury secretary from another party (Alexander Hamilton) in a duel. We've had a Republican president, Richard Nixon, threatened with impeachment, and a Democrat, Bill Clinton, actually impeached. The number of times in this country's history when sound economic policy was made by trustworthy, rational politicians and experts can be counted on one of old-time pitcher Mordecai "Three Finger" Brown's hands (and not the one that had the full complement of digits).

But where will the jobs come from? By the end of 2011 the United States had 6.3 million fewer payroll jobs than it had in December 2007 and the same number it had in September 2004. Until the economy puts people back to work in larger numbers, the crisis won't fully pass. From the nadir in February 2010 the private sector added a respectable 3 million jobs through the end of 2011. That's not nearly enough. The short, and honest, answer to the question of where the jobs will come from is: I don't know.

But we never do.

It's difficult to project which firms will be big employers three or five years from now because companies rise and fall quickly. In 1980 Exxon topped the Fortune 500 as the largest U.S. company by revenue. Thirty years later, in 2010, it was second to Walmart, the nation's largest private sector employer, a company that barely charted in 1980. Of the other top-ten members of the Fortune 500 in 1980, five no longer exist in their earlier form: four oil companies were merged into other firms, and General Motors went through bankruptcy. Besides, as I've argued, economic growth and employment growth are now less dependent on the ability of companies and industries to create jobs directly than on their ability to create platforms and systems that encourage and enable others to create jobs. Does the U.S. economy still provide such a platform? Absolutely.

Many skeptics believe, with good reason, that conditions in the United States are so fundamentally broken that only a revolution and complete reinvention can get the country back on the right trajectory. And since calls for fundamental reform tend to be greeted with silence or founder on the shoals of politics, there's little hope for the country to avoid decline. From Occupy Wall Street to the Tea Party, the call rings out that this is no time for incremental measures. But a look under the hood of the U.S. economy leads to a contrary conclusion. The private sector is in the throes of a permanent revolution. Slow, steady, incremental efforts to change do lead to significant results. Indeed there are signs that progress is already being made in tackling some of the most thorny problems America faces—without explosive, fundamental change.

Take housing. Falling house prices, excess supply, and the mortgage mess have been a millstone around the economy's neck since 2007. The crisis has destroyed household wealth, ravaged banks' balance sheets, and sapped consumers of their desire and ability to consume, borrow, and invest. The housing crisis turned out to be like Hanukkah: we were told it was going to last for a year, but it will probably last a good eight years. Residential investment morphed from a force that supercharged growth between 2001 and 2006 to one that sandbagged it. In its reports the Commerce Department points out how much each sector contributed to or detracted from growth. In 2008 declining residential investment reduced growth by 1.62 percent, and in 2009 the reduction was 0.72 percent. Our fervent wish is not that housing will return to bubble-era levels, but that it will simply stop acting as a major buzzkill.

Six years into the housing decline there were signs that this was starting to happen. Prices continued to fall in 2011, and the wrenching, shambolic foreclosure process continued apace, but other metrics began to point upward. New home construction starts bottomed in 2009 at 554,000, and rose to 587,000 in 2010, then ramped up sharply in the second half of 2011. For the full year, construction started on 607,000 housing units, and as 2011 closed starts were running at an annual rate of 680,000—a pace not seen since the fall of 2008. In 2011 the volume of existing home sales rose for the first time since 2005, rising to 4.26 million from 4.19 million in 2010. While prices continued to fall, inventory came down, from 4.04 million in July 2007 to 2.38 million in December 2011. That constituted a 6.2-month supply at the prevailing sales rate.[1] These levels aren't healthy by a long shot, but they're much closer to healthy and represent a vast improvement. Price stability and appreciation don't just stop the pain; they add to wealth and improve banks' balance sheets. Keep in mind that this improvement has come in the absence of any serious change in government policy.

There will come a day when housing isn't a drag. In fact, that day may be here. In the third and fourth quarters of 2011 residential investment contributed 0.03 and 0.25 percentage points to the rate of economic growth, respectively. This is just the beginning. In its report "The Long View on Housing—There's a Boom Out There Somewhere," the consulting firm Macroeconomic Advisers makes a convincing case. At the end of 2010 the United States had 130.8 million housing units, of which 112.5 million were occupied. Some 18.4 million were empty, leaving a vacancy rate of 14 percent, above the boom-era rate of 12 percent. Because Americans continue to grow up, leave home, get married, form families, and have children, it's likely that some 14 million new households will form over the next ten years. To accommodate them, assuming the vacancy rate dips a bit, "the housing stock will have to expand by about 12.5 million units over the next 10 years." But each year about 0.8 percent of the housing stock withers away, through collapse, fire, condemnation, or redevelopment. Crunching the numbers, the report concludes that the nation will need "16 million housing starts over the next 10 years. That's an average of 1.6 million starts per year." Now consider that in 2011 starts were made on only 607,000 units. Even if Americans adapt to straitened circumstances by having smaller families or living with multiple generations under a single roof, à la the Waltons, or simply make more use of existing homes, we will still need about 1.2 million new homes per year for a decade to meet demand. Housing may not return to its levels of 2006 and 2007 for a generation, but housing will begin contributing to economic activity sooner rather than later.[2]

What about the deficits? A host of scolds in Washington and on Wall Street have been fretting for years about the nation's budget and trade deficits. The United States has to borrow trillions of dollars each year to finance government operations and consumption. That leaves us at the mercy of foreign lenders and fickle markets that can suddenly push interest rates up to untenable levels. The political system's demonstrated inability to make deficit-reduction deals adds to the pessimism. The fears, of course, have been overblown. Interest rates have fallen as deficits spiked in the post-Lehman era. That speaks to one of the enduring advantages of the United States and a sign of its superiority: the world regards our government assets as the safest, most protected, most liquid assets available, the ultimate safe harbor in stormy seas.

But, as with housing, there are signs and portents that there may be improvement. In fiscal 2009 the deficit came in at $1.4 trillion. The deficit checked in at $1.3 trillion in both fiscal 2010 and fiscal 2011. The deep recession drove revenues off a cliff—tax receipts fell 18 percent between 2007 and 2009—but revenues have bounced back. Growth, it turns out, is a miracle deficit cure. Even with the tax cuts and easily gamed system, federal receipts rose from $2.1 trillion in 2009 to $2.16 trillion in 2001 and $2.3 trillion in 2011. At the same time, the fiscal discipline imposed by congressional Republicans and the fading of the stimulus have reduced the rate of spending growth. Federal spending actually fell 1.8 percent in fiscal 2010 and rose only 4.2 percent in 2011. Through the first four months of fiscal 2012, with revenues rising 3.5 percent and spending falling 5.3 percent from the levels of the first four months of fiscal 2011, the deficit for the first third of the fiscal year had fallen by 15 percent. Thanks to economic growth, the deficit is shrinking and is likely to shrink further.[3]

It's true that the efforts to tackle the debt head-on have failed. The bipartisan Bowles-Simpson Commission, impaneled in 2010, couldn't get the congressional members on both sides to sign off on its recommendations for $3.9 trillion in deficit reduction over ten years. The "grand bargain" talk between President Obama and House Speaker John Boehner reached a level of $4 trillion before foundering. Next the Super Committee, tasked with coming up with a mere $1.2 trillion in deficit closure over ten years, failed in spectacular fashion. But here's the thing: all these failures may be good for deficit reduction. Given the structure of policy, a much larger amount of deficit reduction is in the works if Congress simply does nothing. According to the Center for Budget and Policy Priorities, if we pursue the "do-nothing option"—if Washington remains gridlocked over vital policy issues—the Bush-era tax cuts on income, investments, and estates will expire; the payroll tax holiday will end; the alternative minimum tax will hit ever larger numbers of taxpayers; spending cuts in Medicare passed in 1997 will finally take hold; the automatic sequestration of spending for defense and social programs envisioned in the Super Committee gambit will take place; and Obamacare will be implemented. All told, the combination of higher taxes and spending that is now the default, no-action option would reduce deficits by $7.1 trillion over ten years.[4]

The trade deficit, which peaked in 2006 at $753 billion, shrank to $381 billion in 2009, and started to grow again as the economy recovered, to $500 billion in 2010 and $558 billion in 2011. But here too existing trends contain the seeds of progress. The United States doesn't so much have a trade deficit problem as it has a China trade problem and an oil dependency problem. In 2011, trade with China accounted for 40 percent of the deficit, and petroleum and petroleum-related products accounted for another 40 percent.

Rising costs and living standards in China, the rising strength of the renminbi, and the rise of reshoring may help bring the China-related trade deficit under control in coming years. Two of the economy's vital post-bust disciplines, tapping into internal resources and efficiency, have the potential to make a significant dent in the petroleum trade deficit. The combination of rapidly increased domestic oil production, energy efficiency in cars, and the use of alternative fuels in automobiles, from natural gas to electricity, together have the makings of a revolution. U.S. crude oil production in 2011 was more than 5.6 million barrels per day, up

13 percent from 2008, thanks in part to the development in unconventional fields in North Dakota. And as the *Financial Times* has reported, there's much more where that comes from: "According to analysts at Credit Suisse, by 2016 the U.S. could be producing an additional 2.5 million barrels per day, with the increase divided between deep water fields in the Gulf of Mexico and new onshore sources." Meanwhile America is slowly but surely weaning itself off oil as a transportation fuel, or at least figuring out how to travel more miles while using less of it. Consider the expansion of mass transit, the rising use of natural gas and electricity to fuel fleets of buses and trucks, corporate efforts to drive more efficiently, and, above all, the rising efficiency of the U.S. vehicle fleet. Each item, taken alone, doesn't do much to reduce oil demand, but taken together they can have a significant impact. Every time the U.S. auto fleet improves its average mileage by a mile, it saves about 150 million barrels of oil, eliminating the need for about $15 billion in imports. Oil imports, which peaked at 5 billion barrels in 2005, fell to 4.3 billion in 2010 and through the first eleven months of 2011 were running at a pace that was 4 percent lower than that. If the industry is able to meet the current standards—that the typical car sold in 2025 will get about 56 miles per gallon—the amount of petroleum used for transportation will fall rapidly.[5]

Although I promised not to rattle off a ten-point plan to guarantee America's economic dominance for another fifty years, there are a few attitudes and concepts worth keeping in mind.

Aim high. The impact of higher mileage standards on energy use points to another feature of the U.S. economy that can help it run better, stronger, and faster in coming years. Providing incentives and subsidies for behavior and innovation is all well and good, but the key is really to focus on standards. A great nation, one that believes in the capacity of its businesses and consumers to adapt, sets high standards for itself. There's a tendency for incumbent businesses, loons, and libertarians to squawk at high standards. But generally U.S. businesses and consumers adapt, accept the changes, get on with it, and reap the benefits. It's easier to be more efficient when efficiency is wired into products when they arrive. Thanks to higher standards, the refrigerators, air conditions, and washing machines sold today all use much less energy than their predecessors in the 1980s, while costing less and working better. Starting in 2012 higher standards will force consumers to make their homes more energy efficient, as the century-old filament lightbulb is phased out and replaced by more efficient bulbs, compact fluorescents, and light-emitting diodes. Standards act as a spur to investment and to the creation of new industries and platforms for growth. The renewable portfolio standards many states have adopted, which require utilities to buy up to 20 percent of their electricity from renewable sources, have done much more to spur solar and wind farms than loan guarantees. Higher standards for auto mileage are stimulating investment in batteries, engine research, and the use of alternative fuels. Imagine the gains that could be reaped if efficiency were built into more products, with, for example, higher standards for housing materials and construction.

Hope for transformation, but settle for improvement. Some of the problems we face are so deeply impacted that many believe only radical surgery or complete reinvention can alter the situation. Others dream of a future deus ex machina as a reason not to do anything. If cars will all be powered by hydrogen in twenty years, what's the point of improving gasoline mileage now? That attitude completely misses the point. As I've noted, amid the serial debacles of the 2008–2009 period, significant innovations that led to marginal and ultimately noticeable improvements in a variety of areas were taking root. And there's no reason to stop. Yes, it would be nice if 250-mile-per-hour bullet trains could cut the travel time from New York to Washington to an hour. But as the Acela has shown, a train that simply goes faster than a car can make a difference. It has carved out a healthy share of the market for all types of travel in the Washington-to-Boston corridor. Rather than pray for super-trains, we should just aim to make existing trains run more rapidly. We may not have the resources to lay down entirely new transportation infrastructure, but we do have the capacity to make the infrastructure that exists more efficient and effective—and hence more valuable. As manufacturers and other companies that rely on repeatable processes have done, Americans have to learn to focus on—and be happy with—continuous improvement.

Light a candle; don't curse the darkness. It's easy to use the absence of rational, nationwide planning as an excuse for inaction. Whether it's education, infrastructure, broadband, or health care, we're not going to get a supereffective McKinsey-designed plan for improvement and national renewal. But it's important not to use the enor-mity of the challenges as an excuse not to do anything. The tolerance for risk and the heedlessness is what got us in so much trouble. But the willingness to try new things, to adapt new ways of doing business, and to take a plunge is a vital attribute. As Americans recover, rebuild, and sober up, it's important not to lose this source of dynamism. Individuals, foundations, institutions, companies, nonprofits, cities, states, and government institutions can do something. Don't wait for a national mortgage modification program; start buying homes out of foreclosure and reselling them to existing residents, as the nonprofit lender Boston Community Capital has done with a few dozen homes in poor neighborhoods. Don't wait for the approval of gigantic solar farms; start attaching solar panels to telephone and utility poles, as New Jersey has done. Don't wait for an infrastructure bank; scrape up some funds and start building and rebuilding commercial infrastructure on your own. In today's economy the simple act of building something can send important signals, inspire action, and turn economic liabilities into assets.

This dynamic can be seen in the High Line, the elevated railroad whose transformation from defunct rail bed to elevated park has in turn transformed the Manhattan neighborhood it runs through. Eighty miles north of Manhattan, another defunct elevated railway performed a similar function for a town that has been starved of capital. Since a fire in 1974, the railroad bridge that spanned the Hudson River at Poughkeepsie stood as an unused, rusting piece of infrastructure. A down-at-the-heels industrial town of about 33,000, Poughkeepsie doesn't have Manhattan's resources. Yet boosters formed a nonprofit, raised $38.8 million from private and public sources, and in May 2008 set to work transforming the Poughkeepsie-Highland Bridge into a 1.3-mile-long elevated walkway over the Hudson. It opened on October 3, 2009, claiming to be "the longest elevated pedestrian bridge in the world." About 300,000 visitors were expected in its first year; instead 750,000 showed up, providing work for local businesses: a restaurant adjacent to an entrance to the bridge, bike rental shops, and snack shops. The walkway has also spurred significant fixed investments as developers have broken ground on a slew of new real estate projects in the area that will inject a multiple of the project's $38 million cost into the regional economy.[6]

Get out more. The drive to double monthly exports from the 2009 low by 2015 relies on a 14 percent compound rate of growth for five years. With more than 70 percent of the world's purchasing power lying outside the United States, it is imperative for American companies, businesspeople, and workers to get more comfortable working with (and for) foreigners, at home and abroad, and selling to them everywhere. The United States racks up impressive export figures — about $180 billion per month — with only the smallest portion of its productive population engaged in the effort. "Less than one percent of America's 30 million companies export," according to the International Trade Administration. "And of U.S. companies that do export, 58 percent export to only one country." If only 2 percent of American companies were engaged in exporting, we'd have twice as many exporters. Meanwhile only about 30 percent of Americans have passports, and in 2010 they took a collective 61.5 million trips outside the country.[7] We simply have to get out more — all of us. One of the few policy prescriptions I do propose is the awarding of a travel stipend for anybody who finishes a college degree in the United States, enough to support a few weeks of travel somewhere outside America's borders.

Traveling costs money, and it can be disorienting and tiring. It takes a good week to recover from the jet lag you suffer when traveling to Asia. But I've always found that it is worth going, even if you have to fly coach and stay in second- and third-rate hotels. Going abroad makes people look at the world, and the place of the United States in it, in new ways. And yes, lots of people return from abroad and find that their travels have simply reinforced their sense of decline. In many ways the world does seem to be running away from us. But if you go with your eyes open, it's also clear that the world is taking us with it. When you pay more attention to CNN International than Headline News, when you read the *Financial Times* more closely than the *Wall Street Journal*, several factors emerge that argue against the decline of U.S. influence. The world really needs the United States—its economy and the products, services, concepts, and business models it creates.

When the global economy slows down, the United States is still capable of serving as an engine of growth. In a year in which the United States grows at a rate of 3 percent and the rest of the world is flat, the global economy will still expand. When it's growing at 3 percent, the United States each year produces an incremental amount of economic activity equal to the entire GDP of Greece. Even when it expands slowly, its businesses and consumers still provide work for hundreds of millions of people around the world.

But there's more to this relationship. Consider how much the world still relies on and looks to the new products and services the United States develops. Visit China, and you can't help noticing how much that country's efforts to develop a consumer society depend on U.S. brands and on domestic knockoffs of U.S. brands. China needs American assets, from George Clooney to Stephon Marbury, from Coca-Cola to Mary Kay, to create a consuming culture. Meanwhile the systems that American companies have invented and scaled up in recent years are being put to vital use. Participants in Iran's attempted Green Revolution communicated with one another on Twitter. Egypt's pro-democracy activists organized on Facebook. Syrian dissidents are courageously making videos of clashes with the army on iPhones and uploading them for the world to see on YouTube. The General Motors Buick plant in China is bringing higher standards of safety, quality, and efficiency to the domestic manufacturing market. Walmart is trying to bring its logistics experience to bear in India, where its involvement in the retail sector could help prevent the spoilage of a large chunk of the nation's food production. Highly productive American farmers are feeding the world. The planes manufactured by Boeing in the Pacific Northwest provide mobility to people in Africa. General

Electric's gas turbines, produced in South Carolina, are bringing light to the many dark places of the world. Then there are the systems and ideas that American wealth makes possible: the Gates Foundation's projects on malaria, the Clinton Global Initiative's work on AIDS. The Endeavor Foundation, a small nonprofit based in New York, is spreading the gospel of entrepreneurship, mentoring, and supporting small-business creation to great effect in Latin America, South Asia, and the Middle East.

The U.S. economy's greatest export is the one it has offered people all over the world for hundreds of years: hope. The hope for a better life, at home or in the United States. The hope for better living standards, greater mobility, and leisure. And the hope of being lifted from the dark pits in which far too many people remain stuck. Whenever someone argues that the United States has run out of things to offer the world, I think of the thirty-three Chilean miners stuck at the bottom of a deep, dark hole. Their salvation ultimately came from the products and services of two small, unheralded U.S. companies that do most of their business overseas. After emerging, one of the miners, Edison Peña, journeyed to New York to engage in one of the most life-affirming things a person can do: run the New York City marathon. That's a pretty good metaphor with which to end this book. The New York City marathon itself provides a perfect example of what the U.S. economy does. It's a major global event that is firmly and undeniably American. It has grown from nothing to an immense scale. Its participants rely on competencies and stamina developed through intense training, and draw on internal resources to power them through. And the whole chaotic event comes off only because of highly coordinated logistics, communications, and infrastructure systems. Most significantly, the competition between nations, like the internal competition of a country to improve its economy, isn't a sprint. It's a marathon.

Acknowledgments

Writing a book is like playing a long solo—a very, very long, frequently dull, but ultimately satisfying solo. The creation of any book, including this one, is necessarily a solitary act. But this one wouldn't have been possible without the financial, editorial, logistic, and emotional support of several people and institutions.

First, the outfits that employed me over the past few years have been remarkably tolerant of all my journalistic efforts, from Tweets on up to books. They have financed my travel, promoted my work, encouraged original reporting, and continually prodded me to look further and deeper at America's place in the world.

Better, Stronger, Faster had its genesis in a *Newsweek* cover story that ran in April 2010. I did a large chunk of the vital thinking, traveling, and reporting that went into this book during the three years I was on staff at the magazine. At *Newsweek* Jon Meacham, Kathy Deveny, David Jefferson, Daniel Klaidman, David Kaplan, Daniel McGinn, and Fareed Zakaria championed and improved my writing. Nick Summers, Matthew Philips, and Jessica Ramirez provided valuable reporting and research assistance.

From 2002 through 2010, when I had the privilege of writing *Slate*'s "Moneybox" column, *Slate*'s editorial team encouraged me to develop a voice and goaded me into pursuing a wide-ranging set of interests, from global growth to the financial bailouts to Broadway's treatment of the money culture. The chapter on the efficient consumer had its genesis in a *Slate* project on home energy efficiency. David Plotz, Jacob Weisberg, and June Thomas consistently forced me to sharpen my ideas and prose, while either subtly ignoring or endorsing my tendency to insert one-liners into eight-hundred-word columns. June Thomas also read every word of the manuscript and provided sage editorial advice.

Yahoo! Finance, my professional home since the fall of 2010, picked up where *Newsweek* and *Slate* left off. As a columnist, and as one of the cohosts of the *Daily Ticker*, I've been able to spend my days learning, talking, and meditating about many of the themes covered in the previous pages. The constant stream of colleagues, friends, and deep-thinking guests who come through our studios and offices have helped inform my work. I'm particularly grateful to Diane Galligan for creating a new post for me and for providing me with the freedom and platform to pursue my interests. My colleagues Aaron Task, Stacy Curtin, Peter Gorenstein, Morgan Korn, Rebecca Stropoli, Elizabeth Trotta, Caroline Kim, Chris Nichols, and Lisa Scherzer have tolerated my foibles, saved me from countless mistakes, and make my day job an easy one. A thankful yodel as well to Robertson Barrett, Mickie Rosen, Chris Hunter, Nicole Slavitt, and Becky Auslander.

I've been fortunate to have grown up in the word trade with a group of friends who offer feedback, support, and hospitality and provide sympathetic hearings to my many gripes. Thanks to David Shuster, Gavriel Rosenfeld, Adam Lashinsky, Jonathan Mahler, and Scott Medintz,

Oh, and a special thanks to the engineers of Metro North, who kept the jostling to a minimum as I pecked away at my laptop while on the train to and from New York.

Several people and institutions made it possible for me to travel and see firsthand much of what I wrote about. Thanks to Susan Kreifels at the East-West Center in Honolulu for including me in the 2009 Japan exchange; to Alison Bradley and Zhen He, intrepid guides and wranglers for two China-U.S. Exchange Foundation fellowships, in 2009 and 2011; to Will Bohlen and Randy Soderquist of the German Marshall Fund of the United States, with whom I traveled to South Africa, Vietnam, and Cambodia. Adrian Monck and Kai Bucher at the World Economic Forum have made it possible for me to attend many extremely useful events. Dean

Acknowledgments

Vance Roley hosted me for a very fruitful week at the University of Hawaii Shidler School of Business. I also spent a week in the fall of 2011 at the Hoover Institution, collecting thoughts and writing, and wondering why I shouldn't move to northern California. Thanks to David Brady and Mandy Macalla for their patience and support.

Sloan Harris, my agent at ICM, has represented me for more than a decade and a half, and has the gray hairs to prove it. Through several paradigm shifts and business cycles he has maintained an even keel and helped me negotiate New York's publishing world with good humor, patience, and wisdom. Thanks too to his assistant, Kristyn Keene.

At the Free Press, Dominick Anfuso believed in this book from the beginning. It was a pleasure to work with him again. Sydney Tanigawa helped shepherd the book through production, Judith Hoover copyedited the manuscript, and Eric Fuentecilla designed the cover.

My parents, Barry and Sandra Gross, my earliest editors and boosters, were, as always, highly supportive. And as I have for forty-four years, I continue to rely on the advice and expertise of my two older brothers, Michael Gross and Leon Gross.

The best part of being a journalist is getting paid to see the world. Over the past few years hundreds of people on five different continents and in a few dozen states have welcomed me into their homes, their offices, their companies, and their businesses. I'm grateful to all of them for sharing their experiences, and look forward to visiting again soon.

There's one particular place to which I cherish returning. It's the home my wife, Candice Savin, and our children, Aliza and Ethan, have created. Whether I'm in New York for the day, in Israel for a few days, or in China for the week, I always count down the hours until I can return to our small haven in the wilds of Fairfield County. Agreeing to write a book is like bringing an unwelcome guest into the house, one that causes agita, ruins vacations, and sucks up time on weekends and in the evenings. I'm sure they'll be glad that the guest has finally left.

The most gratifying part about finishing a book—other than

being able to pick up phone calls from your editor without fear or guilt—is to be able to dedicate it. For nearly eighteen years Candice Savin has been a constant source of support, optimism, companionship, love without reservation or condition, and inspiration. She is a better and stronger person than anyone I know.

Notes

Unless otherwise noted, direct quotes are from interviews I conducted with individuals and corporate sources.

Chapter 1. The Rise of Decline

1. The transcript for Niall Ferguson's speech at the Peterson Institute of International Economics is available at http://www.petersoninstitute.org/publications/ papers/niarchos-ferguson-2010.pdf.
2. Stiglitz quoted in Anthony Faiola, "The End of American Capitalism," *Washington Post*, October 10, 2008. Krugman's February 2009 speech at Wharton School is available at http://knowledge.wharton.upenn.edu/article.cfm ?articleid=2167.
3. IPO data provided by Dealogic and by Renaissance Capital, http://www .renaissancecapital.com/ipohome/review/2011Review.aspx.
4. On Japan's suicide rate, see the World Health Organization website, http:// www.who.int/mental_health/media/japa.pdf.

Chapter 2. The Myth of American Decline

1. Francis Sisson quoted in Arthur Schlesinger, *The Coming of the New Deal* (New York, 2003); Richard Whitney quoted in John Brooks, *Once in Golconda* (New York, 1969).
2. Data on nations' GDP in 1875, compiled by Angus Maddison, can be seen at www.ggdc.net/maddison/Historical . . . /vertical-file_02-2010.xls.
3. Tsongas quoted in Maureen Dowd, "Voters Want Candidates to Take a Reality Check," *New York Times*, February 17, 1992.
4. All data on job gains and losses can be accessed at the Bureau of Labor Statistics website, www.bls.gov/bls/employment.htm; data on poverty can be seen in the Census Bureau's "Income, Poverty, and Health Insurance Coverage in the United States: 2010."

Notes

5. The Philadelphia Federal Reserve forecasts can be seen at http://www.phil .frb.org/research-and-data/real-time-center/survey-of-professional-fore casters/.
6. Ross DeVol, "From Recession to Recovery: Analyzing America's Return to Growth," Milken Institute, October 2010.
7. Information on the recessions' and expansions' length and depth is from National Bureau of Economic Research, http://www.nber.org/cycles.html.
8. The McKinsey report can be seen at http://www.nyc.gov/html/om/pdf/ny _report_final.pdf. Floyd Norris, "Resentment Is Rising in Euro Zone," *New York Times*, April 15, 2011.
9. The calculation is from the *Financial Times*, http://www.ft.com/cms/ s/0/2dacd064-0ece-11e0-9ec3-00144feabdc0.html#axzz1je03UHlK.
10. Data on permanent resident status are from "DHS Yearbook of Immigration Statistics: 2010," available at http://www.dhs.gov/files/statistics/publications/ LPR10.shtm; data on fertility rates are from CIA Factbook, https://www.cia .gov/library/publications/the-world-factbook/index.html
11. Meeker's report, *USA Inc.*, can be seen at http://s3.amazonaws.com/kpcbweb/ files/USA_Inc.pdf.
12. Data on global stock market capitalization are available at http://www.world -exchanges.org/statistics/annual/2010/equity0markets/domestic-market-cap italization.

Chapter 3. Faster: Policy

1. The White House report "The Economic Impact of the American Recovery and Reinvestment Act of 2009" can be seen at http://www.whitehouse.gov/ sites/default/files/cea_5th_arra_report.pdf. The CBO report is titled "Estimated Impact of the American Recovery and Reinvestment Act on Employment and Economic Output from January 2011 through March 2011." Zandi and Blinder's report is available at http://www.economy.com/mark-zandi/ documents/End-of-Great-Recession.pdf.
2. Data in this chapter on the Federal Reserve's Maiden Lane transactions can be seen at the New York Fed's website, http://www.newyorkfed.org/markets/ maidenlane.html.
3. All data in this chapter on the Federal Reserve's balance sheet come from the series "Factors Affecting Reserve Balances" at http://www.federalreserve.gov/ releases/h41/.
4. Data on the Treasury's money market fees come from http://money.usnews .com/money/blogs/planning-to-retire/2009/09/18/treasurys-money-market -guarantee-program-ends; data on the Temporary Liquidity Guarantee Program are at the FDIC's website, http://www.fdic.gov/regulations/resources/ TLGP; data on the Fed's commercial paper funding facility can be seen at http://www.newyorkfed.org/research/epr/11v17n1/1105adri.pdf; data on the TALF come from http://www.newyorkfed.org/aboutthefed/annual/annual 10/FRBNY_Financial_Statements_2010.pdf.
5. Data on the Fed's profits can be seen in the Fed's annual reports, http://www .federalreserve.gov/publications/annual-report/default.htm.

6. Information on the AIG bailout comes from AIG's press website, http://www.aigcorporate.com/newsroom/index.html.
7. Data in this chapter on banks taking and repaying TARP funds come from releases and reports available at http://www.treasury.gov/initiatives/financial-stability/briefing-room/Pages/briefing-room.aspx.
8. Data on U.K. bailouts come from U.K. Financial Investments, http://www.ukfi.co.uk/releases/1396.pdf.
9. Data on bank failures can be seen at the FDIC's website, www.fdic.gov/bank/historical/bank/index.html; and in FDIC Quarterly Banking Profiles at http://www2.fdic.gov/qbp/.
10. Data on Chrysler, GM, and Ford market share, employment, and profits come from corporate public relations sources and the companies' investor relations websites. Data on TARP returns come from TARP updates. Data on employment come from the report "The Resurgence of the American Automotive Industry," issued by the White House.
11. Data on Fannie Mae and Freddie Mac come from releases on the companies' investor relations websites, http://www.fanniemae.com/portal/about-us/investor-relations/index.html, and http://www.freddiemac.com/investors/.
12. Data on the size of the savings and loan bailout come from a 2000 FDIC report at http://www.fdic.gov/bank/analytical/banking/2000dec/brv13n2_2.pdf.

Chapter 4. Better: Restructuring the Nation

1. Bankruptcy statistics cited here and elsewhere in this chapter can be seen at http://www.uscourts.gov/Statistics/BankruptcyStatistics.aspx. Data on corporate bankruptcies cited here and elsewhere in this chapter supplied by Diane Vazza of Standard & Poor's.
2. Jack Willoughby, "On the Road to Redemption," *Barron's*, October 9, 2010; CIT information from company's pressroom and investor relations portal, http://news.cit.com/portal/site/cit/media/, and http://ir.cit.com/phoenix.zhtml?c=99314&p=irol-IRHome.
3. Information on the Hancock Tower comes from the author's interview with the principals. On the Bain lease, see http://www.boston.com/business/ticker/2010/05/bain_capital_wi_1.html; on the sale of the building, see http://dealbook.nytimes.com/2010/12/29/john-hancock-tower-sells-for-930-million/.
4. Ford data and information come from the company's pressroom and investor relations website.
5. All data on U.S. corporate profits, debt, and cash holdings in this and other chapters come from the Federal Reserve "Flow of Funds" report, available at http://www.federalreserve.gov/releases/z1/; and from the Commerce Department, http://www.bea.gov/national/#corporate.
6. All data on consumer credit come from the Federal Reserve series on consumer credit, available at http://www.federalreserve.gov/Releases/g19/current/default.htm. All data on retail sales come from the Census Bureau, http://www.census.gov/retail/. Data on mortgage equity withdrawal cited here and elsewhere in this chapter are provided by Moody's/Economy.com. Data on the personal savings rate cited here and elsewhere in this chapter can be seen at

the Commerce Department's website, http://www.bea.gov/national/index
.htm#personal. Data on household debt can be seen in Federal Reserve reports,
http://www.federalreserve.gov/releases/housedebt.
7. Cardhub.com's data on credit card delinquency and charge-off rates can be
seen at http://www.cardhub.com/edu/credit-card-statistics.
8. Data on U.S. consumer debt are from the Federal Reserve data series, http://
www.federalreserve.gov/releases/housedebt/.
9. Target's earnings can be seen at http://www.cardhub.com/edu/credit-card-sta
tistics/; Capital One's earnings reports can be accessed at its investor relations
website, http://phx.corporate-ir.net/phoenix.zhtml?c=70667&p=irol-irhome;
JPMorgan Chase's third quarter 2011 earnings can be seen at its investor relations portal, http://investor.shareholder.com/jpmorganchase/index.cfm.

Chapter 5. Stronger: The Efficiency Economy

1. Data on productivity can be seen at Bureau of Labor Statistics website, http://
www.bls.gov/lpc/.
2. Material on BigBelly Solar came from the author's interviews with company
executives and users and BigBelly's online pressroom, http://bigbellysolar
.com/newsinfo/inthenews/.
3. Information on Waste Management's electricity generation can be seen at
http://www.wm.com/sustainability/renewable-energy.jsp.
4. Material on Empire State Building efficiency efforts came from the author's
interviews with Malkin Properties executives and http://www.esbnyc.com/
sustainability_energy_efficiency.asp.
5. The McKinsey efficiency report is available at http://www.mckinsey.com/en/
Client_Service/Electric_Power_and_Natural_Gas/Latest_thinking/Unlock
ing_energy_efficiency_in_the_US_economy.aspx.
6. Data on EnerNOC's operations can be seen at www.enernoc.com.
7. Information on Walmart is from its investor relations website, http://inves
tors.walmartstores.com/phoenix.zhtml?c=112761&p=irol-irhome; and its
sustainability website, http://walmartstores.com/Sustainability/9071.aspx.
8. The Deutsche Bank report is cited in *Business Insider*, http://www.business
insider.com/ups-productivity-2011-5.
9. Data on miles driven and gasoline consumption are from the Environmental
Protection Agency, http://ww.bts.gov/publications/national_transportation
_statistics/html/table_04_23.html.

Chapter 6. The Myth of International Irrelevance

1. Data on foreign direct investment used here and elsewhere in this chapter
come from the Department of Commerce report "Foreign Direct Investment in the United States" at http://www.esa.doc.gov/Reports/foreign-direct
-investment-united-states, and from reports of the Organization for International Investment at http://www.ofii.org/docs/FDIUS_3Q_2011.pdf.
2. On the Ecclestone purchase, see http://online.wsj.com/article/SB1000142405
27023037147045763840137982288854.html.

3. On the Milner purchase, see http://blogs.wsj.com/developments/2011/03/30/russian-investor-buys-silicon-valley-mansion-for-100-million/.
4. On the Rybolovlev purchase, see http://www.observer.com/2011/12/na-zdaro via-dmitry-rybolovlev-fertilizer-kingpin-buys-sandy-weills-88-m-penthouse/.
5. On Prokhorov purchase of Nets, see: http://www.bloomberg.com/news/2010-05-11/prokhorov-s-200-million-purchase-of-nets-gains-approval-from-nba-owners.html; on sale of Miami Herald building, see http://www.mcclatchydc.com/2011/05/27/114898/mcclatchy-sells-miami-herald-land.html; on Slim investment in New York Times Compay, see http://phx.corporate-ir.net/phoenix.zhtml?c=105317&p=irol-newsArticle&ID=1246109&highlight=.
6. On foreign company purchases of U.S. shale properties, see "CNOOC Buys Chesapeake US Shale Oil, Gas Assets for $570 Million," Dow Jones, January 30, 2011.
7. Data on auto production provided by the Auto Alliance http://www.auto alliance.org.
8. Reports on foreign takeovers of failed U.S. banks are available at the FDIC's "Bank Failures in Brief," http://www.fdic.gov/bank/historical/bank/index.html.
9. Toledo quoted in http://en.mercopress.com/2011/04/26/banco-do-brasil-moves-into-the-us-and-buys-florida-based-bank.
10. Williams quoted in *Wall Street Journal,* March 1, 2011.

Chapter 7. The Myth of Not Making Stuff the World Wants

1. Data on imports and exports for this chapter come from the Bureau of Economic Analysis section on international trade, http://www.bea.gov/newsre leases/international/trade/tradnewsrelease.htm. Data on U.S. rank as a global exporter come from http://www.dlc.org/ndol_ci.cfm?kaid=108&subid=9000 03&contentid=255203.
2. Nuts data are available at www.nytimes.com/2010/06/29/business/media/29nuts.html.
3. Data on food production by country can be seen at the website of the Food and Agricultural Organization of the United Nations: http://faostat.fao.org.
4. All data on U.S. agricultural exports come from the U.S. Department of Agriculture, http://www.ers.usda.gov/Briefing/FarmIncome/nationalestimates.htm.
5. Data on coal production, use, and exports can be seen at the Energy Information Administration's coal page, http://www.eia.gov/coal/; on electricity generation, see http://www.eia.gov/todayinenergy/detail.cfm?id=2391.
6. Thomas Power, "The Greenhouse Gas Impact of Exporting Coal from the West Coast," http://www.sightline.org/research/energy/coal/Coal-Power-White-Paper.pdf.
7. American Petroleum data can be seen at API's statistics page: http://www.api.org/en/publications-standards-and-statistics/industry-statistics.aspx.
8. On ethanol exports, see Renewable Fuels Association, http://www.ethanolrfa.org/news/entry/november-ethanol-exports-set-record/; Ed Crooks and Greg Meyer, "Brazil Imports of U.S. Ethanol Soar," *Financial Times,* May 5, 2011, http://www.ft.com/intl/cms/s/0/f1486874-775d-11e0-824c-00144feabdc0.html.

9. Yergin quoted in "Firms Plan to Export Gas," *Wall Street Journal*, January 25, 2011.

10. Natural gas data can be accessed at Energy Information Administration, http://www.eia.gov/naturalgas/. Information on Cheniere transactions is available at the company's investor relations page, http://phx.corporate-ir.net/ phoenix.zhtml?c=101667&p=irol-news. "Firms Plan to Export Gas," Russell Gold, *Wall Street Journal*, January 25, 2011.

11. Data on ferrous scrap exports can be seen at the website of the Institute of Scrap Recycling Industries statistics section, http://www.isri.org/iMIS15 _Prod/ISRI/_About/Scrap_Recycling_Industry.aspx?hkey=1c15f9cb-6f70 -4130-a053-ceba7a327c7f.

12. James R. Hagerty, "U.S. Drilling Companies Get Moment in Spotlight," *Wall Street Journal*, October 14, 2010.

13. Martha White, "How Can America's Biggest Exporter Get Foreign Airlines to Buy More Planes? And What Can the U.S. Government Do to Help?" *Slate*, November 1, 2010, http://www.slate.com/articles/business/exports/2010/11/ the_boeing_co.html.

14. Information on U.S. arms exports is available in "Gulf States in \$123 bn U.S. Arms Spree," *Financial Times*, September 2, 2010. On the Pentagon arms backlog, see "Pentagon Has \$327 Billion Arms Backlog, Sees Drone Demand," *Bloomberg*, June 10, 2011, http://www.bloomberg.com/news/2011-06-10/ pentagon-has-327-billion-export-backlog-sees-drone-demand-1-.html.

Chapter 8. The World of New Exports

1. The National Foundation for American Policy report can be seen at http://www .nfap.com/pdf/DAYOFRELEASEImmigrantFoundersInVentureFunded Companies.pdf.

2. Information on the number of foreign students, their point of origin, and their impact is in the Institute for International Education's "Open Doors" report, http://www.iie.org/Research-and-Publications/Open-Doors.

3. Jacques Steinberg, "Recruiting in China Pays Off for U.S. Colleges," *New York Times*, February 11, 2011, http://www.nytimes.com/2011/02/12/education/ 12college.html?pagewanted=all.

4. Information on New York City tourism can be seen at http://www.nycgo .com/articles/nyc-statistics-page; on the fifty-millionth tourist, see http://city room.blogs.nytimes.com/2011/12/20/as-city-closes-in-on-50-millionth-visitor -british-couple-to-be-feted/.

5. Information on incoming tourism to the United States can be seen at http:// tinet.ita.doc.gov/tinews/archive/tinews2011/20110316.html; data on exits and economic impact can be accessed via the portal of ITA's Office of Travel and Tourism Industries, http://tinet.ita.doc.gov/.

6. On the first Chinese charter to Hawaii, see http://www.hawaiinewsnow.com/ Global/story.asp?S=13935812.

7. Author interview with Nahoopii; data on Hawaii tourism come from the Hawaii Department of Business, Economic Development and Tourism, http://hawaii.gov/dbedt/info/visitor-stats.

Notes

8. Elizabeth Holmes, "Stores Push for Chinese Tourists," *Wall Street Journal*, June 9, 2011, http://online.wsj.com/article/SB10001424052702304563104576361270343556278.html.
9. On the Saudi king's visit to New York, see http://www.nypost.com/p/page six/saudi_king_takes_york_the_entire_EypM45miPSYGsOHd9OLfVO#ixzz 1YQaxOHJo.
10. On Marbury, see Wells Tower, "Welcome to the Far Eastern Conference," *GQ*, May 2011.
11. On sales of the Jobs biography in China, see http://micgadget.com/16976/ steve-jobs-biography-launch-in-china-draws-crowds-250000-copies-sold/.
12. For data on box office receipts, see http://www.mpaa.org/Resources/93bbeb16 -0e4d-4b7e-b085-3f41c459f9ac.pdf; for data on the *Transformers* box office, see http://latimesblogs.latimes.com/entertainmentnewsbuzz/2011/07/box -office-transformers.html.
13. On Bruce Willis's deal with the Russian bank, see http://www.reuters.com/ article/2010/11/23/us-russia-bank-willis-odd-idUSTRE6AM3OL20101123.

Chapter 9. Inports

1. For data on companies' split of foreign-U.S. revenues, see http://www .prnewswire.com/news-releases/foreign-sales-by-us-companies-tick-down -in-2010-463-of-all-sales-were-derived-outside-of-the-states-125804878.html.
2. Information on projections of global auto sales is available at Global Emerging Markets Forecast Update, http://www.jdpower.com/news/pressRelease .aspx?ID=2011042.
3. On the Credit Suisse pension report, see http://www.ft.com/intl/cms/ s/0/1adc855a-d567-11e0-bd7e-00144feab49a.html.
4. Data on Disney's Russian movies come from http://www.nytimes.com/ 2009/11/14/movies/14masters.html?_r=1, and http://www.hollywoodreporter .com/news/disney-begin-production-two-russian-180575. Information and details on Disney's theme parks come from Disney's corporate website.
5. On the growth of Pulpy, see http://www.thecoca-colacompany.com/dynamic/ press_center/2011/02/pulpy-joins-roster-of-billion-dollar-brands.html.
6. KFC and Yum data can be accessed from Yum's investor relations portal, http://www.yum.com/investors.
7. Kraemer, Linden, and Dedrick's paper can be seen at http://pcic.merage.uci .edu/papers/2011/Value_iPad_iPhone.pdf; Apple store data come from the company's store locator, http://www.apple.com/buy/locator/.
8. David Barboza, "Gap Joins U.S. Retail Rush to China," *New York Times*, November 11, 2010.
9. The Millward Brown study can be seen at http://www.millwardbrown.com/ BrandZ/Default.aspx.
10. For information on Cleveland Clinic see http://my.clevelandclinic.org/loca tions_directions/locations-index/abu-dhabi/default.aspx.
11. Information on Cornell's medical school in Qatar comes from its website, http://qatar-weill.cornell.edu/.

Chapter 10. More Like North Dakota

1. Information on North Dakota's labor market can be seen at the Bureau of Labor Statistics State and Local Employment portal, http://www.bls.gov/sae/.
2. The Poppers' article can be seen at https://wesfiles.wesleyan.edu/home/ pletourneau/web/ees_116/bison/buffalocommons-doc%20copy.pdf.
3. Data on North Dakota's oil production are provided by the North Dakota Industrial Commission, https://www.dmr.nd.gov/oilgas/.
4. Information on Bank of North Dakota can be seen at http://banknd.nd.gov/.
5. Information on North Dakota's Legacy Fund is available at http://bis marcktribune.com/news/opinion/editorial/legacy-fund-gets-its-start/ article_65cef2e0-dd56-11e0-983a-001cc4c03286.html.
6. On North Dakota's status as a revenue-receiving state, see http://www.tax foundation.org/files/ftsbs-timeseries-20071016-.pdf; data on the state's budget can be accessed at http://www.nd.gov/fiscal/budget/state/.
7. Kevin Helliker, "Frigid North Dakota Is Hot Draw for Out-of-State Students," *Wall Street Journal*, July 16, 2011.

Chapter 11. Reshoring and Insourcing

1. Alan S. Blinder, "Offshoring: The Next Industrial Revolution?" http://www .foreignaffairs.com/articles/61514/alan-s-blinder/offshoring-the-next-indus trial-revolution.
2. "China's One-Child Plan Faces Fire," *Wall Street Journal*, April 29, 2011.
3. BCG's report can be seen at http://www.bcg.com/expertise_impact/publica tions/publicationdetails.aspx?id=tcm:12-84591.
4. John Bussey, "Analysis: Will Costs Drive Firms Home?" *Wall Street Journal*, May 5, 2011.
5. A list of the most expensive cities can be seen at http://money.cnn.com/ 2011/07/12/pf/expensive_cities/index.htm.
6. Immelt's speech is available at http://files.gereports.com/wp-content/uploads/ 2011/04/03-31-11-Jeff-Immelt-@-The-Economic-Club-of-Washington-DC .pdf.
7. Paul Glader, "As Indian Companies Grow in the U.S., Outsourcing Comes Home," *Washington Post*, May 20, 2011.
8. Jeremy Lemer, "GE Plans to Return to U.S. Made Products," *Financial Times*, October 18, 2010.
9. On Whirlpool's investments in Tennessee, see "Whirlpool to Invest in Tennessee Plant," *Wall Street Journal*, September 1, 2010.
10. "GM Deal to Hire More at Low End," *New York Times*, September 20, 2011; on the Chrysler-UAW deal, see http://www.tulsaworld.com/business/article.aspx ?subjectid=461&articleid=20111013_461_E6_WARREN989907&rss_lnk=5.
11. Adriana Gardella, "A Company Grows, and Builds a Plant Back in the U.S.A.," *New York Times*, October 12, 2011, http://www.nytimes.com/2011/10/13/ business/smallbusiness/bringing-manufacturing-back-to-the-united-states .html.
12: On Peerless Industries, see http://www.prnewswire.com/news-releases/peer

Notes

less-industries-to-create-new-illinois-jobs-with-move-to-aurora-85750847
.html.

Chapter 12. The Efficient Consumer

1. Ken Auletta, "You've Got News," *New Yorker,* January 24, 2011. Data on AOL's earnings can be seen at the company's investor relations website, http://ir.aol.com/phoenix.zhtml?c=147895&p=irol-irhome.
2. The breakdown of consumer expenditures in the Consumer Price Index can be seen at the Bureau of Labor Statistics website, http://www.bls.gov/cpi/data.htm.
3. For data on historic homeownership rates, see http://www.census.gov/hhes/www/housing/hvs/historic/index.html. Moody's data on housing being cheaper to rent are cited in http://www.huffingtonpost.com/2011/05/24/new-generation-of-renters_n_866032.html.
4. Data on housing starts and completions can be seen at the U.S. Census residential construction portal, http://www.census.gov/construction/nrc/.
5. AAA "Your Driving Costs 2011" can be seen at http://newsroom.aaa.com/wp-content/uploads/2011/08/YourDrivingCosts2011.pdf.
6. Data on Zipcar's membership growth, membership, and business development was taken from press releases at the company's media site: http://zipcar.mediaroom.com.
7. Data on student debt come from The Project on Student Debt, http://projectonstudentdebt.org.
8. Data on Airbnb's growth, size, and fundraising was taken from press release at the company's media site: http://www.airbnb.com/home/press.

Chapter 13. Supersize Nation: Scale, Scope, and Systems

1. Data on the number of Apple, Google, and Facebook employees come from the companies' SEC filings. See also Greg Linden, Jason Dedrick, and Kenneth L. Kraemer, "Innovation and Job Creation in a Global Economy: The Case of Apple's iPod," http://pcic.merage.uci.edu/papers/2011/InnovationJobCreationiPod.pdf. Timothy Noah's comments can be seen at http://www.tnr.com/blog/timothy-noah/95877/steve-jobs-job-creator.
2. Data on Amazon.com's revenues can be seen at http://money.usnews.com/money/blogs/flowchart/2011/06/30/why-us-companies-arent-so-american-anymore; information on LivingSocial and HomeAway's expansion can be found at the companies' websites; Lynn Cowan, "HomeAway IPO Opens at 34% after Pricing Well," *Wall Street Journal*, June 29, 2011, http://www.marketwatch.com/story/homeaway-ipo-opens-up-34-after-pricing-well-2011-06-29.
3. Larry Summers's remarks can be seen at http://tech.fortune.cnn.com/2011/07/19/brainstorm-tech-video-larry-summers-transcript/.
4. The American Society of Civil Engineers "Infrastructure Report Card" can be seen at http://www.infrastructurereportcard.org/.
5. Raul Katz, "Estimating the Economic Impact of the Broadband Stimulus

241

Plan," http://www.gcbpp.org/files/BBSTIM/KatzBBStimulusPaper.pdf; the ITU's broadband rankings can be seen at http://www.websiteoptimization .com/bw/1109/; Pando Networks' download speed rankings can be seen at http://dl.dropbox.com/u/33013/pandoglobalstudy.pdf.

6. The Brattle Group, "Transforming America's Power Industry: The Investment Challenge, 2010–2030," http://www.brattle.com/_documents/Upload Library/Upload725.pdf.

7. Author interview with Henrik Fisker. Details of the Ford/Sunpower relationship can be seen at http://media.ford.com/article_display.cfm?article_id =35036; for Google's solar-powered parking structures, see http://pluginbay area.org/fileadmin/materials/zero_emissions/EV_and_PHEV/Solar_Fuel_ Station_Brochure.pdf.

8. On Governor Christie's rejecting tunnel funds, see http://www.cnn.com/2010/ US/10/07/new.jersey.tunnel.project/; the Regional Plan Association's study can be seen at http://www.rpa.org/2010/07/arc-to-raise-home-values-by-18 -billion.html.

9. The "superstar cities" paper can be seen at http://papers.ssrn.com/sol3/papers .cfm?abstract_id=921741; Dana Rubinstein, "Rail Stations Drive Demand," *Wall Street Journal*, June 13, 2011.

Conclusion. The Myth of American Decline

1. Data on home starts are available at the U.S. Census residential construction site, http://www.census.gov/construction/nrc/; data on home sales volume are from www.realtor.org.

2. The Macroeconomic Advisers report can be seen at http://macroadvisers .blogspot.com/2011/05/long-view-on-housing-theres-boom-out.html.

3. Data on spending and receipts are available at Financial Management Service, http://www.fms.treas.gov/index.html.

4. On the do-nothing option, see http://www.washingtonpost.com/blogs/ezra-klein/post/the-do-nothing-plan-now-worth-71-trillion/2011/08/25/gIQAmf IIYN_blog.html.

5. Ed Crooks and Sheila McNulty, "U.S. Oil Production Revives Despite Offshore Disruption," *Financial Times*, March 2, 2011, http://www.ft.com/intl/ cms/s/0/8698ae80-4503-11e0-80e7-00144feab49a.html; oil imports and production data come from the Energy Information Administration at http:// www.eia.gov/dnav/pet/pet_move_impcus_a2_nus_ep00_im0_mbbl_a.htm.

6. On the Walkway over the Hudson, see http://walkway.org/.

7. Data from the International Trade Administration are at http://trade.gov/cs/ factsheet.asp.

Index

Index

Index

Index

Index

Index

Index

Index

Index

About the Author

Daniel Gross, economics editor and columnist at Yahoo! Finance, is a veteran journalist and best-selling author. In a career spanning more than two decades, he has worked as a reporter at the *New Republic* and *Bloomberg News*, written the "Economic View" column in the *New York Times*, and penned cover stories for *Newsweek*, *New York*, *Fortune*, and the *New York Times Magazine*. From 2007 to 2010 he was jointly employed by *Slate*, for which he wrote the "Moneybox" column, and *Newsweek*, where he was a senior editor and columnist. Gross appears regularly on media outlets such as MSNBC, CNBC, and National Public Radio. His previous books include *Forbes Greatest Business Stories of All Time*, *Pop! Why Bubbles Are Great for the Economy*, *Dumb Money*, and *Bull Run: Wall Street, the Democrats, and the New Politics of Personal Finance*. He lives in Connecticut with his wife and two children.